Images of Schoolteachers in America

Second Edition

Edited by

Pamela Bolotin Joseph
Antioch University Seattle

Gail E. Burnaford
Northwestern University

2001

LAWRENCE ERLBAUM ASSOCIATES, PUBLISHERS
Mahwah, New Jersey   London

Lawrence Erlbaum Associates, Inc., Publishers
10 Industrial Avenue
Mahwah, NJ 07430

Cover design by Kathryn Houghtaling Lacey

Library of Congress Cataloging-in-Publication Data

Images of schoolteachers in America / Pamela Bolotin Joseph,
   Gail E. Burnaford, editors.—2nd ed.
        p. cm.
   Rev. ed. of: Images of schoolteachers in twentieth-century America,
c1994.
   Includes bibliographical references and index.
ISBN 0-8058-3087-1 (pbk : alk. paper)
1. Teachers—United States. 2. Teachers in literature. 3. Teachers in motion
   pictures.   4. Teaching.   I. Title: Images of schoolteachers in America.
   II. Joseph, Pamela Bolotin.   III. Burnaford, Gail E.   IV. Images of
   schoolteachers in twentieth-century America.
LB1775.2 .I52   2001
371.1'00973—dc21   00-041071
                                                              CIP

Books published by Lawrence Erlbaum Associates are printed on acid-free
paper, and their bindings are chosen for strength and durability.

Printed in the United States of America
10   9   8   7   6   5   4   3   2   1

To our students—our colleagues

Contents

Images in Textbooks, Literature, Television, and Film

Epilogue

Preface

In our lives, we have collectively known a multitude of schoolteachers. They have recited multiplication tables with us, attended class picnics with us, and shared Shakespeare with us. They have pleaded, coaxed, scolded, and cared for us as we made our way from childhood to young adulthood. If we take a moment, we can all summon images of teachers in our own experiences, most notably those who made some sort of impression on us.

Yet our images of schoolteachers stem from more than private memories. In the first place, depictions of teachers emanate from the history of schooling and the teaching profession—from the decisions made by teachers and required of them within the social-political context in which they lived and worked. In addition, representations of teachers come forth from the memories and imaginations of others throughout various media of American culture such as literature, film, and television. Also, for those of us who are teachers or want to become teachers, we have images of ourselves and the kind of teachers we believe we are. We strive to define ourselves, even though we know that images of schoolteachers—real teachers who have come before us, public images, imaginary characters, and perceived roles defined for us by society—influence how others view us and perhaps how we portray ourselves.

This book explores images of schoolteachers in America from the beginning of the 20th century to the present. We hope that it will be a valuable resource for all who have curiosity and concern about teaching and schooling. Especially, it is intended for both experienced and aspiring educators to use as a springboard for discussion and reflection about the teaching profession and for contemplating these questions: What does it mean to be a teacher? What has influenced and sustained our beliefs about teachers?

Overview

Images of Schoolteachers in America is the second edition of *Images of Schoolteachers in Twentieth-Century America: Paragons, Polarities, Complexities.* As in the first edition, this book contains a wide range of approaches to scholarship and writing. As before, many of the essays demonstrate the potency of the experiences of teaching and schooling through narratives. This edition similarly makes known human feelings, hopes, and concerns that reports and commissions cannot reveal.

The modification of the title, though, suggests some of the changes in the second edition. First, we want to consider portrayals of the teaching profession as the 21st century unfolds and do not want to limit the focus of this text to the preceding century. Also, although we continue to explore teacher images by conceiving of this book as a composition of various genres—oral history, narrative, literature, and popular culture—we place somewhat more emphasis on the social-political context that has shaped not only images of teachers but the daily experiences of teachers and the teaching profession itself. The provocative questions and implications of this research are rooted in the traditions of feminist research methods because our contributors often substantiate and emphasize the voices and interpretations of women; it is impossible to understand the teaching profession without deeply acknowledging women's experiences. The authors also draw from the critical tradition in educational inquiry to probe the issues of power and authority, race, social class, and gender in their study of teacher image and schooling.

Finally, a focus on normative characterizations of teacher images—the good, the bad, and the complex—no longer seems a cogent way to characterize this project. All schoolteacher images have elements of complexity because teachers are not just caricatures—not merely mothers, or saints, or tyrants. Rather, teachers are people and workers involved in the complex pedagogical and moral craft of teaching and trying to survive and succeed in complicated environments. The classroom presence in itself does not portray teachers' lives within their profession and their communities. It particularly does not represent the early activists who fought for teachers' entitlement to a decent livelihood, better working conditions, and academic freedom, or those who, in recent times, work for the betterment of students' lives in a more equitable society. Moreover, teachers themselves—collectively and as individuals—hold a multitude of metaphors and interpretations about what it means to be a teacher. We wish to emphasize the multidimensionality of teacher images.

In this book, several of the authors who wrote for the first edition revised their chapters in accordance with timely scholarship and their evolving knowledge and interests. We have chosen to begin this text with a chapter that is a historical overview of the teaching profession emphasizing gender, unionism, and professionalism—told through an imaginary interview with a teacher who describes her "100 years of schoolteaching." Several other new chapters have been added: portraits of progressive activist teachers; a retrospective of the satirical cartoon show, *The Simpsons*; a study of crusading and caring teachers in films; and an overview of progressive classroom practices in "the new millennium." Unfortunately, we needed to delete several fine chapters from the first edition to hold this text to a manageable length and for coherence among the essays.

This is not a neutral book offering a plethora of images presented with equanimity. Scholarship and analyses often are infused with personal response. Together, the authors take strong positions on the nature of teaching in classrooms and teachers' roles in their communities and in the greater society.

We have organized *Images of Schoolteachers in America* in four parts. The first, the prologue, chronicles the history of the teaching profession in the 20th century; it endeavors to consider teacher images amidst the historical circumstances that have influenced the profession. The second part focuses on images in oral histories and narratives from retired teachers to contemporary teachers—who describe their classrooms and schools, their relationships with students, and their work in a larger social and political sphere. In the third part, we have glimpses of teacher images held by those who are outside the classroom, drawn from diverse genres—textbooks, literature, television, and film. The fourth part, the epilogue, portrays dynamic images of today's teachers—giving hope that schoolteachers can be leaders for creative and significant classroom and school reform.

The Continuing Dialogue

In the second edition, we have excluded the "continuing dialogue" activities that previously came after each section to make the text a better "read." We hope, nonetheless, that readers will examine the complexity of teacher imagery through their own investigations and analyses. Certainly, this book could be read as a basis for further studies. We urge readers to actively pursue connections, integrate knowledge from past and present, and embark on different paths to learn more about teacher images in history and those held presently in popular culture, school, communities, and American society.

Readers may want to examine how memories and experiences in their own lives inform their images of teaching. Continuing the dialogue about teachers and their place in society warrants taking a close look at what readers think about the teachers they have met in their own lives. Our experiences in classrooms shape our views and our attitudes about learning have been at least in part influenced by teachers in and out of school buildings. That seems like a reasonable place to begin an inquiry into images of schoolteaching. As readers develop their own analyses of teacher images, we invite them to reflect on the meaning of images for themselves, to hold conversations with their colleagues, and to bring images of teachers before the public and encourage their critical examination.

Readers may also want to continue the forms of research suggested by authors who approach the study of images through qualitative methods which are, by their very nature, autobiographical, historical, and reflective. The voices of teachers are crucial to our knowledge of the teaching profession and our understanding of schooling, children, and reform. There also are elders in our communities who have stories to tell us about being schoolteachers and schoolchildren. Teachers may continue to invent and share metaphors for themselves, their roles, and their work. Readers may wish to ask students in schools to give their impressions of novels, films, and television shows that have teacher characters. Young children may share their drawings and writings about imaginary or real teachers in their lives.

Even as a text such as this is printed, it becomes "dated" as newer pieces of literature, more recent films, and innovative means of inquiry appear. Each day we encounter yet another schoolteacher metaphor—this text would never be complete if we included them all. There also are areas of study that—for lack of time, space, and expertise—we could not develop and examine in this text. Cartoons, works of visual art, poetry, Saturday morning television programming for children, and a study of teacher images across diverse populations and countries are media that deserve analysis. We suggest that readers intrigued with the popular culture surrounding teaching develop their own interpretive questions and design studies that further the dialogue about teachers' self-definitions and how they are informed by cultural contexts.

We invite readers to correspond with the editors and contributors to this text. We will, in turn, facilitate connections with others who have contacted us and who are interested in similar areas of study. The dialogue continues ....

Acknowledgments

During a faculty retreat at Lake Geneva, Wisconsin, shortly after daybreak on a cold December morning, a small group of colleagues attended a breakfast meeting to discuss writing a book about schoolteachers in America. As this core of potential authors identified colleagues who had similar interests, a book project had begun—eventually becoming the first edition of this work.

Quite a few years later, authors and editors had moved on to other universities and other parts of the country and new authors joined the project for the second edition. However, the mainstay of the initial endeavor—teacher educators passionately interested in best practice, school reform, the teaching profession, and the cultural and societal norms that influence schools and the lives of teachers—continues. We are grateful to have the opportunity to work with these wonderful friends and colleagues who have created this book with us and we thank them for their contributions.

In addition, we want to express our appreciation and affection to our editor, Naomi Silverman, who has steadfastly believed in this project and shared with us her enthusiasm and friendship. We wish to thank the reviewers, Patricia L. Anders and Patricia Cantor, who commented on the manuscript for the second edition and not only gave useful advice, but provided a wealth of information about resources to deepen our scholarship.

We also acknowledge Stephanie Bravmann (Seattle University) who gave so much of her time and hard work during the editing process. Thank you, also, to Daniel Joseph for his emergency intervention by rescuing his mother's computer and the production deadline, and to Mark Windschitl (University of Washington) for continued support and encouragement on the Seattle front.

—Pamela Bolotin Joseph
—Gail E. Burnaford

Prologue

1

One Hundred Years
of Schoolteaching:
An Invented Interview

Pamela Bolotin Joseph

I n learning about American schoolteachers in the 20th century from oral histories, historical and sociological analyses, and contemporary descriptions, I have come across many images—some familiar and others less well known to me. I read about girls, scarcely older than their pupils, keeping school in one-room schoolhouses; young women and men from immigrant and working-class families choosing teaching as a career because it offered the status of an educated profession; teachers as timid employees not only afraid to defend their own rights for fear of losing their jobs, but also reluctant to speak up for the rights of others; teachers as social activists who fought for their own freedom and livelihood, defended suffrage for women, demanded support for schools during economic crises, and fought against racism in American schools and society.

As I began writing this chapter about the history of teachers from the past to the present, I grappled with the questions: How do I portray 100 years of teaching without creating a voluminous mosaic? How do I bring in the perspectives of schoolteachers whose voices are silent in histories written by others? How do I represent the image of a teacher consonant with demographic reality and yet include the teachers who do not fit the dominant image? And finally, how do I deal with contradictions inherent in this collection of images?

At first, I began to picture various teachers at different times throughout the 20th century and considered writing portraits of several of them. But, then, I conceived of portraying a history of teachers through a literary device—the story of

3

an imaginary teacher who taught for 100 years. I began to perceive images of a woman: a young girl in a rural community needing to support herself and help her family; an independent career woman working in the city during the Jazz Age and then facing life in the Depression; a more mature teacher working in contemporary suburbia, perhaps tired from cycles of changes and top-down reform, but still loving to work with children. It did not take long for her voice to emerge, telling me her story based on historical recollections and mediated by my own knowledge and experiences as a pupil, schoolteacher, community member, teacher educator, and researcher.

"Teacher" in the following invented interview is a composite that embodies the experiences of many teachers in the 20th century in view of demographics, education, social-political attitudes, and life in classrooms. In trying to develop a somewhat representative narrative based on the history of the teaching profession and the predominant schoolteacher image, her story is told through the lens of a White female elementary teacher. I have attempted to include, to some extent, the teacher's knowledge of the experiences of others who do represent more of the diversity of the profession.

I have used many informative sources in writing this chapter. Rather than interrupting the flow of the conversation, I have not acknowledged specific citations, but have listed the major references at the end of the chapter and organized them according to topics.

§

Interviewer:	Thank you for agreeing to participate in this interview and taking time from your busy retirement to meet with me.
Teacher:	My pleasure.
Interviewer:	I am particularly glad to have the opportunity to talk with you because of your important perspective on the history of schoolteaching in 20th-century America.
Teacher:	Well, it is a shame that it has taken nearly all of that time for scholars to come to feel that way. Except for a few exceptions, it has been just in the last few years that people have taken the time to ask teachers about what schooling was like and about their lives as teachers. Had they asked us, I think that people would have some different images about teaching and teachers.
Interviewer:	Do you have an idea about why teachers' perspectives, for the most part, were ignored?
Teacher:	I think their viewpoints were fairly unimportant to historians and to the people who had power in schools and communities, first, because the majority of teachers were women and, second, because teachers (both men and women) worked with children and adolescents. I hate to say this, but I just do not think America has valued women and children very much. I believe that those social values in-

fluenced perceptions of the teaching profession over the years and the nature of scholarship.

Interviewer: It would really help me to get some understanding about how you came to your viewpoint. Could we "begin at the beginning"? I would like to get a picture of your own history as a teacher.

Teacher: That would be fine.

§

Interviewer: I want to start by asking you to tell me about why you became a schoolteacher.

Teacher: I think there were several reasons. I guess some of these reasons are "noble" and others just practical, and maybe some in-between. I grew up on a farm and was educated in a small town nearby. Although sometimes we had teachers who just drilled us in the three "Rs," a few of my own teachers were wonderful women who really cared about the students, took us outdoors for exciting nature-study projects, read to us from marvelous books, and encouraged us to love literature. I really admired those first-class ones and thought that I would feel good about my life if I similarly encouraged children. Also, as a child, I really enjoyed reading and I remember my mother and father wondering aloud about how I could be a good farmer's wife if I always had my nose in a book. I think that in due time it dawned on them and eventually on me that I might make a good teacher.

Interviewer: Do you have an opinion about why so many women entered teaching?

Teacher: It was considered an acceptable thing to do. You know, the great battle for women in the 19th century was to have a profession that would be of value. Communities began to accept the idea that women should be teachers because women would nurture children and, without a doubt, because they could be counted on to work more cheaply than men and be more easy to control as employees. So, in the 20th century, more and more young women were becoming teachers.

Interviewer: If I am understanding you correctly, it seemed natural for women to be schoolteachers?

Teacher: Keeping school and keeping house were thought to be close to one and the same. I think the female teachers really kept their roles as daughters both in helping their families and in being obedient to their supervisors or to the community. They also began their role as mothers by taking care of children and the schoolhouse. But, in a nice way, schools seemed like families; often I felt like a sister to the other teachers and the more experienced teachers became the big sisters and the new ones the little sisters, and so forth.

§

Interviewer: Did your parents have expectations that you would get married or did they encourage you primarily to become a teacher?

Teacher: It was not one thing or the other. I think my mother felt that her life was hard and that I would increase my opportunities for a better life and social position if I worked for awhile as a schoolteacher. Many of the women who taught eventually did marry, but in the meantime, they brought in money to the family and developed reputations of being respectable, energetic, and bright. Of course, we were not allowed to keep teaching if we did get married. It did not dawn on me at the time to challenge that rule. Maybe I would have been more inclined to confront the school board if I met someone who I really wanted to marry at that time.

Interviewer: Based on what you said about being controllable employees, do you think that the women who became teachers were particularly docile individuals?

Teacher: That's an image that certainly is open to debate. You know, we all felt a lot of pressure to be ladylike, and that meant not showing anger or making challenges. I suppose that in the first decades of the century—especially before suffrage was achieved and the 1920s brought more social independence for women (such as being able to drive cars and get a little more freedom)—there weren't a lot of rebels. A few exceptional women left the rural and small town communities and went off to the city to seek different types of employment such as journalism or theater, but that was very unusual and certainly not "respectable." At any rate, women who were perceived as rebels probably would not have been hired even if they wanted to be teachers, no matter how intelligent they might have been.

Interviewer: Would you say that teachers were respected?

Teacher: Well, I think there is a difference between respectable and respected. By respectable I mean that we were in an occupation that was fitting and proper for women, especially as long as teaching did not become a real career that we chose instead of being wives or mothers. As for respected, if you mean were we respected as the banker or the school board member or a lawyer? Definitely not. We did not really have money or power, except perhaps over children. I am not saying that parents did not appreciate us, but at that time, we were never given authority in the community.

Interviewer: What about the men who taught, were they respected or respectable?

Teacher: I think a better description would be that they were "suspect." By working with children and even adolescents, the public impression was that they were not "real men" or that they were clearly doing schoolteaching until something better opened up for them. Unfortunately, male teachers today suffer such stereotypes. Still, there is some truth to the notion that teaching was a stepping stone for men. For example, male teachers in elementary schools often became administrators. Yet teachers reserved judgment about respecting them. Oh, we would act deferential, but in truth, those administrators would have to earn our respect by really knowing what went on in classrooms and by giving constructive evaluations, not just useless or unwarranted negative comments.

§

Interviewer: So you decided to become a career teacher. How did that happen?

Teacher: For many years I loved teaching and was content to be a teacher. Despite the fact that our little school had very few resources and I wound up doing so many chores that I guess today we would consider "janitorial," I do think that in those ungraded rural schools teachers often had a lot of room to be creative. The creativity and independence was the best part of my work. I had many positive reasons for staying in that community and continuing to be a teacher, but in a small town I also felt constricted by the image of being a schoolteacher

Interviewer: So, you eventually left the small town?

Teacher: Yes, I was attracted to the idea of working in an urban community because salaries were much better and I just was ready to move on to something more interesting. The idea of living in a city and going to concerts and museums and meeting new people drew me there. Nevertheless, to a great extent, I left because I became unhappy with my image as a "schoolmarm." I think the community thought about me differently when I became more of a career teacher.

Interviewer: Can you tell me about how the community's attitude became different?

Teacher: In the beginning, I was just one of the girls who kept school, but had a social life that intermingled with the other young people in town. However, as the other young women left teaching to become wives and mothers, I was not invited to be a part of their social worlds. I always had a sense that people thought there was something wrong with me because I preferred to remain single and teach. It was somewhat different for the men who taught at the high school because they were allowed to be married and integrated more into the community, but they never were considered eminent, as would men from other professions. And definitely, both men and women teachers had to operate under certain social constraints.

Interviewer: Please tell me about these constraints.

Teacher: All the time that I taught in the small town, there was a lot of pressure on teachers to be more "virtuous" than most other people. Sometimes the pressure was overt, taking the form of rules issued by the school board or the checklists used by administrators to evaluate us, but also you just knew what lines you could not cross. For example, schoolteachers' jobs would be in jeopardy if they were seen having a cocktail or going dancing or, of a more serious nature, getting involved in politics or teachers' unions. It's not that I had anything against being a good role model for students. I believed in that. It is just that it got to the point that I wanted to feel like an independent adult. I wanted to leave because I felt that I had no freedom. Career teachers who remained longer in small towns probably stayed because of their family obligations. When my brothers and sisters became adults, I didn't feel that my parents needed me as much any more.

§

Interviewer: So, what was it like to teach in the city?

Teacher: It was as good as I had hoped in some ways and, in other ways, there were some unpleasant surprises.

Interviewer: What did you like about teaching in the city?

Teacher: Many things. First, the pay was much better than in the small town. And there were more teachers and a bigger population, so I did not experience that "fish bowl" environment anywhere as much as living in the small town—although I surely didn't have a situation of perfect freedom. For example, I was not able to sign a lease for an apartment until my brother showed up to sign on my behalf. But I loved having quite a bit of independence. I had some grand times traveling with my teacher friends during summer vacations. I also took advantage of educational opportunities available in the colleges and universities in the city. I met teachers who had a great deal of pride in their profession because they came from immigrant backgrounds and their families felt that becoming a teacher was a wonderful thing. Of course, that applied more to the women than the men who had so many more career options. And, although there were children who did not have much use for school, I taught many children that were immigrants or second generation who just seemed to worship us teachers. So many families believed that the future depended on education and I was considered a heroine to them. And I loved to teach these children about America, its traditions, and its possibilities.

Interviewer: And what didn't you like in the urban school?

Teacher:	Most of all, it was so difficult to have such large class sizes. When I first began teaching in the city in the early 1920s, there could be as many as 50 children in my room. So, although the city had such interesting places to see—architecture, museums, and factories—it was very difficult to enjoy what the community had to offer when I had to deal with so many students.
Interviewer:	How did the administration affect you?
Teacher:	The bureaucracy of the school was very frustrating. There were so many men making decisions about what and how I should teach who were in the central office.
Interviewer:	Were there female administrators when you taught in the city?
Teacher:	Only a few elementary principals, but no principals of high schools or women in the central office except in clerical roles. I saw more female administrators in the rural areas before I left—many were county supervisors—but in the first two decades of the 20th century, there were quite a few woman administrators in urban systems including a female superintendent of schools, Ella Flagg Young, in Chicago. But, by the 1920s, schools became under the rule of a centralized administration and men seemed to lock in their power. Before I came to the city, I was really influenced by stories I read about Grace Strachan from New York City and Margaret Healy from Chicago who fought for female teachers' rights and equal pay. These women were strong role models. And there was such hope that as women had the vote, they would become partners in democracy and democratic institutions.
Interviewer:	What did teachers think of the male centralized bureaucratic system?
Teacher:	Most teachers hated this turn of events. For one thing, as administrators kept expanding their power, teachers were increasingly presumed to be workers in the factory and not considered as educated professionals. And, for another, those administrators' salaries must have drained quite a few resources from the school system, taking money away from resources for children and teachers' pay. But what I remember most during that period was the strong anti-women sentiment in just about everything. There were caricatures of the old maid schoolteachers that were incredibly obnoxious. Furthermore, I read editorials in newspapers and magazine articles about how female teachers harmed the upbringing of boys.
Interviewer:	Such opinions must have been hurtful to you personally. Did the male-dominated administration affect your classroom?
Teacher:	There were some exceptions, but often I thought that all the administrators cared about was efficiency and standardization. They wanted schools to be like well-run machines. If the children were

quiet, the room was orderly, the teacher looked acceptable and had a presence before the children, and we didn't use up too many supplies, they seemed to be content. It became particularly difficult when orders were given to teachers in the same grade to more or less be on the same page of the textbook at the same time, no matter what the children were interested in or how they were doing.

Interviewer: Did you feel that you always had to conform to the administrators' rules?

Teacher: Yes and no. The other teachers and I usually shaped the classroom as we saw fit and incorporated other than the "sanctioned" methods when we could. Naturally, in both rural and urban schools, a teacher's repertoire would depend a great deal upon her education, her exposure to more progressive methods, and sometimes just to her intuition about children and learning.

Interviewer: What kind of education did you get to prepare for teaching?

Teacher: Well, that is a long story. At the turn of the century, rural areas did not have many high schools and so when I finished eighth grade, I enrolled in a summer institute for teacher training. However, that was one tough summer. I was expected to know so much in 8 weeks—about how children learn, different subjects to teach, and methods of teaching. At the end, the state required an examination in content areas and pedagogy that was quite rigorous. I never felt comfortable just having such a brief education, especially as many more young people were getting a high school education. I kept studying in the summers and eventually finished the equivalent of high school. Later I enrolled in a 2-year normal school and was exposed to more modern methods of education. Later in life, I finished college at a liberal arts college and now have my master's degree. You know, educational expectations for teachers changed throughout the century. Now where my education wound up is considered the place to start!

Interviewer: Did the school district help pay for your education?

Teacher: I always had to pay for my own professional advancement.

§

Interviewer: Were there social constraints upon teachers when you moved to the city?

Teacher: Well, you still had to appear as an upstanding member of the community, but no one expected you to teach Sunday school or, for that matter, paid attention to whether or not you attended church. The city in which I worked still had the no-teach rule for married women. Some cities had the rule and others did not. I believe that the variance can be explained mainly by economics; if teachers were really in short supply, the rule was disregarded. However, in New

York, the teachers union was tenacious in opposing the rule and married women were allowed to teach there.

Interviewer: But that rule didn't affect you?

Teacher: On the contrary, it affected my life profoundly. The first year that I arrived, I met a wonderful man who taught at a high school in another neighborhood. We became great friends and eventually wanted to be partners in life. As a man, he was free to marry, whereas as a woman, I was not. Several years later, we were secretly married with just a few friends and family attending, and those friends—many of them teachers—knew that our future would depend on their secrecy. We found a neighborhood to live in that was not close to either of our schools. We both had a long commute and, in the winter, I really hated it, but I didn't dare think of moving closer to my school. But the worst was feeling like I was involved in a conspiracy. Imagine, having to hide your marriage! We did not have children, but other women in my position who became pregnant hid their pregnancies until they no longer could and then had to quit or were fired. It was not until the district had a major teaching shortage with the war effort in World War II that the rule was abolished. We had to live this weird, secretive life for many years. The no-marriage rule was just so socially accepted. Then there was the popular image of the teacher practically as a saint; she should deny herself and live just for her students.

Interviewer: I was under the impression that especially in the 1930s it was considered a terrible thing to have two incomes in one family when so many people were suffering because of the economic depression.

Teacher: This was a hard time for us despite our incomes, which were very, very low in the Depression. I was trying to help my family survive by giving them money to keep their farm, and my husband had relatives totally dependent on him. We kept hoping that the federal government would step in and give some support to school systems, but that never happened.

Interviewer: What about political constraints?

Teacher: What do you mean?

Interviewer: Did you feel free to express your ideas about politics or economic issues, for example?

Teacher: Well, I never considered myself a very political person. For the most part, I really supported many of the values that I think we were supposed to be teaching in school—such as respect for each other and the belief in America as a wonderful country. But I have to tell you that those loyalty oaths were galling.

Interviewer: What loyalty oaths are you talking about?

Teacher: There were loyalty oaths required of teachers during many periods of time in the 20th century—World War I, the Red Scare of the 1920s, the Depression and fear of social upheaval, and World War

II. It was so demoralizing. Imagine anyone thinking that I could be disloyal to my country! In more recent times, the Cold War hysteria and Senator McCarthy's witch hunt to find communists swayed many districts to make teachers take loyalty oaths. What an insult to people who had taught with great devotion all their careers. Some of the people who had served their countries in the war were forced to do so, too!

Interviewer: What were the effects of these loyalty oaths?

Teacher: I think that the people insisting on them, often from very conservative political groups, really wanted to keep teachers intimidated. The teachers who wanted to teach critical thinking, for example, to offer information about different social and economic systems—even when the teachers weren't particularly interested in swaying students with radical ideas—were afraid to offer challenging curriculum. But there also were teachers who lost their jobs, especially those who wanted to band together to fight such coercive practices. Then, there were other awful things that happened to some of my colleagues.

Interviewer: What sorts of things?

Teacher: Mainly unfair practices and discrimination. For instance, I had a friend who was beloved by her students and their families. I really think that the principal at the time felt threatened by her popularity. In fact, he was afraid that if he "got on her case" the community would go against him. He made a request to have her transferred to another school and that meant that she had to leave her neighborhood and family, and find other housing or have a very long commute. Her students' families protested, but since this was a poor immigrant neighborhood without a lot of political clout in the district, she couldn't come back.

Interviewer: Do you have other examples?

Teacher: I cannot remember specifics, but I remember that there was always favoritism or prejudice. I may have been from a poor farming family, but I was a Protestant and the same ethnicity as most of the administrators. The Catholic and Jewish teachers seemed to be hired only as substitutes or got the hardest assignments. Or they were treated with open hostility by some administrators. But schools are just like the greater society. There were virulent anti-Catholic sentiment, anti-Semitism, and racism throughout those decades. I never even met Asian American or Latino teachers when I worked in the city. I never worked with the African American teachers in my school, although they certainly worked in the district. I heard stories, however, that the administration mainly hired them as substitutes so that many never did get tenure.

Interviewer: Didn't anybody speak out about the treatment of these colleagues?

Teacher: I think that the reaction of those of us who did not face discrimination was "that was really a shame" and we didn't like it. It just did not occur to us that we could disturb the social order.

§

Interviewer: What can you tell me about African American teachers? Do you think their experiences were similar to yours?

Teacher: We all were teachers and believed that we were doing important things with our lives and for students, but there were some profound differences. First of all, throughout the majority of the 20th century, African American teachers were only allowed to teach Black children. Schools were segregated in both the North and the South—one region through custom and the other through law. A Black teacher did not have the same freedom as I had to move into any city and get a job where she would like to teach. Although schools in the northern cities sometimes were integrated, only White teachers were hired to teach in them. In addition, in many places, urban and rural, there were dual pay schedules. Districts would pay African American teachers less. Later on, during the days of school integration, there were devastating effects on the African American teachers—30,000 teachers lost their jobs in the southern and border states. Think about all the role models for Black youngsters that were swept out of school systems.

Interviewer: Were African American teachers respected in the communities in which they taught?

Teacher: I think that they were given more respect from parents in their schools than I ever had, except sometimes from immigrant families. I believe that this respect was richly deserved. So many African American teachers took it upon themselves to ensure the future of their students through the power of literacy and trying to "uplift" their race. The Black teachers had high expectations for their children and they worked closely with parents and their communities. Nevertheless, they had to do their work under the most terrible circumstances—with no resources for schoolhouses, books, and all the other things that make schools function. I remember hearing how only when a White school was about to throw away their worn-out textbooks did a Black school get these "new" books.

Interviewer: How did African American teachers feel about working in segregated schools with lower pay?

Teacher: You are talking about two different issues. Many Black teachers worried—and rightfully so—that integrated schools would mean the end of their careers, as well as putting their children in the hands of a White-dominated school where the teachers would not have the same ambitions for Black children to succeed. Furthermore, African American teachers were concerned that White teachers could not teach their children racial pride. The second issue—unequal pay—was a major focus of African American teachers' associations. Under the leadership of Thurgood Marshall in the 1930s, many of the districts' practices were challenged successfully in court. However, as of the late 1940s there still were pay differentials in southern cities—it went on even longer in rural areas. But you have to remember how risky it was to fight unfair practices for Black teachers when their jobs would be in jeopardy. And, although militant White teachers could lose their jobs, it was downright dangerous for Black teachers to be militant because they could also meet with violence.

§

Interviewer:	What was your experience with teachers unions?
Teacher:	When I worked in the city, our teachers' association was a local of the NEA, the National Education Association.
Interviewer:	Did you belong to it?
Teacher:	I became a member soon after I began teaching in the city.
Interviewer:	Why did you join?
Teacher:	I had admired the women in the early 20th century who were leaders in the union movement and I think I was naturally sympathetic toward the idea of union membership because my roots were from working people and not the business class.
Interviewer:	How did you find out about the union? Did someone recruit you?
Teacher:	It was a funny thing. The principal of my school actually signed me up. He was on a campaign to enroll all the teachers in his building into the association. At that time, all the NEA leadership—those who really had some power to influence things—were male and were mostly principals, superintendents, high school teachers, and some education professors. I was told that joining the association was a professional thing to do.
Interviewer:	Wasn't being in a teachers association more like being in a union for workers than a group of professionals?
Teacher:	Absolutely not. We were encouraged to think of ourselves as an association of professionals. We never were allowed think of ourselves as workers, despite a school organization that certainly had its managers. In several other cities, the AFT (the American Federation of Teachers) represented teachers in a different way. That group was adamant that teachers were workers and sought out alliances with labor organizations. During the most anti-labor times in this country, teachers often were either afraid to join the AFT or were

actually unsympathetic to it. That tension between being a worker and being a professional was always an issue for teachers.

§

Interviewer: I would like to know more about the teacher association you belonged to at the time.

Teacher: The teaching association in my city was not exactly militant. Yet it did bring me a little more peace of mind as to job security in specific instances, such as if a principal or superintendent just wanted to give my job away to a relative. You knew there were people looking out for you if you came up against some unfair situations. Overall though, the association usually was interested in "the bread and butter issues" such as salary, job security, and pensions.

Interviewer: Did the association fight the no-marriage rule or against loyalty oaths?

Teacher: It did not take a strong stand on those issues. Remember that the leadership was male, so it was not interested in supporting women's causes. It also was not very political or militant. If a teacher lost her job and it was because of religious discrimination, the association did not protest. When a teacher received a poor evaluation because she really wanted to teach about democracy and had her students vote about controversial current-event issues in class, it did nothing to protect her. To its credit, the association did bring up time and time again the importance of having a safe and habitable environment for the children and the importance of smaller class sizes, not just for the sake of teachers, but for the students' benefit as well.

Interviewer: Did your association protect African American teachers?

Teacher: Not really. The association didn't say boo as African American teachers were routinely assigned only to schools where only Black children attended and never to the White schools. Add to that the fact that for many years, the association just encouraged membership of White teachers and the African American teachers had their own association affiliated with state's Association of Teachers of Colored Children. You have to remember that it was not until way into the civil rights movement that the NEA spoke out against dual locals, separate unions for Black and for White teachers. The history of the NEA contrasted quite a bit with that of the AFT whose leaders were more likely to tackle social issues such as racism. The NEA leadership did what they could to portray the AFT as "gadfly" union way outside the mainstream.

Interviewer: Was there antagonism to unionism, that is, affiliation with labor unions during the decades that you taught in the city?

Teacher: Unionism, the way you are describing it, was never welcomed. Moreover, there were times that anything that resembled worker coalitions and teacher activism was dealt with in drastic ways and other times that were a little more conducive. In the 1920s, business had such a big influence in American culture and on schools that the idea of teachers unions smacked of Bolshevism. In the 1930s, most teachers were too scared to do anything to jeopardize their jobs because having a job was just so much a blessing. The decade of the 1940s was a better time for teachers to get a little more power because for the first half of the decade, there were many more jobs—people were either at war or working for war-related industries. There seemed to be more-varied occupational opportunities for women then, too. Quite a few of the men who came back from the service went to school on the G. I. bill and became teachers, and they were more assertive about dealing with administrators and school boards. But, then, the 1950s were very difficult. In some of the big cities, teachers who had been interested in communism when they were young (before they were disillusioned by totalitarianism) or those who admired socialism were "devoured" and lost their jobs and pensions without recourse.

§

Interviewer: I'm interested in knowing more about professionalism. What was your sense of the importance of teachers being considered as professionals?

Teacher: I think the issue is complicated. Certainly, many of us viewed our social position as being higher than that of working-class people. We thought we did better than our friends and relatives who stayed on farms or worked in factories. Despite the fact that many administrators wanted to "manage" us, we really were very uncomfortable with the idea that teaching is technical. It just seemed like nonsense to me to equate the teaching profession with the medical profession—which was often how the discussion about this issue was phrased. I mean, there were many ways to teach a child—so many possible choices in curriculum and methods, but just how many ways are there to take out a gall bladder?

Interviewer: How did you picture your role as a teacher?

Teacher: Teaching just always struck me more as a craft than as an exact science. I remember several discussions my teacher friends had about whether a teacher was an artist or a scientist. The artist-teacher would draw upon her creativity and artistry and the scientist-teacher would continue to experiment to understand children and find the best ways to teach them. And the classroom is just a community brimming with energy and different interests. A teacher's craft means fluidity, intuition, and a wealth of experience. Then, too, teachers generally have had a moral calling to help children learn and perhaps to help children to grow up to be better people. That certainly made us different from those entering most professions.

§

Interviewer: There have been some awful images of teachers. What do you think about the depictions of teachers as heartless disciplinarians and classrooms as stifling places where only rote learning takes place?

Teacher: I cannot deny that there were many terrible classrooms, but also there were some excellent ones. The worst situations generally were brought about by the lack of resources and extreme overcrowding. Classrooms could really be a nightmare to children that today we say have special needs. So often, the "sink or swim" rule applied, especially for immigrant children who could not speak English. Children, particularly the older ones who didn't learn language as easily as the little ones, had miserable experiences because the teacher had too many students on her hands to give them enough help and often they just dropped out of school. Then you have the legacy of order and uniformity so that all the seats and desks were bolted to the floor—it's hard to imagine a dynamic classroom in that environment. In addition, there never was enough encouragement for new teachers to get out of the "drill and control" routine. Finally, I can think of some bad situations when schoolteachers who were not happy teaching, but had very few other career options, continued to work but were, as they say in more modern times, "burned-out."

Interviewer: Tell me about the wonderful classrooms.

Teacher: Well, those could happen almost anywhere when a teacher was really gifted and devoted to her students and scholarship. There have always been a scattering of wonderful classrooms where teachers capture the excitement I experienced as a child going outdoors for nature study. Some teachers really encouraged children to explore their communities, do science experiments, and even to create really useful and beautiful things—such as planting and caring for gardens around their schools. Some teachers, through teacher training or because they sought out professional development, had been exposed to progressive methods, such as the project method, rather than following a rigid curricular content. Even some of the urban districts developed progressive schools that were much more like private schools.

Interviewer: It sounds as if the reforms in teaching have been some of the same ones throughout the century.

Teacher: That's for sure. The old ways in most public schools always consisted of rote and isolated learning, memorization, and coercion.

The new ways emphasize reasoning, discovery, cooperation, and learning as intrinsically valuable. There seems to be a never-ending cycle as teachers and the public rediscover the "new" ways.

Interviewer: What is your response to the notion that the main duty of the urban teacher was to Americanize their students, even if that meant disregarding students' own cultures?

Teacher: Early in the century, Jane Addams took teachers to task for turning immigrant children against their parents and the wisdom of their cultures. I think that her criticism for the most part was accurate and we often encouraged immigrant children and the first generation to reject too much of their cultures. I believe that many teachers felt that Americanization was what parents wanted for their children and would lead to successful entry into society. Still, there were exceptions. Some teachers asked children to bring in examples of their cultures and encouraged parents to come to school and help teach about traditions. I have heard about White teachers in Harlem who developed curriculum units to teach African American history and teachers who went west to teach in Bureau of Indian Affairs schools who encouraged the Native American children to learn their language and history. However, for the most part, White teachers were not sensitive to diversity in very meaningful ways. We still have not examined how our "Whiteness" has affected the children we teach.

§

Interviewer: But you didn't stay in the city for your whole career.

Teacher: I took a job in a suburban system in the 1960s.

Interviewer: Why did you make this change?

Teacher: There were various factors that influenced my decision—"push and pull" circumstances.

Interviewer: What pushed you out?

Teacher: I left my position in the city because of my feelings of frustration and the increasing sense I had of disillusionment. My colleagues, the parents, and the even the children did not have faith any longer that schools could be the hope for the future. There were just too many years of neglect of city schools and I felt that all of us, especially the children, were paying the price of the negligence. School buildings were getting even more dilapidated, class sizes were still extremely high, and the children—who were facing such difficulties because of increasing poverty—could have used more attention from the teacher, not less. Parents and community leaders were demanding better schooling for the children, and rightly so. But the confrontations between the school board and the community were very angry and sometimes the issues seemed more political than educational.

Interviewer: Do you think that race, ethnicity, and social class were factors in those confrontations?

Teacher: Let me just say that school integration should have been an opportunity for people to come together and make the schools better, but instead, many of the better-off White parents moved to the suburbs or enrolled their children in private schools. The parents who remained and other community members recognized the racism and were very frustrated because children were receiving even fewer resources than before. To make matters worse, I think we were affected by the popular image of schools as "blackboard jungles" in which chaos reigned. I believe that image only hurt the schools more by doing an injustice to children and teachers and made the powers that be—in local communities and on the state level—even less willing to provide resources. It was demoralizing. Fortunately, there were teachers who did stay in the city systems and tried to rise to the challenges, and there were new teachers who came in who also cared a great deal about the urban schools and the children. And yet, often the teachers who were the most altruistic left the profession because they felt the most frustration because they couldn't measure up to their ideals.

Interviewer: How did you feel about the "White flight"?

Teacher: I always thought that racism was more of a southern phenomenon, yet that clearly was not the case. It was very unsettling to have my assumptions confronted. We always taught that the American dream could be realized by all our children through education, but the racism and poverty around us made such sentiments seem hypocritical.

Interviewer: What pulled you toward the suburbs?

Teacher: First, there was opportunity. The combination of the baby boom and the great push to the suburbs created many new jobs. And I perceived the suburbs as having new schools, smaller class sizes, better resources, and less bureaucracy. In the 1960s and 1970s, ideas about open classrooms and interesting curriculum projects were prevalent and the districts that had more money often tried out the new curricula and strategies. I had worked for so many years in the city system and felt that it would be wonderful to work with more resources and with fewer uphill battles. But I have to admit that I just didn't have the heart anymore for the confrontations continually taking place in an urban district and all the politics. I also questioned my effectiveness as a White educator as the city became more diverse.

§

Interviewer: So, you finished you career in the suburbs. I would like to know about your experiences teaching there. Were your suburban classrooms when you began your work there in the early 1960s greatly different from the city classrooms?

Teacher: There were some differences. In those early years, the school population was pretty homogeneous—White and middle class. And there were far more resources and community support. Although many city parents cared about their children's education, in the suburbs the teachers were scrutinized if we didn't provide the kind of education that would lead to prestigious colleges. Those parents were often more educated than the parents in the city neighborhood where I taught. The suburban moms and dads challenged teachers more about curriculum or assessment. Naturally, the parents who were the most insistent seemed to have the most influence. You know, "the squeaky wheel ...."

Interviewer: What stayed the same?

Teacher: Male administrators, male union leaders, and male school boards. We had just gone through a very conservative decade, the 1950s, and the repercussions of the barriers that kept women from taking leadership roles in schools and society were with still us. There were very few leadership models for female teachers and little encouragement to change this situation. Not until the 1980s did we see a real entry for women into administration or leadership in the community.

Interviewer: What about the conditions in the school?

Teacher: The population growth in some of the suburbs was so tremendous that class sizes were just as high as in the city in times of population booms. There were years that I had an enormous number of pupils. But, then, most of the time the suburbs had resources from property taxes to build more schools and enough land for building additions and for a quick fix, mobile classrooms. It has mainly been in the last few years that we have seen tax revolts that have threatened the resources of these schools.

Interviewer: During the time that you taught in the suburbs, did the school population stay the same in terms of ethnicity and social class?

Teacher: In the last few decades before I retired, the student population became increasingly diverse. There were students who had immigrated to America from all around the world—Russia, the Middle East, Mexico, India, and Taiwan. In addition, African Americans moved from the cities to give their children a better education. Some suburbs continued to have predominantly middle- and upper-middle-class families living there, but as industry moved to some suburbs and apartments were built, there were also families who moved to the suburbs who were not as well off.

§

Interviewer: What about the demographics of the teacher population?

Teacher: The majority of the teachers continued to be women, although there were more men in the higher grades and in the last decade or so, most elementary schools had quite a few male teachers. The racial composition of the teaching profession did not change much, except that there was a steady decrease in teachers of color. The suburbs never did have much of a tradition of minority hiring. I did notice that many more teachers were coming from middle-class backgrounds themselves, not just entering the profession as a way for social mobility, like those of us whose families were more working class earlier in the century. Many of the teachers lived in the suburbs and were married to businessmen and other professionals, so their status was also derived through marriage. Our social status in the suburbs seemed different from what I experienced in the city or earlier in the small town; quite a few parents were very successful and educated, and we teachers occasionally were looked down upon. I did enjoy how much the parents who came from other cultures respected teachers—that was nice for a change.

Interviewer: I would like to return to the subject of teacher unionism especially in the last several decades of the century. Did teachers' opinions of unions change?

Teacher: Unions continually gained acceptance throughout the century. Collective bargaining became more acceptable and then routine. The NEA went from being horrified at the idea of teachers striking to eventually accepting the fact that teachers would have to take a stand to protect their own interests. However, that development went hand in hand with teachers taking control of the NEA from administrators. In fact, in the last few years, the NEA and AFT have come very close to merging. I really think that many teachers today take unions for granted.

Interviewer: How do you see the effect of taking unions for granted?

Teacher: For one thing, some teachers just assume that they are getting a good deal on salaries when, in actuality, the teaching profession has lost a lot of economic ground at different times. When there weren't teacher shortages, school boards just hired the most inexperienced teachers to bring down salaries. And teachers' lukewarm support of unions allowed the profession to fall behind when the cost of living greatly escalated. I also think that, for the most part, teachers want their unions to be pragmatic but not ideological; they don't want unions to champion political and social causes, such as confronting inequity in school funding and resources—especially when that means taking resources from your own pot and giving them to less well-off districts, defending the security of teachers who are sexual minorities, or taking on controversial cases relating to academic freedom.

Interviewer: There have not been many public images of activist teachers.

Teacher: We ought to give serious thought to why there are not more public images of teachers as intellectuals, as creative forces, or as activists who work with others to bring about serious changes in schools and society. And it's too bad that children do not have images of teachers as defenders of justice and equality.

Interviewer: And you said you weren't political?

Teacher: Well, all and all, I have become more political. Maybe that's the wisdom of experience. Or thinking this way is a luxury I now enjoy because I'm not busy all the time with children's problems, lesson plans, assessment, and meetings.

§

Interviewer: What were classrooms like in the suburbs?

Teacher: Not always very different than they were in small towns or cities earlier in my career. For many years, the textbook was the primary method of instruction, although in the suburbs there was more of a chance for the textbooks to be up-to-date and we would have enough for each child. Later, many teachers stopped using textbooks as their main instructional tool, but relied heavily on work sheets. Teachers sometimes created their own topics for curricular content, and so children studied fish, or Japan, or some such thing, but seldom was there really collaborative development of a scope and sequence of the curriculum. In the past few years, efforts to make curriculum more uniform came about because of school reforms that emphasized state and national student assessment.

Interviewer: Didn't you get the support in the suburbs to work with innovative curriculum, and didn't you have better resources?

Teacher: I found that support for innovation was "a mixed bag." Sometimes the administration gave us directives to teach in new ways and provided some in-services and planning time for us to learn new ways—but usually not enough. Then, often in a few years, something else was "hot" and the old "new" methods were discarded. I think that teachers became cynical, especially because they seldom were the initiators of change, but had to go along with pressures for change. But that's not the whole picture about teachers' professional growth because throughout the century we also

Teacher: learned so much about best practice and innovation from other educators outside of our schools.

Interviewer: What do you mean by educators outside of your schools?

Teacher: Quite a few of us took advantage of numerous educational organizations. You could go to conferences and get ideas for innovation and support from, for example, The International Reading Association, the Middle School Association, and The National Councils for Teachers of English (or Social Studies, Science, etc.). Through affiliations with those and other groups, teachers have advocated for more professional autonomy and more practitioner influence in the management of schools, higher standards, and professionalism, and the strengthening of credential requirements. There were groups that were particularly influential in helping teachers to become innovators and agents of change. Earlier in my career, the Progressive Education Association gave me some wonderful ideas, and I have really appreciated the publications and ideas coming from newer teacher networks, such as the Rethinking Schools. If teachers took a little initiative, they could always find support for improving practice and changing schools.

§

Interviewer: How did recent school-reform movements in the last two decades of the century affect you?

Teacher: For the most part, they were just examples of top-down change. In the last part of the century, empowerment became a popular word that we used when we talked about students becoming more in charge of their own learning. We teachers surely did not feel empowered when that report in the 1980s, *A Nation at Risk,* said that we were all doing a mediocre job and that schools are so bad that you would think that an enemy conquered the United States and put in these terrible schools. In the 1990s, *Goals 2000* and state reform movements stemming from this national legislation began to influence teaching tremendously. We all felt the pressure to teach to the various tests that were being created in all subject areas.

Interviewer: Did you think the latest reform in the century that emphasized learning outcomes was a bad thing for children and teachers?

Teacher: The jury is still out, but my impression of the good parts of the reform is that teachers often were encouraged to have a great deal of dialogue with each other and administrators about what they were teaching and why. I know that many professional organizations see these reforms as a way of doing significant curriculum alignment, so that, for example, children are not just learning about fish one year without any apparent connection to anything else that they are learning. And I believe that people in these organizations see the possibilities of teaching becoming more of a profession with a special knowledge base. Personally, I think that the opportunity to ask hard questions and to be reflective was a marvelous result. The implication that all children must know the same thing and at the same time and that all teachers must teach the same way, though, reminds me of what I told you about attempts at professionalism earlier in the century. Required conformity is always stifling to teacher and child. I also wonder what would have happened if each school district gave teachers the opportunity—time and education—to be leaders for reform and not followers?

Interviewer: Are there any changes in teaching that make you feel hopeful about the role of teachers and schooling?

Teacher: Well, in some ways "everything old is new again"—that is, many of the exciting classrooms in recent years would have been similar to excellent classrooms very early in the century. As for me, I am happy to see classrooms as learning communities. My goal is for teachers to see their students as fellow learners and really to value their ideas and insights. Such teachers have to be very knowledgeable and flexible, so they can guide students toward more educative experiences. It's also very exciting when teachers collaborate with their colleagues to pool their expertise, try out team-teaching with integrated curriculum, and share their knowledge about resources in their communities. Most of all, I want all of us—children and teachers—to know the joy in learning.

§

Interviewer: What thoughts would you like to share about teachers and teaching as we begin the next century?

Teacher: First, that I loved being a teacher, enjoyed the children, took great pleasure in sparking enthusiasm about learning, and loved being in a school community where I didn't have to go to work each day feeling as though I was in competition with my colleagues but rather we were all in the educational endeavor together. I have a great deal of pride in my 100 years of service.

Interviewer: During all your years of teaching, what do you most wish could have been different?

Teacher: What I would have changed is the attitudes about schoolteachers. I despised how noneducators patronized me when I met them in social situations. Earlier in my career I would hear, "How nice; that's a good job for a women"; or people would say, "Lucky you; you don't have to work in the summer"; or more lately I have heard, "I don't know how you do it." Even worse is having our image represented by those negatively foolish caricatures of teachers in cartoons, commercials, and movies.

Interviewer: So, you think that the public has some preconceived notions of who you were because you were a schoolteacher?

Teacher: Yes, and those notions never addressed who I really was as a professional. Furthermore, I think that this country ought to be giving attention to the public image of schoolteachers and the status of the teaching profession. I truly believe that teaching still appears merely "respectable," but is not seen as a profession that grants respect and power. I am less concerned about the images in popular culture because I think they just pander to adolescent sensibility to be profitable. Those caricatures are not reason enough to answer the question why many young people and, in particular those who are not middle-class White females, do not see themselves as teachers.

Interviewer: What would you say to people to attract them to teaching?

Teacher: What can we say to them? Yes, it's a wonderful thing to help children learn and teaching has such great intrinsic rewards such as intellectual satisfaction and altruism. And we can say that the teaching profession is working hard to make itself more like other professions, undoubtedly not only to improve teaching, but to counter the common perception that "anyone can teach." But shouldn't we also tell them that education has been a low priority in this country and therefore if you become a teacher, in all likelihood, you will contend with many of the same obstacles that teachers faced throughout the 20th century? That teachers have some control, but less and less all the time, over what and how they will teach? That schools with great resources and that encourage teachers' creativity and empowerment are remarkably unusual?

Interviewer: So, from your perspective of 100 years of schoolteaching, do you interpret this as a century of a progress for the teaching profession?

Teacher: I see cycles of progression and regression throughout the century. It's disquieting to realize that there were activists at the turn of the century who understood and spoke out about the conditions of teaching that disempower teachers as well as children and those who imagined the exciting democratic possibilities of classrooms and schools. And at the end of the century there were the "experts" who offered solutions for schools that would, in effect, turn teachers into robots using a standardized curriculum and paying little attention to students' curiosity or what happens to the children who fail the tests.

Interviewer: Well, you have given me a great deal to think about. I want to thank you for the time you have given me for this interview. Perhaps you would like to end this interview with a concluding thought?

Teacher: Yes, I would. I just want to say that if history tells us anything, teach-
                  ers in the 21st century must know that they cannot rely on school
                  systems or society to ensure their status, freedom, creativity, and the
                  condition of work. To a great measure, the future is in their own
                  hands.

REFERENCES

Teacher Demographics

Archer, J. (1997, July 9). NEA's portrait of a public school teacher: White, female, aging. *Education Week on the Web.*
Meek, A. (1998). America's teachers: Much to celebrate. *Educational Leadership, 55,* 12–16.
Rury, J. L. (1989). Who became teachers?: The social characteristics of teachers in American history. In D. Warren (Ed.), *American teachers: Histories of a profession at work* (pp. 9–48). New York: Macmillan.

Teacher Images

Cohen, L. M., Higgins, K. M., & Ambrose, D. (1999). Educators under siege: The killing of the teaching profession. *Educational Forum, 63*(2), 127–137.
Giroux, H. A. (1989). *Schooling as a form of cultural politics: Toward a pedagogy of and for difference.* In H. A. Giroux & P. L. McLaren (Eds.), Critical pedagogy, the state and cultural struggle (pp. 125–151). Albany: State University of New York Press.
Grant, G., & Murray, C. E. (1999). *Teaching in America: The slow revolution.* Cambridge, MA: Harvard University Press.
Hofstadter, R. (1962). *Anti-intellectualism in American life.* New York: Random House.
Rallis, S. F., Rossman, G. B., Phlegar, J. M., & Abeille, A. (1995). *Dynamic teachers: Leaders of change.* Thousand Oaks, CA: Corwin Press.
Shannon, P., & Crawford, P. (1998). Summers off: Representations of teachers' work and other discontents. *Language Arts, 75*(4), 255–264.

History and Historiography: The Teaching Profession

Altenbaugh, R. J. (1992). The history of teaching: A social history of schooling. In R. J. Altenbaugh (Ed.), *The teacher's voice: A social history of teaching in 20th century America* (pp. 191–194). London: Falmer.
Altenbaugh, R. J. (1997). Oral history, American teachers and a social history of schooling: An emerging agenda. *Cambridge Journal of Education, 27*(3), 313–330.
Beale, H. K. (1936). *Are American teachers free?: An analysis of restraints upon the freedom of teaching in American schools.* New York: Scribner's.
Dougherty, J. (1999). From anecdote to analysis: Oral interviews and new scholarship in educational history. *Journal of American History, 86*(2), 712–723.
Elsbree, W. S. (1939). *The American teacher: Evolution of a profession in a democracy.* New York: American Book.
Quantz, R. A. (1992). Interpretive method in historical research: Ethnohistory reconsidered. In R. J. Altenbaugh (Ed.), *The teacher's voice: A social history of teaching in 20th century America* (pp. 174–190). London: Falmer.

Tyack, D. (1989). The future of the past: What do we need to know about the history of teaching? In D. Warren (Ed.), *American teachers: Histories of a profession at work* (pp. 408–421). New York: Macmillan.

Waller, W. (1932). *The sociology of teaching.* New York: Wiley.

History of Women Teachers

Hoffman, N. (1981). *Woman's "true" profession: Voices from the history of teaching.* New York: The Feminist Press.

Holmes, M., & Weiss, B. J. (1995). *Lives of women public schoolteachers: Scenes from American educational history.* New York: Garland.

Quantz, R. A. (1992). The complex vision of female teachers and the failure of unionization in the 1930s: An oral history. In R. J. Altenbaugh (Ed.), *The teacher's voice: A social history of teaching in 20th century America* (pp. 139–156). London: Falmer.

Weiler, K. (1988). *Women teaching for change: Gender, class & power.* New York: Bergin & Garvey.

Weiler, K. (1997). Reflection on writing a history of women teachers. *Harvard Educational Review, 67*(4), 635–657.

History of African American Teachers

Foster, M. (1992). The politics of race: Through the eyes of African-American teachers. In K. Weiler & C. Mitchell (Eds.), *What schools can do: Critical pedagogy and practice* (pp. 177–202). Albany: State University of New York Press.

Foster, M. (1997). *Black teachers on teaching.* New York: The Free Press.

Fultz, M. (1995a). African-American teachers in the south, 1890–1940: Growth, feminization, and salary discrimination. *Teachers College Record, 96*(3), 196–210.

Fultz, M. (1995b). African American teachers in the south, 1990–1940: Powerlessness and the ironies of expectations and protest. *History of Education Quarterly, 35*(4), 401–422.

Perkins, L. M. (1989). The history of Blacks in teaching: Growth and decline within the profession. In D. Warren (Ed.), *American teachers: Histories of a profession at work* (pp. 344–369). New York: Macmillan.

History of Rural and Western Teachers

Carter, P. A. (1995). "Completely discouraged": Women teachers' resistance in the Bureau of Indian Affairs schools, 1900–1910. *Frontiers, 15*(3).

Fuller, W. E. (1989). The teacher in the country school. In D. Warren (Ed.), *American teachers: Histories of a profession at work* (pp. 98–117). New York: Macmillan.

Vaugh-Roberson, C. A. (1992). Having a purpose in life: Western woman teachers in the 20th century. In R. J. Altenbaugh (Ed.), *The teacher's voice: A social history of teaching in 20th century America* (pp. 13–25). London: Falmer.

Weiler, K. (1998). *Country schoolwomen: Teaching in rural California 1850–1950.* Stanford, CA: Stanford University Press.

History of Urban Teachers

Addams, J. (1908/1985). The public school and the immigrant child. In E. C. Lagemann, (Ed.) *Jane Addams on education* (pp. 136–142). New York: Teachers College Press.

Altenbaugh, R. J. (1992). Teachers and the workplace. In R. J. Altenbaugh (Ed.), *The teacher's voice: A social history of teaching in 20th century America* (pp. 157–171). London: Falmer.

Fraser, J. W. (1989) Agents of democracy: Urban elementary-school teachers and the conditions of teaching. In D. Warren (Ed.), *American teachers: Histories of a profession at work* (pp. 118–156). New York: Macmillan.

Markowitz, R. J. (1993). *My daughter, the teacher: Jewish teachers in the New York city schools.* New Brunswick, NJ: Rutgers University Press.

Nelson, B. E. (1988). *The good schools: The Seattle public school system, 1901–1930.* Seattle: University of Washington Press.

Rousmaniere, K. (1997). *City teachers: Teaching and school reform in historical perspective.* New York: Teachers College Press.

Tyack, D. (1974). *The one best system: A history of American urban education.* Cambridge, MA: Harvard University Press.

Weiss, B. J. (1982). *American education and the European immigrant 1840–1940.* Urbana: University of Illinois Press.

History of Unions and Activism

Casey, K. (1993). *I answer with my life: Life histories of women teachers working for social change.* New York: Routledge.

Fraser, J. W. (1989) Agents of democracy: Urban elementary-school teachers and the conditions of teaching. In D. Warren (Ed.), *American teachers: Histories of a profession at work* (pp. 118–156). New York: Macmillan.

Gitlin, A. D. (1996). Gender and professionalization: An institutional analysis of teacher education and unionism at the turn of the 20th century. *Teachers College Record, 97,* 588–624.

Murphy, M. (1990). *Blackboard unions: The AFT and the NEA 1900–1980.* Ithaca, NY: Cornell University Press.

Newman, J. W. (1992). Religious discrimination, political revenge, and teacher tenure. In R. J. Altenbaugh (Ed.), *The teacher's voice: A social history of teaching in 20th century America* (pp. 90–106). London: Falmer.

Schultz, M. J., Jr. (1970). *The National Education Association and the black teacher.* Coral Gables, FL: University of Miami Press.

Urban, W. (1982). *Why teachers organized.* Detroit, MI: Wayne State University Press.

Urban, W. (1989). Teacher activism. In D. Warren (Ed.), *American teachers: Histories of a profession at work* (pp. 190–209). New York: Macmillan.

Weiner, L. (1996). Teachers, unions, and school reform: Examining Margaret Haley's vision. *Educational Foundations, 10*(3), 85–96.

Gender and Status

Blount, J. M. (1996). Manly men and womanly women: Deviance, gender role polarization, and the shift in women's school employment, 1900–1976. *Harvard Educational Review, 66*(2), 318–338.

Carter, P. (1992). The social status of women teachers in the early 20th century. In R. J. Altenbaugh (Ed.), *The teacher's voice: A social history of teaching in 20th century America* (pp. 127–138). London: Falmer.

Clifford, G. J. (1989). Man/woman/teacher: Gender, family and career in American educational history. In D. Warren (Ed.), *American teachers: Histories of a profession at work* (pp. 293–343). New York: Macmillan.

DeCorse, C. J. B., & Vogtle, S. P. (1997). In a complex voice: The contradictions of male elementary teachers' career choice and professional identity. *Journal of Teacher Education, 48*(1), 37–46.

Gamble, R. J., & Wilkins, J. (1997). Beyond tradition: Where are the men in elementary education? *Contemporary Education, 68,* 187–193.

Kaufman, R., Westland, C., & Engvall, R. (1997). The dichotomy between the concept of professionalism and the reality of sexism in teaching. *Journal of Teacher Education, 48*(2), 118–128.

Recruitment and Attrition

Jones, D. L., & Sandidge, R. F. (1997). Recruiting and retaining teachers in urban schools: Implications for policy and the law. *Education and Urban Society, 29*(2), 192–203.

Joseph, P. B., & Green, N. (1986). Perspectives on reasons for becoming teachers. *Journal of Teacher Education, 37*(6), 28–33.

McLaughlin, M. W., Pfeiffer, R. S., Swanson-Owens, D., & Yee, S. (1986). Why teachers won't teach. *Phi Delta Kappan, 67*(6), 420–425.

Miech, R. A., & Elder, G. H., Jr. (1996). The service ethic and teaching. *Sociology of Education, 69*(3), 237–253.

Newman, J. W. (1994). *America's teachers: An introduction to education* (2nd ed.). New York: Longman.

Sedlak, M., & Schlossman, S. (1986). *Who will teach? Historical perspectives on the changing appeal of teaching as a profession.* Santa Monica, CA: Rand Corporation.

Recruitment of Minority Teachers and Race

Goodwin, A. L. (1995). Asian Americans and Pacific Islands in teaching. *ERIC/CUE Digest 104.* (ERIC Document Reproduction Service No. ED379389)

Gordon, J. A. (1994). Why students of color are not entering teaching: Reflections from minority teachers. *Journal of Teacher Education, 45*(5), 346–353.

Jones, W. D. (1999). Enormous teaching career opportunities flourish in the new millennium. *Black Collegian, 30*(1), 124–127.

McIntyre, A. (1997). Constructing an image of a white teacher. *Teachers College Record, 98,* 653–681.

Mitchell, A. (1998). African American teachers: Unique roles and universal lessons. *Education and Urban Society, 31*(1), 104–122.

Murmane, R. J., Singer, J. D., Willett, J. B., Kemple, J. J., & Olsen, R. J. (1991). *Who will teach? Policies that matter.* Cambridge, MA: Harvard University Press.

Rong, X. L., & Preissle, J. (1997). The continuing decline in Asian American teachers. *American Educational Research Journal, 34*(2), 267–293.

Summerhill, A, Matranga, M., Peltier, G., & Hill, G. (1998). High school seniors' perceptions of a teaching career. *Journal of Teacher Education, 49*(3), 228–234.

Professionalism

Bradley, A. (1997, March 26). Standard board touted for elevating teaching profession. *Education Week on the Web.*

Burbules, N. C., & Densmore, K. (1991). The limits of making teaching a profession. *Educational Policy, 5*(1), 44–20.

Labaree, D. F. (1992). Power, knowledge, and the rationalization of teaching: A genealogy of the movement to professionalize teaching. *Harvard Educational Review, 62*(2), 123–154.

Lortie, D. C. (1975). *Schoolteacher: A sociological study.* Chicago: University of Chicago Press.

Provenzo, E. F., Jr., & McCloskey, G. N. (1996). *Schoolteachers and schooling: Ethoses in conflict.* Norwood, NJ: Ablex.

Welker, R. (1992). *The teacher as expert: A theoretical and historical examination.* Albany: State University of New York Press.

Classrooms and Schools

Cohen, D. K., & Grant, S. G. (1993). America's children and their elementary schools. *Dædalus, 122*(1), 177–207.

Cuban, L. (1993). *How teachers taught: Constancy and change in American classrooms 1890–1990* (2nd ed.). New York: Teachers College Press.

Goodlad, J. (1984). *A place called school.* New York: McGraw-Hill.

Jervis, K., & Montag, C. (Eds.). (1991). *Progressive education for the 1990s: Transforming practice.* New York: Teachers College Press.

McGrath, D. J., & Kuriloff, P. J. (1999). "They're going to tear the doors off this place": Upper-middle class parent school involvement and the educational opportunities of other people's children. *Educational Policy, 13*(5), 603–629.

Mead, M. (1962). *The school in American culture.* Cambridge, MA: Harvard University Press. (Original work published 1951)

Sirotnik, K. (1983). What you see is what you get: Consistency, persistency, and mediocrity in the classroom. *Harvard Educational Review, 53,* 16–31.

Tyack, D., Lowe, R., & Hansot, E. (1984). *Public schools in hard times: The great depression and recent years.* Cambridge, MA: Harvard University Press.

Tyack, D., & Tobin, W. (1994). The "grammar" of schooling: Why has it been so hard to change? *American Educational Research Journal, 31*(3), 453–479.

Westheimer, J. (1998). *Among schoolteachers: Community, autonomy, and ideology in teachers' work.* New York: Teachers College Press.

School Reform

Battistich, V., Watson, M., Solomon, D., Lewis, C., & Schaps, E. (1999). Beyond the three R's: A broader agenda for school reform. *Elementary School Journal, 99*(5), 415–432.

Goodlad, J. (1999). Flow, eros, and ethos in educational renewal. *Phi Delta Kappan, 80*(8), 571–578.

Sheldon, K. M., & Biddle, B. J. (1998). Standards, accountability, and school reform: Perils and pitfalls. *Teachers College Record, 100*(1), 164–180.

Windschitl, M. A., Mikel, E. R., & Joseph, P. B. (2000). Reculturing curriculum. In P. B. Joseph, S. L. Bravmann, M. A. Windschitl, E. R. Mikel, & N. S. Green, *Cultures of curriculum* (pp. 161–174). Mahwah, NJ: Lawrence Erlbaum Associates.

Images in Oral Histories
and Narratives

2

Good Women and Old Stereotypes:
Retired Teachers Talk
About Teaching

Nancy Stewart Green
Mary Phillips Manke

I n the quintessential women's profession, how have women interpreted their role and their work? We looked for an answer to this question in interviews with 12 retired women teachers and in the images they communicated of their lives and careers. To give readers some sense of these women's personalities and motivations, and of the social and historical contexts within which they made their choices, we begin with brief biographies, in order of seniority, of the teachers we interviewed.

All of these women were elementary school teachers who taught in the Chicago or Milwaukee area. We contacted them through currently working teachers and through the Chicago Retired Teachers' Association. They were not selected systematically, except that we purposefully selected an equal number of African American and White teachers for interviews. The women did share, however, a number of characteristics. All but one were in the first generation of their families to be educated beyond high school. (This is not surprising, given our time frame, as they were all born before 1930, the years in which high school attendance became common in the United States, but college attendance was still relatively rare.) All held bachelor's degrees, although three earned them during their careers, having attended one or two years of normal school before beginning to teach. Three had earned master's degrees.

Most taught and lived in the same city or community in which they were born. All but one were married, and 8 of the 12 had children. Three of the teachers began teaching in rural schools in an area outside of Milwaukee that became suburban/industrial during their careers. The others taught in the city schools of Milwaukee or Chicago in working-class, immigrant, poor, or lower-middle-class communities.

Beyond these demographic facts, we found few generalizations that could be made about these women. Placing them in categories, such as "the rural White teachers" or "the older African American teachers" seemed unproductive to us. We could only say that, as a group, the 12 women displayed remarkable similarities in their images of themselves as teachers. These commonalities seem to transcend economic, racial, and demographic backgrounds, but exemplify pervasive cultural expectations of women in a women's field.

Biographies

Leo Sparks, born in 1910, is an African American from Carbondale, Illinois, and the only one of our teachers who had a parent who was a college graduate. Her mother was a teacher; her father was "the only Black contractor in Carbondale." She graduated from Indiana State Teachers College at Terre Haute in 1932 and came to Chicago looking for work as a teacher. She explained that, at the time, district regulations limited elementary teaching positions to graduates of the Chicago Normal School so as an "alternative" she worked as a playground supervisor and taught adult evening classes. When hiring regulations changed, she was assigned to the first of three all-Black elementary schools in the city in 1950 and taught until 1975. Fiercely independent and not reticent about her conviction that she was a born teacher, Leo Sparks stressed the importance of love and involvement with children's families, as well as having high standards for children's work. (All the teachers in this chapter are referred to by pseudonyms, except for Leo Sparks, who preferred that we use her actual name.)

Emily Downer is an African American, born in 1911, whose family was "poor as Job's turkey" but strong, united, and devoted to reading. After graduating from Chicago Teachers' College in 1932, in the depths of the Depression, she waited 6 years for a permanent placement in a city where Black teachers were allowed to teach only in all-Black schools. She taught for 35 years, first in primary grades, then as an elementary librarian, and then again in primary grades. She retired in 1971 because her principal moved her to the eighth grade. One of the oldest of the teachers we interviewed, Emily Downer emphasized most strongly the importance of order and of "sticking to the curriculum."

Martha Corey was born in 1914 in Morgan Park, Illinois, an African American community on the edge of Chicago. She still lives there in the house where she grew up. Her father worked in the post office, and all the members of her family were great readers. She graduated from Illinois State Normal College in 1937, one of the few African Americans in her class. Because of Chicago's policy of hiring only Chicago Normal School graduates, which was in effect until the late 1940s, her first position was as a substitute at the all-Black DuSable High School. Later, she taught physical education at two all-Black elementary schools and finished her 30-year career in the central office in the research and evaluation department. An avid student, Martha Corey completed 40 hours beyond a master's degree and calls herself a "pseudo-intellectual." She retired early, in 1972, frustrated by cutbacks in programs she believed were effective and the uselessness of the compliance evaluation work she was doing.

Pat Barnes, a White Chicago teacher, was also born in 1914 and graduated from high school during the Great Depression. She took care of children in people's houses for 5 years, and then married and attended Chicago Teachers' College, graduating in 1943. She began to teach only after her son began kindergarten in 1949. For most of her 30-year career, she taught at just one school, on the southwest side of the city. At first, her pupils were from European immigrant families; later, her classes included children from Latino and Arab families. She particularly enjoyed the experience of teaching in a small school, where teachers supported one another and could teach as they wanted to. She retired in 1976.

Sally Tate, a White teacher, was born in 1914 in West Bend, Wisconsin. She attended a county normal school for 1 year, and began teaching at age 18 in a one-room school. She taught for 4 years before marrying. She had three sons, and it was to "do things for them" that she returned to work when the oldest was 10. She taught in a two-room school and studied at night and during summers for a bachelor's degree. After 5 years in a two-room school, she moved to the four-room Amy Bell School, where she remained for 20 years. During her time there, the school grew to be a large modern elementary facility. Sally Tate retired in 1981 because of her husband's illness. After his death she substituted regularly for several years and still does so on occasion. She now volunteers regularly in the classroom where her granddaughter is the teacher.

Georgia Tunney had the most varied career of all the teachers we interviewed. Born in Alabama in 1915, she moved at age 6 to Pasadena, California, where she was the only African American child in her elementary school. She was sent on a scholarship both to high school and to Spelman College in Atlanta. After earning a master's degree in early childhood education from Atlanta University, she taught in Thomasville, Georgia, and in Indianapolis before settling with her husband in Milwaukee. She taught first grade and kindergarten in the Milwaukee Public Schools. After a few years as a professor of education at the University of Wisconsin at Milwaukee, Georgia Tunney initiated, and eventually directed, the Head Start program in Milwaukee. Retired in 1979 after 40 years as a teacher, she continues to be active as a volunteer and community leader.

Ellie Varney, an African American teacher, was born in Springfield, Missouri, in 1918. Although she had not expected to go to college, the National Youth Administration, a New Deal program, gave her the opportunity to attend Lincoln University in Jefferson City. The program ended before she graduated, but with help from her soldier brother, she was able to graduate in 1946. She taught for 3 years in the high school she had attended in Springfield, Missouri. Then, urged by friends who had opted for big-city life, she moved to Chicago, where she substituted during the day and took courses at Chicago Teachers College at night. Her first regular assignment in an elementary school began in 1951. After a 2-year leave when her son was born, she taught at Shoup School in Chicago for 26 years until she retired in 1981.

Cora Ulm, a White teacher, was born in 1922 in a rural area north of Milwaukee. She studied for 2 years at Dodge City Normal before teaching for 4 years in a two-room school. Married to a returning soldier after World War II, she raised her children until 1962, when she resumed teaching. She took a job at Amy Bell Elementary School, near the family farm where she still lives. The school grew as nearby Germantown changed from agriculture to industry and suburban residences, and finally had enough children for a graded school. From then on, Cora Ulm taught third grade. She earned a bachelor's degree in 1968 and retired in 1986.

Dot Miller, another White teacher from Amy Bell Elementary School in Germantown, was also born in 1922. She had 2 years of normal school before beginning to teach in a one-room school in Golden Dell, Wisconsin, where she remained for 7 years. After 1 year at a bigger school, she married, but continued to teach until her first child was born. Taking off only a year and a half with her first child and less than 6 months with her second, Dot Miller taught a total of 45 years before retiring. Once Amy Bell had become a graded school, she taught either second grade or grade 1–2 or 2–3 combinations. Like Sally Tate, she took courses at night and in the summers to complete her bachelor's degree in 1957. She retired, reluctantly, in 1991.

Norah Krupar, a White teacher who was born in 1928, grew up in a poor Chicago neighborhood. She attended DePaul University, graduating in 1955. She was recruited by an elementary principal for his school in a poor neighborhood near the County Hospital. She enjoyed teaching there because she believed that, having grown up poor, she could relate well to the children she worked with. She took off 7 years to have two children of her own and then returned in 1967 to teach in another working-class school, this time working with "brain-injured children." The designation was later changed to "learning disabled," and Norah Krupar earned a master's degree in special education. She stayed in the same classroom for nearly 20 years, but was forced to retire early, in 1986, because of illness.

Kate Turner was born in Chicago in 1929 and attended first a junior college and then Chicago Teacher's College. Hearing that jobs were available in Milwaukee, she moved there and began a kindergarten teaching career of 34 years. She began as the first African American teacher at a mostly White school and taught at four schools in the city, including one for 12 years and another for 18. Kate Turner earned a master's degree at the University of Wisconsin at Milwaukee in 1977. She had to retire in 1989 because of arthritis.

Frances Schmidt, a White Chicagoan, was born in 1929 and graduated from Chicago Teachers College in 1950. She says proudly that her class was the last of the selectively admitted classes in the college; after that, the rules were changed in order to get enough teachers to serve the first of the baby-boom children. She taught first at a school on the West Side, then at Pasteur School, and finally, for 22 years, at Seward School in the "Back of the Yards" neighborhood, where she worked primarily with children from Mexican immigrant families. Like Pat Barnes, she enjoyed the experience of teaching in what she said was "like a small country school." Teachers shared and supported one another, especially in minimizing any discipline problems that might arise. Like Kate Turner, she retired, with regret, because of arthritis in 1991.

Methodology

Our unstructured interviews with these teachers, which were tape-recorded and later transcribed, were usually conducted in the homes of the teachers. We began by describing the nature of the project and our wish to focus on the images people have of teachers. The first question we asked called for the teacher to give us a history of her career, including how she chose to become a teacher and the schools and settings in which she taught. When this "tour" (Spradley, 1979) of her career had been brought up to her retirement, we used a list of questions to elicit information that had not already been discussed.

These questions focused on the teachers' changing images of their profession, as well as their beliefs about what others thought. We also asked whether they believed they were typical teachers and whether they would recommend that a young person today become a teacher.

Looking back on careers that began between 1930 and 1955, the teachers told us of their personal histories, the children and parents with whom they had worked, and their concerns about teaching and schools. In keeping with our ethnographic intent, we tried to let the concerns of the retired teachers surface in the interviews with a minimum of shaping on our part. Then, after the interviews had been transcribed, we read and reread them until recurrent themes began to stand out. From our discussion of these themes and their meanings and interconnections the focus of the chapter emerged.

Themes

Our search for common elements in the stories told by our teachers revealed three interrelated themes that appeared in almost all the interviews. The first of these, the importance of dedication in teaching, arises from questions we asked about images of exemplary teachers. "Dedication" is a word that some of the teachers used more than did others, but all agreed that the desire to serve was vital in the lives of teachers. Most emphasized the caring, loving side of this work as service; others stressed commitment and hard work in the service of students' learning.

The second theme that emerged was that of the many intrinsic rewards that the teachers derived from their profession. Again and again, the interviewees mentioned the satisfaction, the excitement, and the positive human relationships that arose from their work as classroom teachers.

The third theme involved the financial rewards of teaching. This theme raised more questions for us (and quite possibly for the retired teachers) than the other two. The retired teachers' understanding of the place of monetary rewards in their lives, and the lives of their fellow teachers, revealed ambiguities in our cultural expectations of schoolteachers and in their own expectations of themselves. There was a clear connection between the first two themes; the greater one's dedication to teaching, the greater the intrinsic rewards one gains from it. However, remuneration does not seem to be linked to either dedication or intrinsic rewards. Does this suggest that good pay is incompatible with the satisfaction derived from teaching? Do women feel ambivalent about demanding higher salaries and remain content with intangible compensation? These interviews suggest that the question of rewards in a "women's profession" merits further consideration by researchers and by teachers themselves.

Dedication to Teaching

Almost all the teachers used the word "dedication" in describing teachers whom they admired; its absence was what they most condemned in teachers they criticized. As aspects of dedication, they emphasized love of children, commitment to children's learning, concern for children's needs—whether academic or emotional—and willingness to work hard. In reflecting on the hard work of teaching, Norah Krupar said, "We used to laugh. We would say teachers are like bag ladies. They are always carrying something to the classroom or carrying something home. I think for anybody that tried to do a decent job it really isn't a short hour job, because it's a lot of preparation time." Describing one of the schools where she taught, Frances Schmidt said, "There were about 21 on the faculty, and they were all such hard workers, such dedicated teachers. My husband used to say, 'I don't see anybody but you bringing all this work home.' That isn't true. Over there everybody brought work home."

In some cases, such hard work may have had an unintended consequence for teachers' own families. Two of those we interviewed commented on their own children's attitude toward becoming teachers. Frances Schmidt said, "I'd like to see my daughter get into teaching. She doesn't want to, and I think I may have spoiled it for her, because she says, 'Mom, I see you staying up at night working on lesson plans and marking papers and doing all this ....'" Cora Ulm also mentioned that "you'd get home and of course you'd always have school work to do—I think that's why none of my children are teachers—you know, Mother always had so much homework. It was kind of a standing joke; none of them ever wanted to be a teacher."

But by the perspective from their own student days, these women saw hard-working teachers as worthy of emulation. Looking back on her early observations of teachers, Martha Corey said, "I began to recognize that the people I admired most were the teachers who gave of themselves and who went the extra mile." Thinking back to her own teachers as she was growing up, Ellie Varney cannot remember them ever missing school, except "maybe some teacher whose mother died or something like that ... I am sure they must have had some illnesses, but mostly they were there, and they were dedicated and loving."

In fact, love and care for children stand out as the most important reasons for all the hard work the teachers described. Norah Krupar said, "It is because you have that feeling for the child that you are there, because there is a lot of work in special ed." Leo Sparks' words reveal the involvement that characterizes the images of these teachers' lives and careers: "I love my [students'] parents, and my parents love me, and my kids love me, and my kids would [say], 'We belong to Miss S., and she calls us her babies, and she tells us she loves us. So you can't tell us anything.'"

Georgia Tunney echoed the theme of loving, but revealed a universal kind of love that transcends love of individuals or even of children: "All my life I've tried to help somebody. I did not do it for recognition; I did it because I wanted to be of service, and because I feel that love goes beyond sexual love. Love is love for humanity."

The teachers' view of the importance of loving children came out strongly in the their responses to the question, "Would you advise a young person today to go into teaching?" Kate Turner replied, "The ones that love the kids I'm not really too worried about." Leo Sparks answered:

> Of course, if they love themselves and if they love children, if they love people. Unless they feel in here, feel that this is their purpose in being on this planet is to be a teacher .... Love is a prerequisite for teaching. That is the reason a whole lot of people have no business there.

Cora Ulm explicitly connected love of children with the desire to help them learn. "If [a young person] likes to work with children I would say yes. The schools need teachers who are caring and concerned and want to help kids learn."

"Helping kids learn" is, of course, implied in teaching, but some teachers stressed the academic side of teaching more than did others. In describing a much admired teacher from her own high school days, Frances Schmidt said, "She tried so hard to have everyone pass her class and really come out with something .... I knew right away that this is what I wanted to do, too."

Academic weakness could even be turned into a strength; Kate Turner claims not to have been a good student in high school, but she thinks that made her a better teacher. She remarked, "Because I wanted children to love to learn, because I feel like if you love to learn on your own, if you can get that across, everything else sort of falls in place."

Emily Downer was unusual among the teachers we interviewed in that she stressed the importance of "covering the curriculum." In fact, she would not now advise a young person to go into teaching because of what she sees as a "flimsy course of study .... It is not concrete enough. There isn't enough of 'this has to be done, and that has to be done.' [In earlier times,] from September to June, you were supposed to accomplish a great deal."

Dot Miller put concern for the children's learning in more individual terms. In describing the characteristics of great teachers, she said, "They certainly have to motivate, and also follow through on that. They have to be willing to go that extra mile, and if you see someone is having a problem, don't embarrass them, but maybe call on them oftener and maybe take them aside and show them how to do things, and say, 'There's something I'd like you to do at recess time for me,' and 'Oh, by the way, you didn't get this, let me show you,' things like that."

For these teachers, sensitivity to the nonacademic needs of children is also an aspect of dedication. Pat Barnes said, "Sometimes things bother children. For example, one boy left the room one day, and I went to see what was the matter, and I think he was embarrassed, because his father was going to the hospital, and he viewed that as sort of a bad thing. Of course, you want them to learn, to achieve the goals they are supposed to for that grade, but I think you have to have empathy."

Leo Sparks recounted an experience with some neglected children. She and some other teachers had been feeding them before school.

> As the weather got cold, when we drove up, those babies were there. I would unfreeze those hands and feet. I would take their socks off, take them down to the janitors to dry out and put the socks on the wall, so they would be dry and let the children sit there with newspaper under their little feet until they could move after I massaged them. I would tell the children, "I am your daytime mama. Whatever is wrong, whatever is bothering you, tell me." I said, "That is why my shoulders are broad." I said, "My lap will hold you."

One might wonder whether contemporary teachers share these feelings. Does a teacher today view herself as a "daytime mama"? Does society expect teachers to cast themselves in this light? What does this suggest about the nature of parents and parenting in American society?

These retired teachers viewed schoolteaching much more broadly than instruction in academic areas and far more demanding than a "nine-to-three" job. Their understanding of rewards, incentives, and gratification suggests to us the complexity of this helping profession—both then and now.

Intrinsic Rewards of Teaching

The women we interviewed had gained rich rewards from their years as teachers. The aspects of teaching that they found rewarding were closely related to what they saw as constituting dedication. Hard work and deep involvement in their jobs translated into pleasure in their autonomy, variety in their daily work, and opportunities for creativity and problem solving. They also found rewards in relationships. They enjoyed their contacts, often over the long term, with parents and other teachers, and were delighted when children, growing up, remembered them over the years. Some of them found that their position as teacher brought them status in the community.

Most of the teachers found their work so rewarding, in fact, that retirement was painful. Dot Miller, after 45 years as a teacher, said she would not have retired if her husband had not taken her by the hand to the district office to do so. Leo Sparks was still angry that her age had forced her to retire, especially since the rule was changed shortly thereafter to let teachers continue to age 70. Two teachers regretted that they had to retire early because of arthritis in their knees; another went from her classroom to the hospital and never came back to get her teaching supplies because it was too painful. Only one retired early because she felt that changing times had robbed her of the satisfaction she had formerly received from teaching.

Teaching is working with children, and Dot Miller said, "To this day I love little kids, they're great .... And if you love to work with children, there's nothing else that compares with it .... You get so much satisfaction out of seeing what they do." She also spoke of the sense that she had helped an individual child or group of children: "... and if you have a little one there that is having a hard time at home, divorce or something, if you can make that child smile and feel secure for the 6 hours she's in school, that's good." Kate Turner agreed: "It's like the little pebble in the water. You know, you're touching so many children."

Some of the teachers derived great enjoyment from the special activities they did with children and from the children's response to those activities. Said Cora Ulm, "They loved to act out things—I remember one time they acted out a wedding. They brought stuff and they acted out the bride and the groom." Pat Barnes told us that she and the children worked with clay once or twice a year and that the children loved it and remembered it years later. "You'd think that we had done this all the time instead of arithmetic or reading or something."

Many of the teachers described what might be thought of as teaching's intellectual rewards. Teaching provided room for autonomy and for creativity, and solving problems was satisfying. As Emily Downer said, "At that time if you wanted a good job, an interesting job where you are learning all the time, being a teacher was it." For Frances Schmidt, "every year is different, and every year you come up with new ideas and new enthusiasm." Dot Miller spoke of the "satisfaction of solving behavior problems and getting the class to help you with that."

Several women recalled that their schools had offered them the rewards of community—joint efforts and positive relationships. Frances Schmidt recalled, "It was like a family. There was a lot of sharing of things, and we never had any discipline problems there. If on occasion we did—we kind of helped each other. It was fantastic." This was also true of relationships with parents. Dot Miller reported that "the parents showed a lot of respect to this day. They call and I've gotten beautiful things from the parents." Frances Schmidt stated that at her school "if you did anything that was extra, the community, the parents really appreciated it."

Among the most powerful long-term rewards mentioned by several of the teachers were continuing relationships with their students. According to Kate Turner, "I have one child [who] was in my first kindergarten, and she still keeps contact with me. She called me in the hospital ... and she's brought her children over." Emily

Downer described her meeting with a former student after he had returned from medical school: "I hadn't seen him for years, and I hadn't forgotten him—and he said 'Well, I just had to come to tell you what I did and what I am now, and I also wanted to tell you that you were the best teacher I ever had, barring none.'" Similarly, Martha Corey observed, "Such a pleasure now ... I meet so many of my former students who are all in different fields. Some of them are principals who have asked me to come and substitute in their schools." Leo Sparks spoke of these continuing relationships with special joy:

> I had a girl call me the other day to thank me. I had her in second grade at Forest School 38 years ago, and a bunch of those second graders have stayed together as friends, and they meet once a month. And she says, "You can't guess what we talk about—Miss S." Because when she called she said, "Miss S., you don't remember me, but I will never forget you. You will never know how much we loved you, still do, and how much you had to do with our lives." And, I was on cloud, what, 210 for a couple of weeks.

Many of our interviewees had continuing relationships with other teachers as well. Pat Barnes noted, "We still get together after all these years ... just for lunch or something." Referring to a school where she began teaching in the early 1950s, Frances Schmidt said, "To this day I have kept up with that friendship. We meet once a month, very nice ladies."

For many of those we interviewed, teaching was an occupation that carried high status. Dot Miller, a White teacher who began her career in a rural setting, said, "When I started teaching, you were something in the community." This theme was even more marked in the interviews with African American teachers. At the time these teachers entered the field (1930–1950), few white-collar jobs were open to African American women. Kate Turner, a light-skinned African American woman, obtained a white-collar job in Chicago after graduating from junior college, but she soon learned that her employers had assumed she was White. She told us, "Being a teacher probably meant more in the Black world than in the White because it was considered a much better job in the Black world."

Georgia Tunney, who first taught in rural Georgia, said, "The teacher in African American culture was really very important. We gave respect; we respected the teacher." Another African American teacher, Martha Corey, broadened the significance of this theme: "A person of my age would come to the teaching field thinking it was a privilege to be a teacher and thinking of the responsibility that we had as teachers and that we had this opportunity to change lives."

Making a difference, witnessing change, being a part of something valuable within a social system—these were the rewards for intelligent, motivated women of past generations who had limited options in other professions for creativity or recognition. Teaching was a gratifying avenue for empowerment and self-expression —and a logical choice.

The Financial Rewards of Teaching

Our interviews did not explicitly raise the question of the remuneration of teachers. In reflecting on this fact, we have considered the possibility that we ourselves share some of the same reservations about financial rewards for teaching that came to light among the women we interviewed. Without being asked, several of them did raise the issue, and a certain ambivalence about payment for "women's work" emerged. On the one hand, the teachers took it for granted that, although, of course, they were dedicated, they in fact worked for money.

On the other hand, one of the worst things these women could say about a teacher was that "she's in it for the money." This ambivalence was expressed by Ellie Varney, who said, "I think most of [the teachers] really loved their work. It wasn't a matter—well, it was a matter of a job, and, of course, as you know, the pay was lower than most professionals, but I think most teachers are very dedicated."

Some of the teachers mentioned in passing, perhaps because it was obvious to them, that they needed to work and to earn money. Dot Miller said that one reason she went to normal school was that she saw that young women who were teaching had clothes that farm girls just did not have. In explaining how she returned to teaching while her children were still young, Norah Krupar said, "A friend died, and left her young children, and she didn't do for them what we had hoped to do for our children. So I said to my husband, 'I have to go back.'" Moreover, Sally Tate observed, "We didn't have very much money, and [we had] the three boys, so I went back to teaching when they were old enough to go to school." Kate Turner was divorced after her children were born, and she depended on her salary to support herself and them.

Most of the women did not mention the better pay that teachers now receive as a positive change for the profession. On the contrary, many of them brought up concerns that higher salaries have a negative effect. None mentioned higher pay as an indication of higher status or as recognition of professional expertise. While they were grateful for the salaries they earned toward the end of their careers, and for their pensions, these teachers worried that higher salaries were bringing people into teaching (or keeping them there) who lacked the dedication that defined teaching for them. As Kate Turner said, "Much as you like having that money, it keeps people in there for the wrong reason." And Norah Krupar noted: "I think some of the people who are in teaching now are only there for the salary they think they can get. I'm sorry to say that. They don't seem to care that much about the children."

Some teachers, especially Emily Downer, mentioned a loss of a serious attitude about the work to be done in teaching:

> For example, I would buy professional books, and one of the younger teachers would say, "You will never catch me spending my money like that," but anything that most teachers felt they could do that could help them do a better job, I think they were willing to do it. I don't even know

how to describe the feeling that many teachers have now, but I'm afraid that in many instances the attitude is "This is a job." I was surprised to find that. They seem to think "if the children get it by the end of the term, fine. If they don't, so what ...." I think it is just one of the general things that is happening in—I started to say civilization, but no, in the United States.

The teachers' ambivalence about the effects of higher salaries on teachers' dedication also reflected their beliefs about the public estimation of teachers. Although aware that some prospective teachers think that salaries are too low, the women believed that in some communities teachers' salaries were perceived as too high. The teachers thought that the public expects schoolteachers to work for low salaries and denigrates them for earning higher salaries.

Most of the women we interviewed, as we noted earlier, taught in communities that could be characterized as blue collar, immigrant, poor, or lower middle class. A number mentioned that people in their communities believed that teachers are paid too much. It should hardly surprise us that people who are insecure about their own future, and whose salaries are relatively low, might see teachers as better off than they are. As Dot Miller said:

> Now teachers are starting to earn more than the factory workers do .... I think when I started, you didn't get an awful lot of money .... But now, hey, teachers are in it a couple of years, they're earning $34,000, $40,000. Secretaries don't earn that .... So they're being paid more than many people now.

In response to a question about public attitudes toward teachers, Norah Krupar talked about how little she was paid when she started teaching in 1955. "People had the attitude that if you were a good person, you were dedicated to teaching, and you didn't need money. I think that is what their attitude was. You know those old stereotypes." The "old stereotypes" of teachers as selfless and above personal ambition not only kept community members from envying any privileges that teachers might have, but also granted them the respect due to "good women," who performed the nurturing tasks of the society without challenging a social order in which women had little public influence.

In an interesting reversal of the usual complaint that in our culture respect is based on income, Kate Turner said, "I think you got more respect because it's almost like volunteer work. When you're volunteering, you know people appreciate you so. But when you're getting all this money they resent you, especially when the taxpayers are paying, but when I was making $3,000 a year, people were grateful." Norah Krupar summarized this point of view and expressed a certain nostalgia for a time when, she felt, teachers were more respected. "I don't think people have as much respect for teachers as they had when I first started, and I think part of it has to do with the salary."

Questions Raised by These Interviews

It has been particularly interesting to us to view the interviews in light of the findings of broader studies of the teaching profession in more recent times. Several generalizations made by Lortie (1975) in *Schoolteacher* and by Lieberman and Miller (1984) in *Teachers, Their World and Their Work* about more contemporary teachers are not reflected by our research. This fact led us to ponder the changing structures of schools, society, and the teaching profession over time.

The themes that emerged from our interviews differed from those found by Lortie (1975), whose study was conducted during the last several years in which our interviewees were teaching. Lortie, viewing teaching from the perspective of sociological studies of professions, found the salient aspects of schoolteaching to be presentism (the lack of emphasis on long-range commitment to career), conservatism (based on the recruitment of people who are comfortable with existing systems of schooling and who have only limited interest in changing the career of teaching), and individualism (reflecting classroom isolation and a preference for singular autonomy). While these issues were raised to some extent by the women we interviewed, Lortie's themes did not emerge as the core meanings of teaching from the retrospective thoughts of the retired schoolteachers.

We also noticed that the 12 retired teachers emphasized issues other than those raised by the teachers interviewed by Lieberman and Miller (1984). Teachers in the Lieberman and Miller study emphasized scholastic achievement and discipline. Though our interviewees by no means overlooked these themes, they were at least equally concerned with the emotional well-being of their students.

In addition, Lieberman and Miller (1984) identified the difficulty of fitting everything they are expected to do into the time allotted as the greatest problem of elementary school teachers. Only a few of the teachers we interviewed mentioned this problem, and then usually in the context of describing problems experienced by younger teachers. We suggest that the relative lack of the time-management theme in the retired teachers' interviews may be due to the fact that school requirements and mandates set by external authorities did not impinge on teachers 30 and 40 years ago, as they set their own daily and weekly expectations.

In the Lieberman and Miller (1984) study, the elementary teachers believed that the only significant rewards of the teaching profession lay in the students' "words, behaviors, expressions and suggestions" (p. 2). Our teachers found numerous other rewards, including relationships with other teachers and with parents. Thus, we imagine that in earlier decades, schools were more collegial and teachers felt more in harmony with parents and their communities.

In addition to our interest in comparing our interviews with the two studies discussed, we looked at the internal logic of the narratives of these retired teachers. Most strikingly, the three themes of dedication, intrinsic rewards, and remuneration overlapped. Unlike the Lortie (1975) and Lieberman and Miller (1984) studies, the themes of dedication and intrinsic rewards of teaching were clearly related. The retired teachers definitely believed that the more dedicated you were, the more satisfaction you felt.

The teaching profession, however, seems structured to provide no connection between dedication and monetary reward. With few exceptions, teachers retain their jobs and move up the salary scale without regard for the level of their commitment. None of our interviewees linked extra pay with extra dedication. In fact, as we indicated earlier, many of the retired teachers we interviewed clearly connected interest in financial rewards with lack of dedication and commitment. They believed that increased pay has not produced better teachers, but rather has led to a decline in commitment on the part of younger teachers. Common wisdom holds that increased salaries will lead to greater professionalism; however, there is an evident tension in these teachers' thinking between the concepts of professionalism and dedicated service.

Historically, professionalism has implied exclusive rights to a body of knowledge and has been associated with male dominance of an occupation. A hierarchical relationship exists between professionals and their clients—those who do not share the professionals' knowledge. This masculine construction of professionalism is, in essence, self-centeredness disguised as wisdom.

Service, on the contrary, implies a selflessness that is an essential component of the traditional stereotype of women's work. The person rendering service, usually a woman, has a supportive role rather than being in a decision-making or controlling position. The ambivalence these teachers express about the relationship between remuneration and respect may reflect this cultural attitude.

Like many other women of their generation, the interviewees seemed to accept assigned gender roles without much question. They felt, for example, that they could not do some of the things that men could do, but they neither protested at the time nor complain even now. Only one (Norah Krupar) mentioned the "old stereotypes" of female selflessness and the accepted traditional notions of the meaning of work for women. Their central goals were caring, dedication, and service rather than financial rewards. In fact, they almost seemed to feel that money was corrupting and would subvert the more important rewards they sought.

Interestingly, Lortie (1975) noted this same aspect of the culture of teaching but—amazingly, from our contemporary point of view—makes no connection to gender expectations:

> The culture of teachers and the structure of rewards do not emphasize the acquisition of extrinsic rewards. The traditions of teaching make people who seek money, prestige, or power somewhat suspect; the characteristic style in public education is to mute personal ambition. The service ideal has extolled the virtue of giving more than one receives; the model teacher has been "dedicated." (I suspect that these values are linked to the sacred [religious] connotations of teaching in early American History.) (p. 102)

These retired teachers seemed unaware that cultural values might be imposed on them. Other chapters in this book (such as Joseph's essay on teacher-education textbooks) suggest that the larger society establishes expectations for the behavior of teachers. Notwithstanding, most of the teachers we interviewed seemed to identify the locus of expectations within themselves. They saw themselves as wanting to, or choosing to, be dedicated, rather than as having that required of them. Moreover, again with the exception of Norah Kruper, they did not connect this expectation with their gender.

Although our teachers did not seem to be conscious of the imposition of cultural expectations, some of them were aware of, and in one way or another had resisted, the imposition of control from the school system. Three teachers (Pat Barnes, Frances Schmidt, and Emily Downer) spoke warmly about their work in small schools where teachers essentially ran the show and there was a "family atmosphere." Although this was not precisely a case of resistance to imposition of control, since it was by chance that they were teaching in those particular schools, it stands as an ideal of teacher control in the minds of those who experienced it.

Michael Apple (1986) has written about the ways, not necessarily linked to "militance and clear political commitment" (p. 48), in which teachers have sought to control their work. Three of the teachers we interviewed spoke fervently of the ways they had resisted change imposed by their superiors. One stuck to her academic standards, resisting what she saw as their dilution; another drew the line at changes she felt limited her ability to respond to the emotional needs of students; a third, being "more of a rebel than some of 'em," as she put it, refused to use the workbooks that were assigned for her first graders.

Emily Downer was outraged when the idea of "social promotion" was introduced in the Chicago Public Schools in the late 1940s and recalled, "I simply did not pass [children who had not completed the work for the grade] and then other teachers would say to me, 'Oh, you are going to have your efficiency grade lowered.' I said, 'Well, that may be. If the efficiency grade is lowered, they are going to have to tell me why.' I was sure that no one was going to say it was because you didn't pass everybody, because to me that was ridiculous."

Leo Sparks was above all else committed to the emotional well-being of her students. She said:

> I am not afraid for the children to touch me and never have been, and even today if they say "don't"—I do. The people that are making these rules are not human. I don't care how many degrees they have. I used to not allow them in my room if they came and said, "I am Doctor So-and-so." I said, "Get out. There is the door. Get out. I don't need you." I even put my principals out. They came up with those initials. I said, "Don't say EMH or LD or whatever it is. Don't say it. Tell me there is a child that has a problem." I will not accept that label.

Sally Tate, the self-described "rebel," was expected to use 12 workbooks with her first-grade students and found that the whole day was, "Well, get out your language book, or get out your math book." She "managed to eliminate them one at a time; nobody ever noticed." Then there was time to do the kind of teaching she thought was best for the children.

It apparently did not occur to any of these teachers to join forces with others of like mind; their resistance was a matter of individual conscience and individual action. Perhaps the most common form of resistance an individual can offer to an apparently unchangeable system is simply to leave. Two of our teachers took this option. Emily Downer left because her principal required her to teach a grade level with which she was uncomfortable; Martha Corey resigned because the successful federal programs in which she had been working were terminated and she was left with unsatisfying work.

As Apple (1986) pointed out, women's resistance to control may have contradictory results. Teachers' responses may represent a victory of principle over policy, yet at the same time their actions may represent a defeat in leaving the system exactly as they found it or, in the case of teachers who quit, depriving children of good teachers. Apple believes that "the important question is how the elements of good sense embodied in [resistant] teachers' lived culture can be reorganized in specifically feminist ways—ways that maintain the utter importance of caring and human relationships without at the same time reproducing other elements on that patriarchal terrain" (p. 52).

We noted that the teachers we interviewed did not look beyond their individual classrooms and schools to see themselves as part of a larger culture. Their focus on the learning and emotional well-being of their students, though admirable, precluded their thinking about how what they taught the children contributed to the larger society. As did the teachers interviewed by Lortie (1975), the teachers in this group concentrated their attention at the classroom level. Though retired, and therefore possibly in a position to take a broader view, they continued to focus on the personal and individual in the educational endeavor. At its best, as they saw it, teaching represents personal commitment to the welfare of a particular group of children.

As a result of this rather narrow vantage point, when some of these teachers tried to explain what they understood as a decline in the dedication and caring of younger teachers, they looked within the profession itself for an explanation rather than considering larger shifts in cultural values or economic realities. The one exception was Emily Downer, who linked a change in teachers' attitudes with a general decline in the work ethic in the United States. For many others, higher salaries, with their hint of selfishness, were the villains. We might suggest that resistance to exploitation in the name of womanly values, positive concern for one's emotional and physical health, the increasing number of single mothers in the workforce, and an increasing emphasis on the acquisition of material goods were social causes of the changes these teachers were seeing. Awareness of such perspectives, however, was not expressed in our interviews.

Given teachers' inward-turning focus as suggested by these interviews, as well as their ambivalence about the relationship between remuneration and service, we believe that the teaching profession could benefit from the insights that might arise from a feminist analysis. On the issue of caring and compensation, Noddings

(1990) has described how feminist theories of nursing have confronted the dilemma of maintaining the service ethic of nursing while retaining nurses' rights to respect for individual judgment and to adequate remuneration. In the case of teaching, discussion of this dilemma is muted because, although women predominate as teachers in elementary schools, men have typically spoken for teachers—as principals, as leaders in teachers' unions, and as researchers. If women had stronger voices and framed the larger issues in teaching, the meaning of professionalism in the field would be changed.

We believe that the themes that surfaced in this study of retired teachers have significance for teachers who are entering the profession. As future teachers think about their careers-to-be, do they see dedication as an important aspect of their work? Will they judge themselves and others in terms of dedication or lack of it? And what rewards do they envision themselves as obtaining from their teaching careers? What personal needs do they expect to fulfill in teaching?

We would also hope that current and prospective teachers might seek a wider perspective on education as a profession than we found in the retired teachers whom we interviewed. What role do cultural gender expectations play in teaching? How can teachers take into account changes in society without using them as excuses? How can teachers work together to gain greater control over how and what they teach? How can teachers give themselves to their particular students and classrooms without losing sight of their larger ideals for society? The words of the 12 retired women elementary school teachers raised these questions for us.

REFERENCES

Apple, M. (1986). *Teachers and texts: A political economy of class and gender relations in education.* London: Routledge & Kegan Paul.

Lieberman, A., & Miller, L. (1984). *Teachers, their world and their work: Implications for school improvement.* Arlington, VA: Association for Supervision and Curriculum Development.

Lortie, D. C. (1975). *Schoolteacher: A sociological study.* Chicago: University of Chicago Press.

Noddings, N. (1990). Feminist critique in the professions. In C. B. Cazden (Ed.), *Review of research in education 16* (pp. 393–424). Washington, DC: American Educational Research Association.

Spradley, J. P. (1979). *The ethnographic interview.* New York: Holt, Rinehart & Winston.

3

Shifting Images Across
the Generations: Conversations
With Beginning, Current,
and Retired Teachers

David Hobson

When the editors of this text first told me they were conceiving a book around the question, "What does it mean to be a teacher?"—and that they wished to produce a book involving a collaboration among many persons and perspectives—I thought immediately that I would like to collaborate with the 37 classroom teachers with whom I was working.[1] Since many educators would be reading this book, it seemed especially meaningful to actively involve teachers in the process of its construction, to invite them to take part in conceiving, conducting, and consuming research about education; and to be guided by them as much as possible.

As the project evolved, the teachers and I planned to interview retired educators—how better to gather insights informed by long years of classroom experience? Also, we chose to talk to aspiring teachers, persons who were just starting out in our profession and who were either completing a period as practice teachers or their first or second years of full-time teaching—who better than persons new to the work to help us see our profession through fresh eyes? By interviewing both aspiring and retiring teachers, perhaps we could get a sense of how images of schoolteaching are changing in our profession as ensuing generations of teachers pass through the schools. By juxtaposing these three perspectives, we hoped to uncover some significant ideas about what it means to be a teacher.

The Study

The teachers and I decided to develop the specific lines of inquiry together, to create a collaborative and exploratory investigation, and to see where it would lead. Interviewers generated a list of the questions they found interesting. Then we formed small groups and brainstormed some more. After we shared what we had generated with larger groups, we organized ourselves into triads and conducted some practice interviews, role playing with one another. For about 30 minutes, one person interviewed, the second person responded, and the third person attempted to record. Then, another round began and we switched roles. Finally, in a third round, we switched again. At the end of the session, we talked about the interviewing experience we had just enacted.

Some interviewers had asked just one or two questions and followed the intriguing path that the respondent forged. Others asked numerous questions, also to good effect. Nearly all agreed that taking notes was next to impossible; we would use tape recorders all around.

Following the organization meeting, each of the classroom teachers agreed to conduct an interview with a retired or neophyte schoolteacher, although some eventually conducted two. Seven of the interviews I conducted myself. In all, 45 teachers were interviewed—32 who were retired teachers and 13 who were just beginning their teaching careers.

After the interviews, the researchers wrote responses to the interviews that they conducted and taped. Subsequently, we exchanged tapes and wrote additional responses to the interviews conducted by colleagues. Finally, I listened to all of the tapes and made transcripts of the conversations. I wondered and pondered. I wrote a draft chapter. Some excerpts were shared with an additional group of classroom teachers and that discussion was transcribed. Finally, another draft of the chapter was put in the hands of the entire group of teacher-researchers with the invitation to respond to it in writing. Further collaborative analysis (see Van Manen, 1990) was conducted in small groups.

Much of the pleasure of this investigation for me was the interactive aspect that I shared with my colleagues. Collaboratively envisioning this project, sharing drafts as they came along, and engaging in discussions of what all this material might mean have been very satisfying aspects of the project.

For all my efforts to involve classroom teachers in the design and implementation of this interview project, and despite all the writings in response penned by many individuals along the way, two central facts remain: First, I am the university instructor and, as such, have had a powerful influence throughout the research process, and, second, I did the actual writing. Still, this is an intentional collaboration. For all its limitations, this was a deliberate effort to amplify the wonderings of classroom teachers in conversation with colleagues who are both more and less experienced in the teaching life. It was my hope that the participation of many teachers in the ways I've described would help this work elicit more response and reflection than if I had done it entirely alone.

This chapter focuses upon the oral histories of 32 retired teachers and 13 neo-phyte teachers identified from the personal and professional networks of the inter-viewers. All but two of the participating teacher-researchers were White, middle class, and suburban—as were all of the retired teachers. All but six of both the inter-viewers and interviewees were female. Most of the retired teachers were in their sixties and seventies, a few were in their eighties, and one was age 92. The 13 aspir-ing teachers were a somewhat more diverse group. Three were changing profes-sions mid-career: one woman in her thirties, and two men in their forties. One woman was African-American, another Latina. Several of the newcomers had done their student teaching or were currently teaching in diverse urban Chicago neigh-borhoods. Most participants, however, were White, middle-class persons who lived and taught in the suburbs.

What follows is a rendering of these teacher-to-teacher interviews with statements from those interviewed serving as frameworks for discussion. The voices of the con-temporary teachers—*the interviewers*—will be presented in *italics* throughout this chapter in order to distinguish them from those of the interviewees. As they looked more closely at the experiences and perceptions of retired and neophyte teachers, the contemporary teachers constructed meanings and pondered questions about the im-ages teachers hold about themselves and their profession. Individually and together, we reflected on the question, what does it mean to be a teacher?

"Teaching One Grade Was a Cinch!"

It wasn't that the information was so surprising—stories of one-room school-houses, of not being able to teach if you were married, and of having to carry in wood for the fire are familiar to teachers who have perused history of education texts. It was more a feeling of incredulity that this very person with whom one was conversing and laughing and meeting in real human terms actually had been there.

> You had to fix the fire in the morning; you had to do your own janitor work. You had to go out and pump water and bring it in. They didn't have indoor toilets then—no flushing. They would clean them out once a year.

> You had to go up on Sunday afternoon and start the fire. You did what they called "banking" it. You put on a lot of coal and shut the draft so it would burn all night. In the morning you kept it going by putting more coal on and you kept it going all week. Every night before going home you had to bank the furnace. That was the worst thing, I think. I probably remember that because I said, "Never again," after I left.

> When I first started it was a rural school with an outhouse and a pump out-side for the water and the big furnace in the room. You couldn't have any plants or anything in the room because it all froze overnight. And you had

the eighth-grade boys take turns bringing in the water in the big cooler. We were all drinking out of the same dipper. They were all farm kids who walked to school, so when they came in they had wet clothes and they put them on the furnace to dry. It smelled like a barn!"

This was not ancient history. These were the stories of a retired teacher, not so different (or sometimes not so very much older) than the interviewer. I heard the genuine respect that the contemporary teachers often had for their older colleagues.

One present-day teacher, upon hearing about the one-room schoolhouse, put it this way: *"It seems incredible to me that just one person was responsible for so many children while doing eight different things at the same time. Do you ever look back and wonder how you ever did it?"* The retired teacher replied laughing: "I do. I do. Especially after teaching one grade. Teaching one grade was nothing after you had taught eight! Teaching one grade was a cinch!"

More taped laughter. Then silence. These small silences occurred with some frequency as I listened to the tapes. Having worked with these present-day teachers for 4 hours once a week for 2 years, I could almost imagine their thoughts as they contemplated the subject matter at hand, in this case the thought of teaching eight grades at once.

There was much about which to feel some astonishment:

> I started teaching in 1930 at the age of 18 for $85 per month. And that included doing the outside chores, which meant throwing in wood. We'd form a line to throw the wood into the basement and then we'd all go in and pile it up. I boarded across the street and the gentleman there started the fire in the morning. And there was sweeping, carrying in the water, and cleaning the outdoor toilet.

Upon listening to this last interview, a present-day teacher commented, *"I can't imagine doing that!"* And the retired teacher replied, "I can't either. I don't know how I did it. Except that I went to school there and so I kind of took over. And I was the last teacher they had before it closed down. Most of the country schools were closing then."

The images of the schoolteacher of the past—teacher as custodian, janitor, day laborer—appeared to be different from those cast by present-day professionals. Those teachers did so many jobs in addition to actual instruction. However, although some of the specific tasks are different, I realized that teachers today also complain about the plethora of nonteaching tasks that call them away from the work of teaching. As one contemporary teacher mused, *"I stopped to think about all the nonteaching tasks I do. If someone interviewed me in 50 years they might also be shocked at the things I do!"*

As I listened to teachers from two generations speak about this issue, I thought it striking how much things have changed in this regard, yet remained the same; the preponderance of nonteaching tasks present in teaching is as much a cause for complaint now as it was then.

"Well, in My Day, Girls Usually Went Into Teaching."

A favorite question employed by the interviewing teachers was *"Why did you be-come a teacher?"* The responses form a pattern similar to Lortie's (1975) research findings about how many individuals became teachers:

> I think I've always known that I would be a teacher. My father had always said to me that he knew I was going to be a teacher because I used to orga-nize the whole neighborhood, put up horses and gave them stools or some-thing to sit on, and then ... played teacher. And I'm the oldest and so I just became the authority figure and the person they looked up to and the baby-sitter ... I've been having schools since I was 8 years old.

> I decided to be a teacher in the second grade, being the oldest; it came kind of naturally with brothers and sisters. I don't remember wanting to be any-thing else. We used to play school all the time, imitating the school rou-tine, sitting at desks at home.

> I always enjoyed school, and we had so many kids so close together that it was a natural thing to come home and share the things I learned. It was a fun thing to do.

The family context was a formative influence. Apparently, teaching was of-ten an activity that emerged out of the "natural" family responsibility of looking after the younger ones, a responsibility that evolved for many into a lifelong ca-reer. For many teachers, it was a loving responsibility. One retired teacher, who continued to work occasionally as a substitute, explained, "I've always wanted to be a teacher from when I was a child. I've always loved school and I still love school. That's why I'm still here." When the interviewer interjected, *"You've re-ally never had any doubts?"* she replied, "No. I've always loved school from the time I was a little 'bitty.' I substitute because I still love teaching; I love the con-tact with the children; the looks on their faces is a reward that can't be matched in any other way."

Nevertheless, memory does not simply reveal the past as a set of facts or as real-ity that can be accepted without analysis. Embedded in the retired teachers' eyewit-ness accounts are clues that warrant additional consideration about the reasons for entering teaching.

> I don't think I thought too much about other possibilities at the time. Cer-tainly most of the females were at school for nursing or teaching, and a lot of the girls I knew were there for the "MRS. Degree." And many of them—that's what they came out with .... Well, there weren't that many choices. I wasn't aware of that many things to do. I wouldn't choose that way now. The people that I knew became teachers.

> All through my childhood and young adulthood it was taken for granted that I would become a teacher because you became teachers or nurses when I was that age. Perhaps if I had been exposed to other vocations, I might have gotten interested, but ....

I believe that the ensuing pause reflected the recognition of how the world had changed during the intervening years, how certain decisions seemed "natural" as the availability of jobs and socially accepted careers for women limited and shaped choices. But one might not be as inclined to choose that way again.

Notwithstanding, the teachers contemplating their vocational choices did not specifically identify the gender structure of jobs as the important factor in many of their work decisions. As a result of research by Weiler (1992), among others, we can read these retired teachers' own portrayals of their decisions to become teachers more critically. We can question how "free" these decisions really were considering the restrictions and limitations on women's roles and work at the time. If a young woman pictures herself as a teacher, a nurse, or a caretaker and if she is able to imagine few other options, then her accepting of such a role may perpetuate that which is familiar—the feminine, the nurturing one, the mother.

I wondered to what extent the entering professionals' choices to become teachers are shaped and limited by forces and conditions operating well outside of their awareness? Will they, 50 years from now, be second-guessing themselves with the considerable benefit of hindsight? The interviews disclosed retired teachers saying over and over words to the effect that, "I didn't think too much about it at the time," and "it seemed the natural thing to do." Their lack of purposeful choice gives credence to how important it is for teacher educators to insure that aspiring and new teachers have real opportunities to think carefully about the full context surrounding the decision to become a teacher.

In contrast to that earlier generation, a new teacher depicted how she came to the profession:

> I did a number of things. First, I thought I wanted to be an attorney. I pursued that vigorously. I was there for a year and I found out that I didn't like it. It just wasn't me. So, I left that, but I learned a lot from that experience. Then I worked as a secretary for a while and that opened my eyes a lot. I saw how people relate to each other and learned about expectations of quality work. I worked as a manager for a dental clinic. So, it was a process of evaluation, of taking a long look at the good and the bad of various choices. Maybe I wouldn't be able to bring to teaching what it is that I do if I had done it right out of college. It is the culmination of all those experiences that have helped me to make this decision to come to teaching.

Another young women came to teaching after working in the corporate sector for a health care company and eventually meandering into the training and development division. Later, when she began to lead training sessions and was teaching adults, she realized, "It was wonderful. I loved it! I realized that teaching was all about me. So, I decided to get my master's in education. And it's worked out beautifully and I'm just tickled about it."

These new teachers described a path to the teaching profession that was chosen actively and thoughtfully from a wider array of occupational possibilities. How were these new and different journeys influencing the self-definitions and professionalism of those who felt more ownership in their careers? Also, what will teaching be like for the many new teachers who enter the profession after having gained experience in a variety of other occupations, many pursuing and then rejecting career paths not available to women who went before?

These new educators were women who had exercised choice denied to their older sisters, who had garnered experience in the world outside of family and school, and who were coming more deliberately to teaching—to a more fully informed and somewhat less-gendered choice. While this trend may seem obvious in today's economy, with its myriad of careers for educated people, seldom have we considered how the teaching profession is shaped and reshaped by the experiences and predispositions of its members.

"It's Nice if You're a Mother Because ..."

The connection between teaching and mothering often explicitly emerged from interviews with retired teachers. However, from their perspectives, it was mothering first, then teaching. Clearly, they saw the profession as a supplement to one's primary mission—raising a family. They defined "normal" life as family life; and teaching was an extension of the familiar in a woman's life.

> I grew up respecting the field of education, realizing what a wonderful thing it is for a married woman to be with her family during vacation time and to have a "normal" life during the summer. Sure you're busy at night, but you are also home with your family, you are there at dinnertime, so I saw many advantages.

> In my instance teaching has been a wonderful supplement to raising a family. I was able to be with my children when they really needed me. I felt it was a wonderful profession to supplement the income, which was necessary, if you wanted your children to go to college ... and for other goodies in life.

> I think there are several occupations that, for females, have the connotation of being a "female job" and one just uses it as a supplemental kind of thing, that it's not really a career. Teaching is like that ....

Some questions were raised, however, by contemporary teachers. On the matter of teaching being supplementary to parenting, one young teacher wrote with strong feeling: *"Oh yeah, says who? Maybe for that "old granny" that was interviewed. Teaching is a legitimate career in and of itself. Sure, it fits in nice with motherhood, but maybe motherhood is a supplement to a strong career!"* Another present-day teacher offered this viewpoint:

> *The interviews perpetuate the idea that teaching is great for a family, a nine-to-three job allowing time for the mother's role. And summers off! Only to a degree is this really true. I've spent too many hours, after my children were asleep, grading papers, planning lessons, doing report cards. And what about the summer spent planning new curriculum? We teachers are hurting ourselves and our image if we don't discuss these aspects as well.*

It was apparent to me that serious questions were being raised and that they came primarily from some of the younger teachers who were single or married but without children. How is the role of teacher being redefined by young women entering the profession who do not see it as supplementary to raising a family? What will be the impact on the teaching profession and communities, many in suburban areas, as an increasing number of teachers do not regard their careers and income as merely secondary? The days when teaching was perceived as a not-so-demanding adjunct to raising children are clearly numbered, if not actually over.

"You Were Almost Like a Mother to These Kids."

As they expressed the theme of the teaching career as a convenient parallel to raising one's own children, the retirees also elaborated on their images of teachers as mother figures. One remembered:

> The one-room school was more like a family atmosphere, a home atmosphere; you were almost like a mother to these kids, especially if you had been at the school very long and I had been there a long time. Some I had for 7 years and you get very attached to these youngsters and they do to you too. And you are almost a mother to them. It was a nice family atmosphere. The older ones become like older brothers and sisters to the younger students. It was really a pleasure. I enjoyed it.

Another recounted: "I still hear from several of the kids at Christmas time who graduated from me. I think it's because you got close to them and they remember you kinda like a mother."

For some, the caring, the emotion of loving, were the primary elements in their mothering relationship. Several retired teachers articulated such sentiments:

> Personally, I just love the children and they love me. I enjoy them tremendously. I want them to know I'm going to do everything I can for them.

> Nurturing and caring is not only done at home. It's an additional part of education. When a child is comfortable, happy, and being accepted, he'll learn more.

These ideas about teaching were supported as well by a teacher as she discussed her own experiences as a child and in her first year of teaching:

> Teachers who have that special relationship with kids may not necessarily be doing the coolest curriculum thing, but the kids really love them and feel like "that was the best teacher I had." And you look at it and there's nothing fancy on the walls, but it's that they felt "she cared" and they walked off feeling that "she is the teacher I had who cared."

In contrast, the interviewers thought that the parallel between teaching and mothering was problematic and called into question the perspectives of several new schoolteachers who believed in the relationship between being a mother and pursuing a career as a teacher. For instance, an aspiring teacher declared that although she had received some valuable knowledge about learning diagnostics and curriculum in her teacher education program, the more important factor was that she was already an experienced mother of three. On hearing that taped conversation, an experienced teacher reacted in this way:

> *I can't think of any other profession besides teaching where people think they know so much about how to do the profession, yet in reality are so clueless. She is being very naïve about thinking she already knows how to teach because she is a mother and is raising three children. As a teacher, she will have 8 to 10 times as many children to "raise" at a time. None of which come from her gene pool, none of which she has had any influence on previously, and many of which will be ingrained with very different values and expectations.*

As the social perception of teaching and mothering as one and the same diminishes, there may be more articulation of just how teaching is different from parenting in very distinct ways.

Moreover, the participants in this study talked about another teacher image, the domineering matriarch whose main realm of power resides in a room filled with small children. One retired teacher proclaimed that the schoolmarm caricature made teaching seem an unattractive choice: "I didn't want to be a teacher. I always envisioned a teacher as a tall skinny woman with her hair up with a knot on top … and I wasn't going to look like that." But she became a teacher. And the stern image that she at first rejected nevertheless influenced her behavior and her understanding of what it meant to be a teacher:

> I used to scare my children half to death on the very first day of school. I'd say, "How many of you children have heard that Mrs. T. is really mean?"

And they would look at you so funny, you know, and nearly all of them would say they'd heard that I was really, *really* mean. And I said, "You wanna know something? I am." And for 6 weeks I was really strict with those kids, until I got them in line .... I think that in this day and age I probably would be considered an old fashioned teacher, a strict disciplinarian, and a "not-smiling-until-Thanksgiving" kind of thing. You set your expectations ... and people live up to them.

A present-day teacher recognized herself and her acculturation into teaching in the retired teacher's description and had concurring memories:

I'm reminded of my cooperating teacher when I was student teaching. One of the first things she told me was not to smile until Thanksgiving. And, believe me, she practiced what she preached! I even find myself in situations today with inexperienced teachers and telling them, "It's always easier to loosen up, than to tighten up." Pretty soon I'll have a bun on the back of my head!

One new teacher spoke of undergoing a yearlong struggle with, as she put it, developing an "attitude."

The only thing I didn't like that happened this year was that I developed an attitude I didn't have when I started. I didn't want to have this attitude, but the kids completely related to it. I went in with a cool curriculum that didn't fly right away. So, I developed an attitude. What attitude? "You're gonna do what I say because you're gonna do what I say—(laughter) *that* attitude."

I was fascinated by the frequency and strength of the mothering theme found in the interviews with the teachers. There was the classic image of mothering: kindly, patient, nurturing—offering a sense of acceptance, approval, and belonging. So, too, existed the image of the mother providing discipline and order. Conceivably, the image of the teacher as mother reflects the influences of images of schoolteachers in American culture upon individuals, even on those who taught. Retired teachers appear to share many of the stereotypical images of teachers that we often see portrayed in television commercials, cartoons, and literature.

The "mothering" image, however, did not sit quite as well among the new teachers. Some of them challenged the gendered stereotype implicit in mothering. Furthermore, two new teachers, one male and one female, protested the image, using exactly the same words: "A man can be just as mothering as a woman." A contemporary teacher, a male, objected to the word "mothering." He instead suggested that *"nurturing would be a better term because both men and women are nurturing of children. I nurture my fifth graders, but I do not mother them."*

We must wonder about the extent to which the meaning of teaching stems from a familiar cultural image (mother), from advice handed down from colleagues (stern matriarch: "Don't smile until Thanksgiving"), or from teachers' understandings of the changing views of their profession and the reality of contemporary classrooms.

"Sometimes You Have a Needy Student … and You're the Only Parent They Have."

As we listened to the teachers' remembrances, I could detect a sense of affectionate nostalgia for the days gone by in the retirees' voices, especially as they made comparisons with their increasingly stark perceptions of teaching today. In their view, American society certainly has changed. The retirees perceive the changes as disruptions of what is normal and proper for children, parents, and teachers.

> In those days, teaching was easy. It was fun. I always felt I had parental support. The children went home for lunch. There weren't as many separated parents. In the last few years that I taught there seemed always to be so many more social and emotional problems.

> The parents were very involved in those days. You never had to ask twice for room mothers or for anyone to come along to be in the classroom. Women did not work as much when I was first beginning, so they were more free to come, I believe.

> At first, the parents were nearly always at home. Later on, both parents worked so the kid would come to school with the key tied around the neck. They would go home from school and there was nobody there. I think that made a difference. And you always found where the parents took an interest in the school, then the children seemed to take more of an interest too.

The emotional tones of the interview responses often conveyed moral judgments. The retirees insisted that schools and children had problems and that parents were to blame, particularly for the frustrations they felt in their later years of teaching. Thus, when asked what they thought was the most significant change that had occurred during their careers, the retired teachers' criticism of parental attitudes emerged time and time again.

> At the start of my teaching career, parents were a little bit in awe of the teacher and when something happened at school, the teacher was right. It was felt that the teacher's solution was the correct one. Nowadays, you hear a child say, "My mother is going to sue you." I think you more often see mothers and fathers coming to school and being irate about what the teacher is doing. I don't think teachers have changed their methods that much. I think it's the attitude of the parents, being a little more belligerent, more likely to have a chip on their shoulders, out to prove something by coming to school and berating the teacher.

I had a lot of respect in the community when I first started teaching, but at the end of the sixties it was starting to go in the other direction. That was one of the reasons I was ready to retire. It became a losing battle, just a losing battle. Even today I overhear things being said in the community about the school and the teachers in the presence of the youths, and it just makes my heart gripe because the children are the ones that suffer. They lose respect for teachers. This is not the way I was raised. This is not the way I was taught.

There are so many things that need to be taught in the home that they're not getting today. What bothers me is that the parents downgrade the school and the teacher, and they let it be known to their children. The child shouldn't be exposed to criticism. If there is something to be corrected, it should be done between the adults and leave the child out of it.

The interviewer engaged in dialogue with the retired teacher about parental criticism, saying, "*I agree. A child came in today and said that his dad said, 'This is dummy work that we're doing,' and I said, 'Your daddy should call me if he has a problem with what's going on in this room.'*" The retired teacher concluded: "I hate to say this, but it's ignorance; it's inadequacy on the part of the parents. What they don't understand, they find fault with."

The retirees also shared their belief that parents today actually seem hostile to schools and teachers. In some emotionally charged interviews, indictments of parents were made. The retired teachers blamed parents not only for mothers being absent from home and poor support of teachers and schools, but for increasing hostility—manifest in strident competition between parent and teacher. They understood such negative parental attitudes as interfering with the education of the child, as overriding the authority and expertise of the teacher.

When I call the television repairman to come over to fix my TV, he tells me to leave the room and he fixes my TV. He gives me a bill for it. I think this is the thing about teaching. The teachers are the experts. Not that I don't want to involve the parents; I think they should be involved, but not to the point where they are dictating the curriculum and all these other things that are happening in schools. It doesn't work. The teachers are the experts. If they would give teachers a chance to do the job, I think the educational system would work.

Well, all you hear these days is that they need more money for education. That's just a lot of bunk. They just need to start in the home and straighten out the parents. I think most of the teachers today are doing the best they can and it isn't the teachers' fault. It's just the training the children are getting in the home. The schools would be what they ought to be if the parents were doing their part.

Ironically, the retired teachers' criticism of parents continued to be juxtaposed with their references to the natural connection between the school and home. "School is a home away from home," one retired teacher said. She then added, "In fact, I think some of the kids have more of a home life in school than in their homes." The retired teachers viewed the natural relationship between family and school as disintegrating, the gulf between the home and the school widening. Yet they also believed that their "tried and true" approaches to teaching are no longer enough, that their way of viewing what it means to be a teacher is no longer sufficient. It is not enough to love children, to want to mother them, and to be a good teacher as well as the classroom expert. It is not enough for today's children. The contributions teachers once felt themselves called upon to give are the very elements perceived to be lacking in the lives of the children.

"I Don't Think It's as Simple as That Anymore."

Many interviews demonstrated the retired teachers' beliefs that not only have parents changed, but, for a variety of reasons, so have children.

> When I started out teaching, it was such fun. You didn't have to spend a lot of time on discipline or emotional problems in the classroom. Now I would say that it's at least a third of your kids. Maybe it was just more fun teaching then … and probably the response that you got from the children was more wholehearted. Now you have kids who have a lot of inhibitions, they have so many other problems, and they don't seem able to free themselves from some of these problems.

> You have to put yourself in the position of the child. The children we have nowadays are not coming from homes that are as stable as they were 30 years ago. We live in a very transient society, and these children have to come in, and they have to learn your way of teaching, and then their parents pack up and leave, and they go to a new school, and they have to learn a whole new regime, all new friends; it's just too difficult.

> I think the children of today [are changing] because of the media they are exposed to—movies and TV. I think they are more worldly than the children I had in second grade many years ago. If this is good, I don't know. But I think they have a wider knowledge than the kids did when I was in the classroom. Today the kids are used to having so much for themselves at home that when a teacher does some nice little thing for them, I don't think they appreciate it as much as they would 25 years ago. The children didn't get out in the world as much then as they do today. I don't think you get the reaction today that you did then. Most children have experienced a lot more things.

> At first it was like a family and the children just loved to come to school. They didn't want to miss a day; even if they were sick, they didn't want to miss. And it seemed that they were anxious to learn; they wanted to do it to please you. I found, as time went on, that the kids didn't seem to care anymore whether they learned anything or not. I know they had a lot of outside interests too. You had TV and everything else that made a difference. But, at first, the children just seemed to want to learn and to do well. They seemed to wish to do well.

Besides hearing the refrain that children are different today, so, too, we heard from the retired teachers another major theme—that teaching also has changed:

> I just think it became harder as time went on. It is easier to get burnout today because it's harder to teach. It takes a lot more skill to analyze what's going on in these kids' heads and why they behave in certain ways and what you can do about it. It seems to me that if you were kind of a motherly person, and affectionate, and anxious for your pupils to succeed, that was enough. I don't think it is as simple as that anymore.

> The kids are not as attentive; they don't care as much as they used to. 'Cause now they have TV and they're entertained and they have all these activities. When I first started, kids just loved to learn; it was a pleasure, a real pleasure. And then, it became harder and harder to keep getting their attention. That's how I think it has changed.

> [Children today] are bored in the classroom because of some of the technology or technical or mechanical things they have at home. They can manipulate those things, you know, at home, and how often can they do that in the classroom? They have to sit and listen. I think that children do not want to listen today. I just don't think most children can learn from listening.

The interviewer reacted to the retired teacher who was concerned that children can't listen by saying, "*Then you have to find a variety of ways to involve them.*" The retired teacher answered back: "I think a teacher's job is to introduce material … and make it as interesting as possible to the kid, but I don't think that teachers today should have to really dwell on methods. I think they should be able to present the material and that's it."

After listening to this taped conversation, another present-day teacher responded:

> *That retired teacher described a fairly typical classroom of 50, 20, 10 years ago, and I'm sorry to say, today it's the type of classroom in which only a specific kind of learner does well. That's great for people like me, but not so great for all those 'other-style learners' out there. I hope that to-*

day we are starting to realize that there are many different ways to learn and our job as teachers is to accommodate ALL children. I don't want to be thought of as the expert by my kids. I don't know everything and certainly do not want to be viewed as if I do. If the children see you as a learner, they will view themselves as learners. That is in essence my job, sharing with kids how to learn.

This seemed a telling dialogue. I could hear the frustration in the retired teacher's voice as the present-day teacher called for a different kind of teaching. The present-day teacher saw her role differently; she has felt the urgency to use what children know and what works for them. The interviewer does not have an image of herself as a teacher elevated on a pedestal, dispensing knowledge to respectful students arranged below. Perhaps she is less caught up in the material to be taught and more attentive to the children who are to be taught, perceiving that not all children learn in the same way. The act of teaching seems to be encountering an evolving set of challenges, as we discover, more about how children learn and develop.

Another interview revealed today's teachers' conception of the complexity of their work. A new teacher, an African-American woman teaching in a primarily Latino community, told her interviewer about how she began to meet the challenges of working in a community unlike the one in which she was raised:

What struck me was how unprepared I was to be in that community. I was just so unfamiliar with that culture. And I felt that lack of understanding was not just mine, but it was the whole school's lack of understanding. We did not connect with the Latino culture; the sensitivity just wasn't there. Yeah, there definitely needs to be a sensitivity toward that. We need to spend a lot of time trying to develop an understanding of what they need, what they want. Not just wait until they get up, complain, and have to fight for their rights.

Some of the changes in children and teaching to which retirees alluded related directly to their experiences in urban schools. Several had taught in the city and moved to the suburbs later. Some had gone into the city to teach for a year or two and returned to the outlying areas. However, It must be remembered nearly all of the retired teachers in the study were residents of suburban and ex-urban areas and had taught in the same or nearby communities. These teachers witnessed in their own lives the movement from one-room schoolhouses in the farm communities of the not-so-distant past to the suburban age-graded consolidated schools of the present.[2] Through this rural–suburban lens they reminisced:

I wouldn't sell my childhood for anything. Living on a farm you know the sources of things. You know processes. You know cause and effect. You just get that in your living. And so, I think I had many advantages. I wouldn't trade my farm experience for the city experience where many things aren't suited for the child. There, it's an adult world rather than a child's world, and they're trying to do away with childhood nowadays.

In the beginning we were all farm families and we were all very closely related to each other and to the school. We were just like a big family. No problems … just nice kids. Then, I went in to the inner city and I had kindergarten kids and they had a lot of problems …. They were much harder to teach.

However, not all the retired teachers attributed problematic changes to urban environments and reserved some criticism for suburban communities:

When I was in Chicago, I had been teaching second grade. When I came out to suburbia I just took what I knew from teaching second grade and moved it down to first grade—the academic difference was horrendous. The children were a little more challenging out here. In the city the children were a little more appreciative than when I came out here … maybe spoiled is the word. But then, my children were raised in the suburbs, too, so I have to say that I produced spoiled children compared to the children I worked with in the city.

Here again was a shift occurring between the generations. The interviewers perceived the classroom as more active and the methods of instruction as more varied. In addition, the contemporary teachers saw a pressing need to be culturally relevant when addressing diverse student populations. Many of the classrooms in which the interviewers work have increasingly become more multicultural. A case in point is one suburban elementary school in the Chicago metropolitan area in which 80 languages are spoken in the children's homes. The contemporary teachers view the current conditions of teaching as the way things are. To the retired teachers, changes in classrooms, schools, and communities seemed troublesome and unwelcome, a huge contrast from their perception of the agrarian communities that many of them had known—where "we were all farm families very closely related to each other."

The image of the American schoolteacher appears to be undergoing some fundamental change, perhaps in response to the profound changes that are occurring in the larger society of which schools are just a part. It became very clear in listening to the voices of current teachers that in modern America "one size no longer fits all." The contemporary teachers in this study recognize these new realities and, accordingly, adjust their visions of what it means to be a teacher.

"Hey, There's a Lot I Don't Miss at All."

Despite their nostalgia, many retired teachers nevertheless brought to light their complaints about their own teaching days. Some noted that parent conferences and testing could easily be added to this "not missed" list. As one retiree commented, "Hey, there's a lot I don't miss at all." She went on to mention:

> A lot of the politics of the school system, I don't miss at all. I don't miss grading papers. I don't miss all the time in preparation, or all the hours of your own time outside of school that you have to put in. I don't miss the last day of school, or the last week, or the week before Christmas vacation, [and] the interruptions at school … there wasn't enough time in the day to teach as it was, and then to have it disrupted for a million reasons was terrible.

Moreover, some retired teacher interviews disclosed some of the sad realities of teaching at the time:

> The only thing that ever bothered me about my teaching was that we were locked in. You teach, you get tenured, you get your insurance, you get your years of seniority, and you can't move around from one school to the next. As a result, you are locked in to a principal and to a school that you're not always happiest at.

I also felt the longing of the retired teacher who experienced changes that kept her from close relationships with children during her own teaching career:

> I felt that inasmuch as I had ceased to have a homeroom, I didn't have the close contact with the children anymore. I had 125 children coming through my classroom and I was teaching reading and science all day long. I felt that was a negative thing in retrospect. At the time I felt it should be that way.

I was particularly intrigued by her response because she said that it was only in retrospect that she realized how much she missed having better relationships with the children. How ironic this seems to me, that so many of the retired said that they went into teaching for the love of children, that the one quality needed above all else was the ability to love the kids. So, here was a teacher, retired—thinking over her career—and she realized that she increasingly missed having these very relationships with children.

The retirees felt concern about the new mechanical developments in schools, but so did a new teacher who worried about the burgeoning of technology and how it could affect human relationships:

> I hope that teaching doesn't become as hands-off as it seems, distance learning with the teacher on a video screen and the students at the computer. I really hope that doesn't happen. I think it would be frightening if that becomes the norm—because you need the personal attention. You

need somebody there. You need the touch on the shoulder. You need the encouragement right there. I don't think there is any replacement for personal contact.

The title of this section, "Hey, there's a lot I don't miss at all," captures very appropriately the musings of the retired teachers. Many of their complaints resonated easily with contemporary teachers: long days, hard work, too many interruptions, and the depersonalization of the school bureaucracy. But, in several other ways, today's teachers challenged the conventional wisdom of the earlier generation. Many of the retirees' complaints have become the very materials with which modern teachers work. Diversity, community, cultural variety, individual learning styles, and technology—these are the exciting challenges for contemporary educators. These challenges increasingly are perceived not as the reasons to get out of teaching, but, rather, as reasons to get in. As a second-year teacher declared:

I think right now is such an exciting time to be a teacher because, in most places and among most people I know in most schools, they really want variety. They want to try all kinds of new things—whatever might work. They want to have teachers who are traditional. They want teachers who are progressive. And they encourage all the different methods. It is so exciting to be a teacher!

"Cooperation and Teamwork and Sharing—With Each Other and With the Kids."

Researchers have long thought of teaching as an isolating kind of work, done "person by person, each working largely in isolation from others" (Lortie, 1975, p. 74). According to research (Johnson, 1990), isolation is maintained because "strong norms of autonomy and privacy prevail among teachers" (p. 179). Working within a cellular structure of schooling, separate rooms, separate buildings, separate districts, it seems that "the very act of teaching is invisible to one's peers" (Lieberman & Miller, 1984, p. 9).

The isolation is especially unfortunate because so many individuals come to teaching with a perception of the family, of belonging, of mothering, of filling the image of the caring helper. Many, unfortunately, wind up cut off from the children and each other.

In these interviews, several new teachers expressed their delight in interaction and collaboration with their peers. One neophyte commented that she gets "such a kick out of my colleagues," that she just loves "the collaborative planning and execution of things." This new teacher had to relocate for the next school year and was sad to be doing so because of the wonderful collegial relationships she would be leaving behind.

> It's such a supportive team—two teachers are quite experienced and the math teacher was also brand new like I am—and I am heartbroken to leave them. We are all getting a little bit weepy because we've worked so well together and we've really enjoyed it, so I guess teaching to me is about cooperation and teamwork and sharing with each other as well as with the kids.

Another novice teacher bemoaned the lack of teaming as one of the reasons she planned to move to another school:

> [The other teachers] have been real supportive when I've had an incredibly bad day more in terms of emotional support, personal kind of stuff, that kind of help, but not professional. We actually never sat down and planned. There was an awareness that it would be a good thing and we even had common planning time, but it never happened. I basically just got irritated with my team. I don't always see that reciprocity. I just got fed up with the fruitless trying: "Hey, let's talk about this ...." or "Let's do this ...." or, "What do you think about that?" and not getting anything really back. So, I just said to myself, "O.K., I'll just focus on my classroom."

In a follow-up interview, she talked more about what she required from her work: "I need to be in a place where you can teach and it's not just you alone and it's not just you giving, but it's other people giving too, and also it's me not feeling that I have to give so much."

Another new teacher, just finishing her first year, contemplated a move to another school, where, she explained,

> They're trying to do it all. They have outstanding teachers. So, like, it's going to be a super-achiever environment of teachers there. On Monday the teachers don't have kids and they are very into group work and you have to work with your team and you're not on your own just to do your own thing. I think when you work with a group of people who are working with kids, you could probably identify things a lot faster and get someplace a little faster too. And I think the quality of the work environment will be better too. I have those days when I come in and I'm too tired to do this all alone.

Expectations about the collaborative nature of work may stem from some of the new teachers' previous work experiences. One woman, who entered education from a career in the corporate world, discussed her experience working as a team member in business and how it helped her as a teacher:

> There were 18 new teachers hired and some of us have been in business and have come into teaching a little later. I have talked to a couple of colleagues who are in my situation and they feel the same way about it as I do. In business you are used to working with other people, maybe even some

you don't really like all that well, but you have different roles, different kinds of expertise, and you really need to work well with each other in order to get a particular task done. So, you are always working in various task groups, and your success in business depends upon your ability to do that well. Lots of teachers haven't had much experience with that and get all "bent out of shape" at the prospect of teamwork. So I think people coming from the business world can contribute a lot in terms of their ability to work with others.

The interviewers responded to the conversations about newer collaborative developments in schools with some mixed emotions:

> *There is real pressure on me, on many of us, to work more closely with specialist teachers who are supporting the special education kids who are being included in our classrooms. We are moving toward the middle school concept and it looks like teaming is on the horizon and block scheduling and who knows what all. I just hope I don't lose what I love about teaching and that is being with the children.*

Another contemporary teacher put it this way: *"There is all this talk about teaming. I don't go near the teachers' room—it is so negative in there. What if I have to team with someone I don't like or can't work with? It's scary!"*

It was very interesting to see how each element—teaming, collegial relations, and the school as an interactive professional community—was perceived differently by these three different groups of educators. Professional teaming hardly comes up at all in our conversations with retired teachers. The experienced teachers, the interviewers, have confronted some new realities of teaching and find themselves wrestling with changes. They contemplate what the changing image of teacher will mean for them and how equipped they were to deal with it effectively. The newest teachers in this study embrace the recent, more collaborative image and look to their relationships with peers as a source of one of the main satisfactions to be found in the profession.

These interviews disclosed that teaching is becoming a much less isolating profession. It is no longer a matter of closing one's classroom door and having satisfying relationships only with the children. Schools are developing into more collaborative enterprises and the image of teaching is changing, too; it is becoming more difficult to envision the teacher in front of the class, standing alone.

"Everyday I Discover Something New About Myself, About Them, About My World—Every Day!"

Although many depictions of teaching given by the retired teachers were supported and affirmed by their interviewers, the present-day teachers' responses also illustrated the profound differences between those two groups. The contemporary teachers seem more flexible, see more possibilities in teaching, and have a greater sense of themselves as professionals.

> *You have to draw on your own resources and come up with something that works. If something doesn't work, you don't throw out the kid.*
>
> *It's not what you are teaching; it's whom you're teaching.*
>
> *What it means to be a teacher is a level of trust—when they start doing it for themselves—when they will let you in.*
>
> *What it means to be a teacher is the ability to allow them to let you into their lives.*

Moreover, teaching is described as a process, as "*snowballing—you have ideas, the kids have ideas.*" For the interviewers, being a teacher means searching within oneself to give children what they need and to respond to children as individuals. It seems clear to the contemporary teachers that children have different needs from students a generation or two earlier and parents create more challenges, yet classroom teachers can discover ways to meet children's as well as their own.

These interviews, and the responses to them, revealed several elements that undergird many teachers' sense of themselves. In this study, the retired teachers indicated the significance of community, of family, and of respect as they generated images of teaching. Present-day teachers expand those reflections to encompass a contemporary world where such values are not necessarily universal or taken for granted. Novice teachers in classrooms today seem have moved beyond the definition of "teacher" that served effectively in former days of schooling to images that encompass the complexity of a profession with an expanded repertoire of skills and an appreciation of a team approach to their work.

One telling example of the new teachers' professional conception of self is their frequently mentioned image of the teacher as a facilitator.

> I think facilitator is probably the best word because it encapsulates everything. I would like to think that a facilitator is sometimes a lecturer. And sometimes she is facilitating a group project. Or helping the students start on independent research. The facilitator does it all. I think I am on my way to becoming one. I don't give myself enough credit to say I'm there yet.
>
> I guess facilitator would come closest to what I see myself wanting to be. My image of teaching is trying to help students accept themselves for who they are, to help them identify and work with their preferred types of learning styles as well as with those they struggle with, helping them get through the developmental stages, helping them to "process"—to make connections of prior knowledge to what we're doing.

New and experienced present-day teachers in this study appear to embrace a more proactive approach to the educative process, one that emphasizes actively engaging students and connecting their energy and curiosity to the tasks of learning. A new teacher described her view of education:

> I don't think anyone is inherently passive. I think we're taught to be passive and that is dangerous because then you let your life happen to you and you don't take an active role in it. The essence of facilitation is to get the students to take an active role in feeling that they are in charge of how things go for them, that they are themselves in charge of their own lives. I don't know if I'm going to be able to accomplish that, but that would be my ideal, my goal for myself.

Another new teacher recalled being told by a professor that the children are the river and the teachers are the banks. "It's nice imagery, but you know, I don't mind being in the water with those guys. I don't mind swimming with them. I don't want to be only on the bank."

Such a rethinking of our profession suggests that the teacher as a person need not be lost. In fact, being a teacher today may require greater personal ownership of the process of growing and learning, one which embraces the student not just as a consumer, but more fully as a collaborator. It seems important that the teachers not just create information or merely impart it to children, but also participate in the reciprocal process of learning. As the contemporary teachers so aptly explain:

> *A teacher is first of all a learner. A teacher who really loves to learn will be able to inspire the students to love learning ....*

> *As a teacher, I have become a more interested learner. I think being a teacher you are a learner all the time. I'm so much more turned on to learning. I am invigorated because I am a teacher ....*

> *Sometimes it is necessary to step out of the curriculum as established in some far away place and use the best that is in us—to draw upon our imaginations at our deepest level and respond as human beings. We must do the best we can, but it really must be the best. The children will respond and the teacher will grow in ways perhaps unimagined.*

> *Every day I discover something new about myself, about them, and about my world—every day! I like to share it too. What it means to be a teacher is sharing, is discovery.*[3]

NOTES

1. Several times a week in the late afternoon, I leave the university behind and head out to various school buildings to meet a group of 15 or so classroom teachers who are experienced professionals. The teachers, graduate students in a 2-year master's of education program in curriculum and instruction, meet for 4 hours once a week with their colleagues and myself, the primary instructor. The centerpiece of this program is the implementation of a classroom-based action research project. The interview project described in this chapter provided these teachers with experience in doing qualitative research methods as well as the opportunity to consider issues significant to the teaching profession.

2. There are many likely sources of the retired teachers' rather negative images about children in schools today. Certainly, these interviews suggest a longing for the past and the rural schoolhouses in farm communities that began the careers of many of the retired teachers. A few retirees had experiences in working in urban areas and several had children who had gone into teaching. However, all had likely been exposed to the chaotic images stirred up by modern mass media.

3. Thanks to my collaborators: Nancy Brankis, Bruce Cramer, Tammy Davis, Sue DeVeirman Vani, Rose Filkowski, Debbie Friedman, Helen Gebler, Jean Glenn, Barbara Halsey, Jill Hancock, Kay Hancock, Barb Henby, Sally Henderson, Dean Hirshman, Karen Kaiz, Gail Kapp, Roberta Kerr, Linda Koolish, Lori Krupka, Tamara Lowy, Annette Lubkeman, Linda May, Terri Mills, Barbara Modica, Richard Moon, Jayne Pedersen, Jim Pergander, Barbara Phillips, Charlotte Renehan, Mary Seaver, Karen Shinners, Herbert Stagge, Phyllis Steffan, Teri Stone, Laura Wiza, Jill Wolf, and Ruth Woodruff.

REFERENCES

Johnson, S. D. (1990). *Teachers at work.* New York: Basic Books.

Lieberman, A., & Miller, L. (1984) *Teachers, their world and their work.* Arlington, VA: Association for Supervision and Curriculum Development.

Lortie, D. (1975). *Schoolteacher.* Chicago: University of Chicago Press.

Van Manen, M. (1990). *Researching lived experience.* New York: State University of New York Press.

Weiler, K. (1992). Remembering and representing life choices. A critical perspective on teachers' oral history narratives. *Qualitative Studies in Education, 3*(1), 39–50.

4

Reflections in a Mirror: Metaphors of Teachers and Teaching

Sara Efron
Pamela Bolotin Joseph

As a teacher, I am like a dentist. The dentist tells you what you have to do to have good teeth, but essentially, you have to do it. Some days it is as hard as pulling teeth. And if they didn't brush their teeth last night, they come back and you can't get near them because they have bad breath. And you have this faint feeling as if they failed you in some way, or you failed because you did not press upon them the importance of doing it. They come with cavities and you have to fix them. They come to you 2 hours before you have to turn in the grades and they ask, "What can I do?" "Well, you really should have brushed. Let's see if I can fill it. We'll stick some silver in there and see if it holds. But next time remember to brush!"

Teacher as a dentist—an unusual description of a teacher—and yet, this metaphor allows us to understand how one teacher views her work, her purpose, her relationship with students. By creating and discussing her metaphor, this teacher reveals how she constructs her teaching reality and what, from this perspective, makes sense in the complexities and dilemmas of her work. Through this image, we see an experienced educator who does not see herself necessarily as a creative power or a dynamic force in the lives of young people. Rather, it is a metaphor of struggle ("pulling teeth"), of compassion ("Come … what can I do?"), of failure and perseverance that expresses her recognition that

75

in the end the responsibility for learning is with the students. It portrays a school-teacher who finds her work difficult and at times frustrating, but who ultimately persists because she cares about the students. This image also recognizes teaching as a practical, demanding profession, and assumes that the teacher is the one who makes decisions and comes up with answers in the ambiguous and complex world of the classroom.

This metaphor and description, told to us several years ago in an interview with a high school teacher (one of our graduate students), make known the complexity in a teacher's practice that is almost never represented in public images of schoolteachers. Images of teachers in popular culture and public discourse, both historically and in contemporary times, have typically been stereotypes and caricatures that may have very little to do with the essence of teachers' work and their understanding of practice (Shannon & Crawford, 1998). These public images give us little meaningful understanding of what it means to be a teacher. We have found that teachers' images of self contrast greatly with public images that obscure the complexity of work and identity, and, at best, reveal only a narrow sense of teachers' professional lives.

In this chapter, we will explore how schoolteachers' metaphors of self depict different facets of their identities and experiences (see Fischer & Kiefer, chapter 5, this volume). Examples of teachers' metaphors and descriptions of practice are drawn from our own work as teacher educators and researchers during the past decade (from interviews, class journals, and papers) in the context of studies about metaphor, curriculum, and the teaching profession by others. We view our contribution not as definitive, but as a way of considering how metaphors can generate themes for reflection about the nature of teachers' work. We will also explore the nature of metaphors and their limitations, how metaphoric inquiry can help teachers to contemplate their practice and to imagine alternatives, and why oversimplified public images must be replaced by a more complex notion of teaching.

Metaphors as Windows Into Teachers' Knowledge

How do schoolteachers make sense of the puzzle of their world—the classroom and its myriad interactions and decisions, "competing goals and actions" (Carter, 1990, p. 302)? How do they acquire knowledge that enables them to work in their environments in what they assume is the best way? Researchers who study new and experienced teachers suggest that teachers develop an "embedded" body of knowledge as they "participate in educational situations" (Connelly & Clandinin, 1988, p. 54). This knowledge cannot be directly taught but must be "worked out experientially over time" (Clandinin & Connelly, 1986, p. 383).

This knowledge is "personal," as teachers remember and draw from images of education and learning events in which they have participated. A perceptual framework of what it means to be a teacher emanates from their integration of experiences, beliefs, and values over time (Bullough, 1991; Bullough, Knowles, & Crow, 1992;

Knowles, 1994; Knowles & Holt-Reynolds, 1991; Lortie, 1975). Knowledge also is "practical," as teachers rely on a framework to meet the demands of their particular situations. The integration of these two forms of implicit theories guides teachers' practice. This is the foundation for their daily actions, interactions, and decisions, not a theoretical or officially sanctioned knowledge base (Briscoe, 1991; Carter, 1990; Clandinin & Connelly, 1986; Cole, 1990; Elbaz, 1983; Johnston, 1992).

One avenue for understanding teachers' personal and practical knowledge is through the study of metaphors. Researchers who study metaphor explain that metaphors influence the ways individuals view the world, act in their world, and form beliefs about what is right (Johnson, 1993; Schön, 1983). Also, metaphors extend beyond language, revealing concepts that may be known only intuitively (Lakoff, 1993; Sfard, 1998). The use of metaphors is a pervasive feature of thinking and discourse; the conceptual system is fundamentally metaphorical (Munby & Russell, 1990; Taylor, 1982).

Metaphors allow teachers' intuitive knowledge base, which is made of beliefs and fragments of meaning, to be synthesized and reorganized into something concrete and public, providing integrated theoretical and practical understanding of the assumptions that govern their teaching (Fenwick, 1996; Munby, 1986; Oxford et al., 1998; Stofflett, 1996). Each metaphorical identification is framed in its own curricular and ethical implication and carries a certain normative image, an alternative set of purposes, and direction of actions (Bauer & Vannice, 1992; Fenwick, 1996; Grant, 1992; Pineau, 1994; Strickland & Iran-Nejad, 1994). The ability of metaphors to be like colored glasses (through which objects of the same color as the tinted lenses are accented and those that are not recede into the background) allows them to be used as thematic organizers (Gradin, 1989). Those thematic organizers enable teachers to name, to give meaning, to categorize (Bowers, 1980).

Teachers' metaphors of self—as well as their representations of students, classrooms, and knowledge—have increasingly become a salient part of the study of teachers and teaching (Bullough & Stoke, 1994; Sears & Marshall, 1990):

- Metaphoric inquiry is a way of looking at practice (Connelly & Clandinin, 1988) and creating windows into teachers' thinking about teaching (Earle, 1995; Fenwick, 1996; Knowles, 1994).
- Metaphors are powerful tools for capturing mental representations of practice, allowing teachers to describe experiential knowledge—activities, thoughts, and feelings—understanding that is difficult, if not impossible, to communicate through literal means. They provide language that bridges the gap between theory and practice (Carter, 1990; Dooley, 1998).
- As metaphors illuminate teachers' perceptions of self, they make complex phenomena accessible through an interpretative framework (see Carter, 1990; Fenwick, 1996; Grant, 1992; Munby, 1986).
- Metaphors are helpful in the construction of professional identities and in reflective exploration of teachers' selves-in-practice (see Briscoe, 1991; Bullough, 1991; Bullough, Knowles, & Crow, 1992; Carter, 1990; Fenwick,

1996; Grant, 1992; Miller & Fredericks, 1988; Munby & Russell, 1989; Provenzo, McCloskey, Kottkamp, & Cohn, 1989).

Metaphors of Identity and Practice

We discovered that schoolteachers' metaphors represent two missions of teachers' work: the cognitive and affective (Lieberman & Miller, 1990). There are some teachers who see their roles primarily in the instructional realm as they describe their beliefs about curriculum and knowledge; others understand that their roles are also affective and express their self-definitions as a composite of academic and personal relationships; still other teachers believe that the pedagogical area may be the least important aspect of their work and derive their core meaning of teaching from moral relationships with students—especially by assuming parental roles. Consequently, in the following examples, we depict the metaphors of teachers who have shared their words with us via two frameworks: the pedagogical and the moral.

Teachers' Pedagogical Roles

Teachers' metaphors of practice illuminate their pedagogical roles and orientations toward curriculum and learning. These examples reflect diverse beliefs and philosophies that illustrate age-old as well as current discussions about knowledge, learning, curriculum, and schooling (Eisner & Vallance, 1974; Joseph, Bravmann, Windschitl, Mikel, & Green, 2000; Pinar, Reynolds, Slattery, & Taubman, 1995). The teachers' positions run the gamut from insistence on strongly teacher-controlled classrooms to beliefs about children's interests and freedom at the center of pedagogical decisions.

We begin our portrayal of pedagogical metaphors with examples of teachers who see themselves as managers and leaders. These educators see functioning, controlling, and leadership at the core of their work. For example, a "ring leader" is the metaphor chosen by a high school teacher who sees himself as the most important component in instruction. Another high school teacher imagines himself as a well-ordered machine: "My job seems to be like an engine that is well taken care of. Everything works the way it is supposed to work. Everything goes the way it is supposed to go. There is a set rhythm and reason to why things work in the way they do. I lead by example." The engine metaphor emphasizes teaching as a systematic plan for achieving predetermined competencies. To this teacher, school is "a time frame in which you have a set of goals and objectives that need to be accomplished. You take a student from this point to that point." From this perspective, he is a technician who keeps the "factory"—the educational machine—operating.

Teachers as controlling managers expect students to conform and to do their work properly and well. They create environments, therefore, in which students are socialized into the role of workers (Bullough, 1994; Marshall, 1988). This view of teaching as a "management- of-learning" strategy does not attend to whether or not learning is meaningful or satisfying for the students (Green, 2000).

There are other metaphors of teachers who are in control, not as managers of classroom factories, but by virtue of their content expertise. Some teachers think of themselves as master teachers—as deliverers of knowledge—who base their authority on their vast knowledge and instructional expertise. They do not give credence to students as constructors of knowledge, but believe instead that teachers can go from student to student and give knowledge as gifts.

A middle school teacher sees her role as the mediator between content and learning: "I have the subject matter knowledge and I can explain things to students in a concise manner so they can understand." She describes herself as "A light breeze, touching the students, maybe bending a little bit this way or that way. I hope it is always light and never bending anybody over. I think it is refreshing—at times cooler, sometimes it's a warm breeze if they need one." The image of a teacher going from student to student also appears in another teacher's metaphor of "the iron butterfly." This elementary teacher explains how she sees herself as having "the sensitivity to flit from flower to flower and draw out what is needed—yet very organized and structured and strong."

Other master teachers believe that being the giver of knowledge is only part of their craft. An elementary teacher declares that conveying knowledge appropriately to children according to their abilities also is important: "I like to see my self as a communicator more than anything else. I like to communicate with them on their own level Knowledge is obviously important, but more important is the ability to break that knowledge down to a level the children can understand."

Knowledge giving also means directing students toward sources rather than simply giving them information. A high school teacher sees himself as a "motivator," sharing his love of history:

> The teacher should be knowledgeable in the content area and be able to present it to the students in a meaningful way. He should look for questions and for answers . . . I am like an encyclopedia of information for which the student has a way to open me up and ask questions. I will gladly not give him the answers, but show him where to go to get answers.

A subsequent metaphor reveals teachers' beliefs that they must stimulate learners who by their nature are passive. The image of the teacher as an "activator" emerges as an elementary teacher who believes "that the teacher is in charge of trying to get basic information to the children" describes her desire to arouse and motivate reluctant or apathetic learners.

> I want to stimulate them .... I don't care if they hate it; I just want them to respond ... I don't see them reacting to a lot of things. I think that they are numbed by just being placid. At times, I feel like I am a television set. I want to say "react!" I don't care if it's good; I don't care if it's bad. I want to see something.

However, when teachers see themselves as stimulators and motivators, the illumi-
nation that students experience is like the metaphor of the light bulb in which "the
control is with the teacher, rather than the students. Light bulbs do not switch themselves on ... the teacher has control, and students are assigned subservient roles
(Tobin, 1993, p. 222).

A different image of a teacher as leader and stimulator is "devil's advocate." This
metaphor, told to us by a teacher working at a Catholic high school, suggests the So-
cratic tradition of critical examination of conventional thinking—asking unsettling
questions that lead to disequilibrium. Although this teacher does not believe that he
always has the ultimate answers to questions, he encourages doubt, guides learners
through their bewilderment, and, at the end, leads students toward meaningful answers and affirmation of values.

> I teach by the Socratic method—posing questions and not giving answers.
> I see myself as a facilitator, an active questioner. For example, when I
> teach religion, I show the kids the supposition that disproves God exists
> and then go on from there—a little knowledge can take you away from
> God and a lot of knowledge can take you back. I rely on my study in phi-
> losophy to give me empowerment and mastery as a teacher. I also help kids
> to become questioners; they learn that it's okay to question and okay to
> doubt.

As in the liberal arts or classical tradition, these examples suggest images of teachers as elders and as masters; neither wishes for learners to passively acquire knowledge but wants them to become intellectually engaged and competent (Joseph,
2000). "Teachers as masters" have the pedagogical expertise to know how to lead
learners to wisdom through inquiry and by personal connection to the content.

Other teachers who see themselves as leaders and stimulators, however, suggest to
us the curricular orientation of critical pedagogy in which teachers are seen as
"transformative intellectuals" and "engaged critics" who play an active role in shaping curriculum (Giroux, 1993, p. 15). The leader metaphor is suggested by an elementary teacher, not as a description of a manager, but as a "leader in addressing
social inequities." She believes, "Views that challenge the conservative status quo
cannot be off-limits, and in fact, may be at the heart of a child's life. If [we] strive to
meet the needs of the child, then does it not follow that we need to help the child confront injustice if he or she sees it in his or her world?" Such teachers stimulate students through their heads and hearts to consider and oppose injustice (Windschitl &
Joseph, 2000). The "stimulator" as provocateur is described by an elementary teacher
who exposed her students to the "blue-eyes/brown-eyes" prejudice experiment in
which the children experienced what it is like to face racial prejudice, as some had
special privileges whereas others had severe restrictions placed on them (see Peters,
1987). This teacher explains that "my students live in such a restricted environment
that without putting our students into disequilibrium, I don't think they would be able
to empathize or speak about any issue, such as discrimination, in any form."

Another teacher working in a middle school has metaphors of herself as "leader" and "spark" as she describes her devotion to democratic education. She characterizes her classroom as a village in which adults have important roles:

> Every community and every society has its elders, counselors, teachers, wise men, and, even in a democracy, there is someone with executive power. While students need to exercise their own powers of autonomy, we should remember that they are children. Careful and respectful adult guidance and supervision does not, in my opinion, destroy the democratic nature of the classroom.

She adds, "I do not want to lead in such a way that encourages others to be followers." For the democratic educator, the teacher is a citizen among many citizens and believes in shared authority for developing curriculum (Mikel, 2000). For those who describe the democratic conception of teaching, the teacher has a powerful role in developing and sustaining a classroom democracy and must be a "catalyst for collaboration" (Kelly, 1994, p. 73). This same teacher also explains her metaphor of herself as a "spark." She says that she "would rather be the spark that initiates an idea so that when all is accomplished, people feel that they did it themselves."

Teachers' leadership roles also appear when teachers hold constructivist images of themselves—as learning facilitators and co-developers of understanding with students rather than a dispensers of knowledge (Windschitl, 2000). Constructivist approaches to teaching depict the teacher as a diagnostician—not for "curing" students, but for accurately assessing what learning experiences are needed to bring them to further understanding. A fourth-grade teacher, in discussing her educational philosophy, brings forth the image of an investigator as she thinks about the ways that her students learn: "I sometimes feel like a detective as I try to look at all the evidence and make a determination of how a child's brain processes information. What pathways should I navigate to try to make learning easier, sometimes just possible, for my students?"

The theme of flexibility—of the tension between planning and spontaneity—occurs as another fourth-grade teacher talks about his selecting appropriate material and activities in conjunction with learners' roles as active constructors of knowledge:

> I am kind of like an actor. Before he goes on stage, he peers into his closet to see what outfit needs to be worn for that specific situation. Depending on the students and their needs, I choose the kind of hat I am going to wear. Sometimes I have to change the act while I am on stage. It depends on the kids you are with. Sometimes you have to be one thing to one group and another thing to another group.

Several metaphors that portray teachers as facilitators of learning embody more of a student-centered philosophy. An elementary teacher describes himself as "kind

of a guide in a forest preserve; [I am] going with them and experience with them."
Such teachers are co-learners who articulate the passion and excitement of learning
(Bravmann, 2000). A holistic child-centered orientation is the basis for a kindergarten teacher's metaphor of herself as "gardener." She epitomizes a view of education
as a natural process stemming from children's inherent curiosity and desire to know
in which teachers are facilitators as children set the pace of learning. This teacher
feels that her students need protection from all those who don't understand their de-
velopmental stage—from the parents who drive their children too much, ignoring
the fact that at times a child needs more time to develop; "you can't force the bloom
to open before its time. Many parents want to transplant it where it should not grow,
and it withers or becomes sick"—or from administrators who keep increasing curricular content. "They push the curriculum more and more. In the two and a half
hours a day that we have with the kids, we can't cover everything. Children still
need time to play; they need time to socialize. The administration does not understand these children's needs."

A middle school teacher also expresses a student-centered philosophy in discussing her pedagogical role. In her eyes, the curriculum in her class should allow
learning "that is applicable to children's lives that will suit their needs." She feels
constricted by district mandates and the tyranny of textbooks and believes that her
students should be taught things other than those proposed by people who do not
know her students: "I am tied to a curriculum that was created by this 'they' who really do not know my kids' needs. I hate to be under the pressure that if it is week 32, I
had better be in unit 32. There is no time to seize the teaching moment and let the
kids go wherever they want to." This teacher's metaphors of self are "mother" and
"friend." To love children, she implies, is to facilitate their freedom to learn.

Teachers' Moral Roles

Metaphors of practice can illustrate teachers' relationships with children and adolescents, reflecting their approaches to moral agency—their beliefs about ethical obligations to their students and their respective actions (Joseph & Efron, 1993; Sockett,
1993; Tom, 1984). In making sense of metaphors that explore moral roles, we suggest
that teachers share similarities with parents who have multiple parenting roles. It is
unlikely that schoolteachers will act out only one parental purpose; their relationships
with students will reflect a composite of social and moral dynamics (see Cutforth,
1999). Although some of these stances seem contradictory, the metaphors may more
meaningfully reflect the complexity of moral relationships.

Metaphors for teachers' moral roles convey their sense of obligation to care
about their students. We often find teachers' metaphors as mother, father, or surrogate parent that reveal how teachers view themselves as loving their students much
as they would their own children. As one first-grade teacher explains, "The
teacher's role is to see the children as her own kids and be concerned about anything
that is going on with the kids." Another elementary teacher affirms that her students
"really become your kids, your second family." Even when parental metaphors are

not explicit, teachers generate complex images of themselves in various forms of parental roles—nurturers, protectors, advocates, and character-builders. In our examples, teachers see themselves—uniquely or in concert—as friends who delight in children and adolescents' blossoming, as caregivers responsible for social and emotional well-being, or as moral guides who inculcate values and habits necessary if one is to survive and flourish in a difficult world. The parental role, despite its wide range of enactments, essentially is a moral one in which adults feel responsibility for meeting students' nonacademic needs and for providing moral guidance. We found metaphors and descriptions of parenting among experienced as well as very young teachers.

We begin by portraying teachers whose approaches to their nonacademic responsibilities go hand-in-hand with their versions of good instructional practice. These teachers believe that, in their parental roles, they should shape the character of children and adolescents. The "ring leader" (mentioned previously), a high school teacher, sees himself leading "in terms of instruction, discipline, and getting along with other people." An essential part of this kind of leadership role is controlling and managing students' behavior "for their own good." Another, an elementary teacher, chooses as his metaphor a "captain who leads the students to new places." He explains, "I like to have control of my class; discipline is important to me. I love my students and I want them to learn."

Some teachers who say they should influence students' moral development think their students have character deficiencies, such as lack of self-control. The image of removing deficits is powerfully expressed in a middle school teacher's metaphor, a "potter": "[I am like] a potter shaping clay, where you try to get the flaws out and you try to bring out the best that is within each student. I shape them into an ideal of what I see. I see certain things each students needs in order to succeed." As this teacher talks more about herself, however, we learned that holding control is not what gives her work meaning. The "potter" emphasizes her excitement and satisfaction when students come back years later, telling her that what they learned in her classroom helped to make them successful.

Acceptance of parental roles may lead teachers to do what they think parents ought to do: teach values by being a moral presence and continually reminding children of right and wrong. A sixth-grade teacher whose metaphor for herself is "surrogate parent" reminisces: "I had a kid write me a poem. Just brought it back when he was in junior high. He wrote: 'Oh, how I loved to watch you when you teach. Oh, how I hated it when you preached.'"

Another teacher working with young adolescents believes that she has to help her students develop moral feelings, to internalize values. She has images of herself as a "mother" and "best friend": "Sometimes I feel like a mother. I am not only giving but also nagging. Nobody ever put guilt trips on some of my kids. They never feel guilty about not doing something—I fill that void. 'You didn't do your homework, but I expected you to'—the Jewish/Italian kind of a mother."

Other teachers believe they can help shape students' character by being role models. A middle school teacher who calls himself a "second father" believes he can be that kind of influence: "I try to keep my life as pure as I can. Not just for the kids. It is my life. I do it for myself. I feel this makes me happy and makes me feel good about myself. And, if I feel good about myself, it will present a light that other people can see, too .... Most of all [I try] to be an example." A first-grade teacher who has an image of herself as "mom" talks about how she teaches her students proper behavior by role modeling, as well as by talking about her expectations.

Teachers who understand the primacy of moral guidance in their practice can have complex perceptions of what those roles entail. As might mothers and fathers, teachers see various ways in which they are moral agents. For example, a teacher who espouses her values to students, describes how she gives "mom lectures" and, as a role model, demonstrates behaviors that she wants her students to imitate. She also sees her role as "mom" by trying to stimulate moral growth through class meetings and group problem solving. An elementary teacher who sees himself as a "juggler" explains that he wants to play "an important role in children's development" by "my presence, the way I behave." He also discusses how he gives "children a chance to analyze" their behaviors and to imagine alternative ways of getting along with each other.

Other teachers focus more on caring or nurturing than upon moral guidance. They believe they must help to meet children's physical and emotional needs. We especially find that teachers who express this sentiment work in communities in which children have experienced hardship and turmoil. The multifaceted nature of the nurturing parental role is apparent in a first-grade teacher's metaphors that describe her relationship with children in her classroom: "I am a helper. You find yourself being a social worker, the teacher, the mother. You have so many roles to play .... There are so many things that influence the kids' lives that you need to be aware of and to be able, as much as you possibly can, to help them." The elementary teacher whose pedagogical metaphor is "detective," also expresses a moral metaphor for herself:

> Learning is a secondary need and a child who is hungry, sleepy, or cold cannot move past those greater needs to the need to learn. Therefore, part of my job is of social worker, making certain my students have had breakfast in the morning ... that they have warm clothes and that they are getting enough sleep.

Nurturing teachers want to protect their students and describe their anguish because they cannot change the conditions that affect children's lives. A middle school teacher laments, "I can't take them home with me every night—they go out to wherever they live and there is reality." She is keenly aware of the dangers her students face and expresses her anxiety and fear for her students' future. This teachers also worries that children lack of love in their lives. She sees herself as a "mother" and a "friend" to her students: "I am giving care and loving that might not be there." The middle school teacher who sees himself as a role model, a "second father," also explains his caring relationship to students:

> I tell the kids all the time that I am like their second father. I try to be more
> like a friend to all, rather than just a teacher. I realize that they have lots of
> problematic situations at home so I treat them with respect so they feel that
> they can come to me and talk with me about things that they would nor-
> mally not talk with teachers about. I want them to feel better while they are
> in the classroom.

Schoolteachers working in communities where children do not face apparent
hardships also may express their roles as nurturers and advocates. An elementary
teacher in a rather affluent suburb also chooses the metaphor of "mother": "In the
first grade, they are so young. All of a sudden, they are thrown into an all-day situation where, during the week, I see them more than their parents do. A lot of the time
kids slip and call me 'mom.'" Moreover, she notes that "you learn to know if there is
an emotional problem or learning problem. A teacher should be very caring and
concerned with the whole child not just his or her academics." This teacher sees her
students holistically and takes social, emotional, as well as cognitive development
into account; she expresses frustration because she believes that the educational
system shows lack of sensitivity and timeliness in responding appropriately to students' individual problems. Another suburban elementary teacher uses the metaphor of "communicator" for her role as instructor and "friend" as the image of her
relationship with students:

> I think that teachers need to show the students that they are on their side
> To me, a teacher is someone that the child is able to come to and say, "Help
> me out." [Teachers] should be able to help out in all areas .... Kids need
> adult guidance—in academic areas as well as social areas. They need
> someone they can trust.

Other teachers believe that their primary moral role is to help students believe in
themselves. For example, the elementary teacher who sees his pedagogical role as a
"guide" and a "co-learner" describes how he cares about "helping [students] see their
potential—I am interested in helping them see themselves in a positive way." The
teacher as "juggler" explains how he tries "to keep everything going and make sure
that it is going successfully," but he focuses on his efforts to help individual students:

> Encourage the children who need encouragement and also recognize chil-
> dren who are doing well. Give them a little spring by saying, "You are do-
> ing a great job, keep going." All through this time you have to know what
> you are doing, have to be attuned and aware of this special balance be-
> tween these different needs.

A high school teacher tries to find something special in every student, to "find
things ... that they can be proud of." His metaphor, "a director of a play," on the surface is a metaphor of control, but instead he emphasizes taking students "with all

the talents and skills they have ... and make each one shine as the leading lady or man on stage." Such teachers want to make students feel strong and cherished—as would loving parents wish for their children.

Implications

While metaphors may provide a useful viewpoint and entry into the thinking of teachers (Knowles, 1994), they can never be perceived as "transparent representations" of teachers' sense of self (Fenwick, 1996, p. 7). Metaphors of schoolteachers and teaching must be considered as representations—but not as the substance of teaching itself. Like windows, metaphors provide only a partial view into individuals' thoughts and feelings—focusing on selective features of complicated classroom realities. A single metaphor, or even several, can never fully depict the world of any schoolteacher because metaphors, by their nature, condense or simplify a collection of experiences into a single vivid communication—a cognitive and emotional snapshot of sorts (Earle, 1994, p. 35).

While we can never take metaphors as the "truth" about teachers' work, we should be especially cautious when the identification of metaphors takes place as an isolated activity—for example as part of "on-the-spot" research that demands immediate responses (see Bullough & Stokes, 1994; Fenwick, 1996; Knowles, 1994). Such situations may not give teachers time to articulate reflective responses or might impel them (especially novices) to give superficial or disingenuous metaphors for the sake of pleasing the researchers and corresponding to the assumed "right" and "favored" images of teaching. As well, people may simply have greater or lesser linguistic gifts for creating elegant metaphoric responses.

Metaphors need to be linked to personal narrative descriptions embedded within the classroom and school context. Schoolteachers' authentic voices—depicting their personal and practical knowledge—can be heard and understood only when their metaphors are an integral part of the detailed story of their social and professional context, "not in the form of abstract explanations, but in terms of the matters that are important" to them (Elbaz, 1991, p. 14).

More important, teachers must have the opportunity to interpret their own metaphors and use metaphors as springboards for perceiving and contemplating the intricacies of teaching. The goal of metaphoric inquiry is reflection:

> Reflection can be summarized as a natural process that facilitates the development of future action from the contemplation of past and/or current behavior. Reflection refers to the ongoing process of critically examining and refining practice, taking into careful consideration the personal, pedagogical, societal ... and ethical contexts associated with schools, classrooms and the multiple roles of teachers. (Han, 1995, p. 228)

As catalysts for reflection, metaphors can be used by teachers for becoming more aware of their beliefs and practice, the contrast between ideal self-definitions and the realities of their classroom actions, as well as of pedagogical and moral dilemmas. Consideration of metaphors provides insight into alternatives of beliefs and actions. Reflection offers the possibility of knowing the benefits and limitations posed by the use of a particular metaphor as well as the problems and possibilities of other perspectives (Bullough & Stokes, 1994; Kloss, 1987; Marshall, 1990; Sears & Marshall, 1990; Tobin, 1993).

For educators, the greatest benefit of metaphoric inquiry may be the possibility of experiencing disequilibrium—the confusion or doubt that leads to questioning of unexamined beliefs. Metaphor (from the Greek *metapherin*) means to transfer, to bear change. When people create metaphors, they join unlike things together. "The essence of metaphor is understanding and experiencing one kind of thing in terms of another" (Lakoff & Johnson, 1980, p. 5). The juxtaposition produced by connecting and contrasting the different images jolts individual anticipation and challenges unaccustomed ways of seeing (Fenwick, 1996). Metaphor can "provide a riddle … which might lead to misunderstandings and bewilderment, but might then allow new knowledge to be produced" (Ricoeur, as cited in Kemp, 1999, p. 88).

Metaphors, as reflections in a mirror, may provide affirming images of teachers and their understanding of practice. Conversely, they can illustrate wide gaps between teachers' ideal selves and the existence of what they know daily. Metaphoric inquiry helps teachers to see conflicts and gain understanding about how they might wish to modify their practice (Tobin, 1990, p. 127). As teachers become cognizant of their own and other teachers' images of self, analysis—of beliefs and expectations that govern practice—and critical confrontation can occur (Farber & Armaline, 1992; Fenwick, 1996; Sfard, 1998; White, 1994). The generative purpose of metaphors is to reframe old problems so they can be "seen" from a fresh viewpoint, in ways that suggest new approaches to the puzzles, leading to new solutions (Schön, 1987). The possibility, then, is for fresh metaphors to be created. "New metaphors open up fresh possibilities of thought and actions" (Scheffler, 1960, p. 48).

Reflection

Metaphors as representations of teachers and teaching are problematic on several levels. First, teachers' metaphors of self can be neither examined nor changed unless there are opportunities for reflection. There may be little opportunity for teachers to have conversations about the possibilities and inadequacies of metaphors of identity and practice when the educational enterprise, considered as a science or as a business, does not value such reflection about philosophies and moral commitments. Second, public images of schoolteachers seem resistant to modification because of stereotypes and caricatures in popular culture, collective memories of schooling (that, at best, are impressionistic and have little to do with the complexity of teachers' personal and practical knowledge), and the social-political ramifications of present-day goals of standardization, efficiency, and technology. The public may never grasp the complexity of teachers' lives and work even if teachers and administrators "put forth a variety of images for the public to consider" (Shannon & Crawford, 1998, p. 262).

For educators to have support for reflective inquiry and practice, and for the public to engage in thoughtful deliberation about the work of teachers, we believe that change must occur in schools and in public discourse. The concept of craft must supersede the notion of image—namely, teaching as pedagogical and moral craft (see Kagan, 1988; Lieberman & Miller, 1990; Oser, Dick, & Patry, 1992; Parks, 1992; Tom, 1984). While we are not calling for teachers to be considered as experts whose practice cannot be fathomed or critiqued, we do believe that teaching must be revealed as a complexity of pedagogical and moral choices and processes. Teaching represented as pedagogical and moral artistry changes the nature of educational and public discourse about teachers and schooling from a focus on superficial images, mechanistic descriptions, and "fixes" to the contemplation of how to create and sustain schools as creative and nurturing environments. Attending to metaphors and images can only be the beginning of such conversations.

REFERENCES

Bauer, D. H., & Vannice, C. K. (1992). Teaching as the art of living. *The Educational Forum, 56*(4), 421–433.

Bowers, C. A. (1980). Curriculum and cultural reproduction: An examination of metaphor as a carrier of ideology. *Teachers College Record, 82,* 264–289.

Bravmann, S. L. (2000). Developing self and spirit. In P. B. Joseph, S. L. Bravmann, M. A. Windschitl, E. R. Mikel, & N. S. Green (Eds.), *Cultures of curriculum* (pp. 73–94). Mahwah: Lawrence Erlbaum Associates.

Briscoe, C. (1991). The dynamic interactions among beliefs, role metaphors, and teaching practices: A case study of teacher change. *Teacher Education, 75*(2), 185–199.

Bullough, R. V., Jr. (1991) Exploring personal teaching metaphors in preservice teacher education. *Journal of Teacher Education, 42*(1), 43–51.

Bullough, R. V., Jr. (1994). Digging at the roots: Discipline, management, and metaphor. *Action in Teacher Education, 16*(1), 1–10.

Bullough, R. V., Jr., Knowles, J. G., & Crow, N. A. (1992). *Emerging as a teacher.* London: Routledge & Kegan Paul.

Bullough, R. V., Jr., & Stokes D. K. (1994). Analyzing personal teaching metaphors in preservice teacher education as a means for encouraging professional development. *American Educational Research Journal, 31*(1), 197–224.

Carter, K. (1990). Meaning and metaphor: Case knowledge in teaching. *Theory into Practice, 29*(2), 109–115.

Clandinin, D. J., & Connelly, F. M. (1986). Rhythms in teaching: The narrative study of teachers' personal practical knowledge of classrooms. *Teaching & Teacher Education, 2*(4), 377–387.

Cole, A. L. (1990). Personal theories of teaching: Development in the formative years. *The Alberta Journal of Educational Research, 36*(3), 203–222.

Connelly, F. M., & Clandinin, D. J. (1988). *Teacher as curriculum planners: Narratives of experience.* New York: Teacher College Press.

Cutforth, N. J. (1999). Reconciling the moral and technical dimensions of teaching: Moving beyond notions of good and bad pedagogy. *Journal for a Just and Caring Education, 5*(4), 386–405.

Dooley, C. (1998). Teaching as a two-way street: Discontinuities among metaphors, images, and classroom realities. *Journal of Teacher Education, 49*(2), 97–107.

Earle, R. S. (1994). In search of teaching metaphors: Images of the classroom. *Educational Technology, 34*(6), 34–37.

Earle, R. S. (1995). Teacher imagery and metaphors: Windows to teaching and learning. *Educational Technology, 35*(6), 52–59.

Eisner, E. W., & Vallance, E. (1974). *Conflicting conceptions of curriculum.* Berkeley, CA: McCutchan.

Elbaz, F. (1983). *Teacher thinking: A study of practical knowledge.* London: Croom Helm.

Elbaz, F. (1991) Research on teacher's knowledge. The evolution of a discourse. *Journal of Curriculum Studies, 23*(1), 1–19.

Farber, K. S., & Armaline, W. D. (1992). Unlearning how to teach: Restructuring the teaching of pedagogy. *Teaching Education, 5*(1), 99–111.

Fenwick, T. J. (1996, June). *Firestarters and outfitters: Metaphors of adult educators.* Paper presented at the annual conference of the Canadian Society for the Study of Education, St. Catherines, Ontario, Canada (ERIC Document Reproduction Service No. ED400463).

Giroux, H. A. (1993). *Border crossings: Cultural works and the politics of education.* New York: Routledge & Kegan Paul.

Gradin, S. L. (1989, March). *English studies and the metaphors we live by.* Paper presented at the annual meeting of the Conference on College Composition and Communication, Seattle, WA (ERIC Document Reproduction Service No. ED306574).

Grant, G. E. (1992). The sources of structural metaphors in teacher knowledge: Three cases. *Teaching and Teacher Education, 8*(5–6), 433–440.

Green, N. S. (2000). Training for work and survival. In P. B. Joseph, S. L. Bravmann, M. A. Windschitl, E. R. Mikel, & N. S. Green (Eds.), *Cultures of curriculum* (pp. 29–50). Mahwah, NJ: Lawrence Erlbaum Associates.

Han, E. P. (1995). Reflection is essential in teacher education. *Childhood Education, 71*(4), 228–230.

Johnson, M. (1993). *Moral imagination: Implications of cognitive science for ethics.* Chicago: University of Chicago Press.

Johnston, S. (1992). Images: A way of understanding the practical knowledge of student teacher. *Teaching and Teacher Education, 8*(2), 123–136.

Joseph, P. B. (2000). Connecting to the canon. In P. B. Joseph, S. L. Bravmann, M. A. Windschitl, E. R. Mikel, & N. S. Green (Eds.), *Cultures of curriculum* (pp. 51–72). Mahwah, NJ: Lawrence Erlbaum Associates.

Joseph, P. B., Bravmann, S. L., Windschitl, M. A., Mikel, E. R., & Green, N. S. (Eds.). (2000). *Cultures of curriculum.* Mahwah, NJ: Lawrence Erlbaum Associates.

Joseph, P. B., & Efron, S. (1993). Moral choices/moral conflicts: Teachers' self-perceptions. *Journal of Moral Education, 22*(3), 201–220.

Kagan, D. M. (1988). Teaching as clinical problem solving: A critical examination of the analogy and its implications. *Review of Educational Research, 58*(4), 482–505.

Kelly, T. (1994). Democratic empowerment and secondary teacher education. In J. Novak (Ed.), *Democratic teacher education: Programs, processes, problems, and prospects* (pp. 70–81). Albany: State University of New York Press.

Kemp, E. (1999). Metaphor as a tool for evaluation. *Assessment and Evaluation in Higher Education, 24*(1), 81–90.

Kloss, R. J. (1987). Coaching and playing right field: Trying on metaphors for teaching. *College Teaching, 35*(4), 134–139.

Knowles, J. G. (1994). Metaphors as windows on a personal history: A beginning teacher's experience. *Teacher Education Quarterly, 21*(1), 37–66.

Knowles, J. G., & Holt-Reynolds, D.(1991). Shaping pedagogies through personal histories in preservice teacher education. *Teacher College Record, 93*(1), 87–113.

Lakoff, G. (1993). The contemporary theory of metaphor. In N. A. Ortony (Ed.), *Metaphor and thought* (2nd ed., pp. 202–250). Cambridge, UK: Cambridge University Press.

Lakoff, G., & Johnson, M. (1980). *The metaphors we live by.* Chicago: The University of Chicago Press.

Lieberman, A., & Miller, L. (1990). The social realities of teaching. In A. Lieberman (Ed.), *Schools as collaborative cultures: Creating the future now* (pp. 153–163). New York: Falmer.

Lortie, D. (1975). *School teacher: A sociological study.* Chicago: University of Chicago Press.

Marshall, H. H. (1988). Work or learning: Implications of classroom metaphors. *Educational Researcher, 17,* 9–16.

Marshall, H. H. (1990). Metaphor as an instructional tool in encouraging student teacher reflection. *Theory into Practice, 29*(2), 128–132.

Mikel, E. R. (2000). Deliberating democracy. In P. B. Joseph, S. L. Bravmann, M. A. Windschitl, E. R. Mikel, & N. S. Green (Eds.), *Cultures of curriculum* (pp. 115–136). Mahwah, NJ: Lawrence Erlbaum Associates.

Miller, S. I., & Fredericks, M. (1988) Uses of metaphors: A qualitative case study. *Qualitative Studies in Education, 1*(3), 263–276.

Munby, H. (1986). Metaphors in the thinking of teachers: An exploratory study. *Journal of Curriculum Studies, 18,* 197–209.

Munby, H., & Russell, T. (1990). Metaphor in the study of teachers' professional knowledge. *Theory into Practice, 29*(2), 116–121.

Oser, F., Dick, A., & Patry, J., (Eds.). (1992). *Effective and responsible teaching: The new synthesis.* San Francisco: Jossey-Bass.

Oxford, R. L., Tomlinson, S., Barcelos, A., Harrington, C., Lavine, R. Z., Saleh, A., & Longhini, A. (1998). Clashing metaphors about language teachers: Toward a systematic typology for the language teaching field. *System, 26*(1), 3–50.

Parks, M. E. (1992). The art of pedagogy: Artistic behavior as a model for teaching. *Art Education, 45*(5), 51–57.

Peters, W. (1987). *A class divided: Then and now.* New Haven, CT: Yale University Press.

Pinar, W. F., Reynolds, W. M., Slattery, P., & Taubman, P. M. (1995). *Understanding curriculum: An introduction to the study of historical and contemporary curriculum discourses.* New York: Peter Lang.

Pineau, E. L. (1994). Teaching is performance: Reconceptualizing a problematic metaphor. *American Educational Research Journal, 31*(1), 3–25.

Provenzo, E. F., Jr., McCloskey, G. N., Kottkamp, R. B., & Cohn, M. M. (1989). Metaphor and meaning in the language of teachers. *Teacher College Record, 90*(4), 551–573.

Ricoeur, P. (1977). *The rule of metaphor: Multidisciplinary studies of the creation of the meaning in language* (R. Czerny, K. McLaughlin, & J. Costello, Trans.). Toronto: University of Toronto Press.

Scheffler, I. (1960). *The language of education.* Springfield, IL: Charles Thomas.

Schön, D. (1983). *The reflective practitioner.* New York: Basic Books.

Schön, D. (1987). *Educating the reflective practitioner.* San Francisco: Jossey-Bass.

Sears, J. T., & Marshall, J. D. (Eds.). (1990). *Teaching and thinking about curriculum: Critical inquiries.* New York: Teacher College Press.

Sfard, A. (1998). On two metaphors for learning and the dangers of choosing just one. *Educational Researcher, 27*(2), 4–13.

Shannon, P., & Crawford, P. (1998). Summers off: Representations of teachers' work and other discontents. *Language Arts, 75*(4), 255–264.

Sockett, H. (1993). *The moral base for teacher professionalism.* New York: Teachers College Press.

Stofflett, R. T. (1996). Metaphor development by secondary teachers enrolled in graduate teacher education. *Teaching and Teacher Education, 12*(6), 577–589.

Strickland, C. R., & Iran-Nejad, A. (1994, November). *The metaphoric nature of teaching and learning and the role of personal teaching metaphors.* Paper presented at the annual meeting of the Mid-South Educational Research Association, Nashville, TN (ERIC Document Reproduction Service No. ED 399208).

Taylor, P. H. (1982). Metaphor and meaning in the curriculum: On opening windows on the not yet seen. *Journal of Curriculum Theorizing, 4*(1), 209–216.

Tobin, K. (1990). Change metaphors and beliefs: A master switch for teaching? *Theory into Practice, 29*(2), 122–127.

Tobin, K. (1993). Constructivist perspectives on teaching learning. In K. Tobin (Ed.), *The practice of constructivism in science education* (pp. 215–226). Hillsdale, NJ: Lawrence Erlbaum Associates.

Tom, A. (1984). *Teaching as a moral craft.* New York: Longman.

White, M. (1994). Metaphor and reflective teaching. *Quarterly of the National Writing Project and the Center for the Study of Writing and Literacy, 16*(4), 23–25.

Windschitl, M. A. (2000). Constructing understanding. In P. B. Joseph, S. L. Bravmann, M. A. Windschitl, E. R. Mikel, & N. S. Green (Eds.), *Cultures of curriculum* (pp. 95–114). Mahwah, NJ: Lawrence Erlbaum Associates.

Windschitl, M. A., & Joseph, P. B. (2000). Confronting the dominant order. In P. B. Joseph, S. L. Bravmann, M. A. Windschitl, E. R. Mikel, & N. S. Green (Eds.), *Cultures of curriculum* (pp. 137–160). Mahwah, NJ: Lawrence Erlbaum Associates.

5

Constructing and Discovering Images of Your Teaching

Joseph Fischer
Anne Kiefer

I believe that the image is the great instrument of instruction. What a child gets out of any subject presented to him is simply the images which he himself forms with regard to it.

—Dewey (1897/1959, p. 28)

We sat on small chairs in Margaret's middle-grade reading lab and talked about the revolutionary school reform being implemented in Chicago. She had been at M. School (a predominantly Hispanic, inner-city school) for most of her 27 years of teaching and was eager to share her thoughts:

> I think a lot of us feel that we can see the end of our career and we would like great things to happen at the schools. I think we are more in control now. Some people feel very frightened and others just want to grab the ring and run with it. So, I think it is a wonderful thing to happen. It is making us all young again.

Margaret began to talk about reading, how she got children to share their experiences and how she hoped they would always love books.

> You have to help children get excited about reading. When you start talking to kids and getting the kid that does not like to read to tell you some

93

> things he knows about whales, then he gets hooked. You do not have to tell
> him to do this, do that. He is already part of the story because he already
> told you he knows about whales.

Helping children "be part of the story" is central to Margaret's teaching. For her, the story does not merely originate from books, but is a lived experience, a relationship she builds with and encourages among her students.

As we talked, Margaret shared her views about her teaching, her students, and her colleagues. These images make up her autobiography of teaching; they seem to say—"this is what I have done; this is what I have created. This is me." We will see that similar imaging is at work for all the teachers described in this chapter.

The teachers we studied talked about how they viewed their work, portrayed their teaching, and thought others saw them. The interviews served as a mirror for reflection and were, largely, an opportunity for mutual explorations of the images that guide teachers in their work. We discovered that teachers not only hold diverse images of themselves, but they actively construct these images throughout their teaching careers. Teachers told how their views about teaching changed during their careers and how the images served them in their teaching.[1]

Another interesting finding was that teachers had multiple images of their work, indicating the multifaceted nature and the complexity of their profession. Moreover, while some images were clear and vivid, others were tentative and emerging, perhaps indicating that the process of creating and capturing images develops with reflection and a deeper awareness of one's interactions with students. Our research revealed that while many images of teaching are given or imposed on teachers, the most profound ones are actively constructed during teaching practice. The images that teachers create of their work appear to result from a process of doing, describing, and naming. We found creative teachers construct images about their professional roles and practices all during their careers.

Given the time and opportunity for reflection, teachers can describe their lives, focusing upon the changing images of themselves that they have experienced over their years of teaching. The complexity of their images reflects the tasks that they have, the jobs for which they receive a salary and, even more important, the roles that they play in the lives of their students, of other teachers, and of the administrators in the system. This chapter will have three major divisions: Images of Teaching: Portraits and Stories, Creating and Discovering Teacher Images, and Interpreting Teacher Images. In our conclusion, we will envision uses, implications, and ramifications of both the images themselves and the process of imaging.

Images of Teaching: Portraits and Stories

> *The world, I said, has its influence as nature and as society on the child.*
> *He is educated by the elements, by air and light and the life of plants and*
> *animals, and he is educated by relationships. The true educator represents*
> *both: but he must be to the child as one of the elements.*

> *In spite of all similarities every living situation has, like a new born child, a new face that has never been before and will never come again. It demands of you a reaction which cannot be prepared beforehand. It demands nothing of what is past. It demands presence, responsibility: it demands you.* (Buber, 1947/1961, pp. 90, 114)

While we captured a multiplicity of images from a wide range of teachers, the following case studies are presented because they represent important dimensions of images and of the process of creating images. The case studies suggest that images are multiple, change over one's teaching career, and grow in meaning and usefulness in informing and even shaping practice. The teachers who spoke to us, furthermore, are witnesses to Buber's belief that teaching demands our presence—"it demands you." A given, contrived, or conventional image of our work usually does not enlighten us. The unique image as self, as personality and character, is worthy of contemplation and brings joy to our teaching and to student learning.

Irene

Irene has been teaching at M. School for the past 21 years, and was working in her computer writing lab, preparing for the next group of students before our interview began. Toward the end of our conversation, she began to describe how her teaching had changed over the years.

> I used to be extremely structured. Everything went by schedule, because that is how I was taught initially. And now, because I feel freer as a teacher I understand more of what I am doing. Now I can let things go and let the children kind of pick up where they would like to work from, whereas before it was only what I felt should be done. I was very strong on discipline, but now I can let them go off in groups and I feel more at ease with my own style than I did in the beginning. I thought that I needed to have everybody's attention at all times. Now I do not feel that need.

Irene's change in teaching style was slow and painful. After observing her colleagues and reflecting upon her teaching, she began to try out new ways of doing things.

> The few times I did let go of the discipline, things did happen anyway. Therefore, it made me feel freer in doing it again. But, it was a good 10 years before I started asking myself, "What is happening to this class?" … It was a very slow process for me. Other teachers were willing to do all these things, and I used to see them doing that, and I thought, "I cannot stand all that chaos in that room!"

Irene's early images of teaching confined her to the role of taskmaster, giver of information; she found it necessary to constantly seek the children's attention. In her desire to change she began to look more closely at what was happening among her students and turned to her colleagues for guidance and new ideas. In her struggle, she began to find herself, her presence among the children. Of significance was her realization that in order to change her teaching, she needed to observe more closely her students and to design her teaching around their interests.

Irene's experiences exemplify a major finding of our research. Teachers need to feel free in their work in order to be creative, grow professionally, and find satisfaction and fulfillment in what they do. If they merely continue to follow given and constricting roles and functions, their teaching will atrophy. Thus, it would seem useful for teachers to examine the images they hold and to sort out and deal with those that do not enhance their growth.

Sarah

Sarah's first job at M. School, 26 years ago, was teaching Spanish to gifted non-Hispanic children. They wrote plays in Spanish, gave presentations at schools with large Hispanic populations, and every year went to the State Fair in Springfield to submit projects about Hispanic culture. She also noted with pride, "I used to take my classes to the university to demonstrate to the student teachers. I would talk to the audience and then my students would actually put on a demonstration of how they would speak in Spanish." Her program no longer exists, but her fluency in her second language serves her well in speaking to her predominantly Hispanic seventh and eighth graders. Sarah reflected on the many changes that have occurred during her teaching career at M. School. What seems constant is her view of teaching as an adventure:

> Every year you have new students, new things to explore with them and I think every day is an adventure. I mean, it is in a constant state of flux and I think this is very important. Working with children gives one a sense of being young and active and always being aware of what is going on in the world. Because children are naturally very curious, they keep you going, more or less.

Sarah's longevity in the same school gives her an intergenerational view of her students and their families. She attends class reunions and weddings of former students. Students and faculty at M. School are like a family.

> It is exciting when the kids come back year after year, you watch the generations go. I mean they come back with their children. We have children of students that we taught, going to our school and you can see that it is a continuing family. The children and the faculty, we're all like a family. There is a great feeling of familial emotion and caring and I think that the children feel comfortable. It is their home away from, and the kids feel that we are their second parents. For the most part, I think the children respect

us, and they understand that we are telling them things for their own good, just as their mother or father would.

Like a counselor, Sarah gets involved with the emotional problems of her students.

> There has to be more than just reading, writing, and arithmetic. There has to be a feeling of emotion, a feeling of the child knowing you care about him as a total human being, not just as a test score on a piece of paper. These kids are filled with problems, they have many concerns, and they need to talk to somebody. The teacher must be involved with the children. You cannot come in and say, "Open your book to page five," and that is the end of the relationship.

Sarah offered that she feels like a "jack-of-all-trades"—that she wears many hats. Teaching can be hectic, and Sarah feels pulled in many directions.

> I am living in a much more mechanized society, a much more rapidly developing one. We work in a very fast pace, we are all pressured, and life seems more complicated. We are all in a hurry; we are on schedule. I feel I have to breathe on a schedule. And people become frustrated with that. I describe myself sometimes like a hamster on a wheel. I never get anywhere. We do not know how to relax and be in tune with nature.

Moreover, Sarah feels that teachers are not valued or recognized in our society. In many societies, she noted, teachers are held with more respect and even reverence.

> The most important thing today is recognition, admiration, someone to pat us on the back and say, "You are important, you made a difference, we need you." People have to have positive strokes. In order to function and to blossom, you need recognition and praise. Just as the children need positive strokes, you make them feel good, so do we.

Sarah sees herself in multiple roles. Like a parent and a social worker, she gets involved with her students, but she feels there is never enough time to do what has to be done, and she is always on a schedule. She finds teaching an adventure; there is something new each day. Like the elder in a village, Sarah rejoices in seeing generation after generation come to school. Some even come back and tell her, "You made a difference in my life."

It is not clear to what extent Sarah has integrated her many roles and whether or not she sees some central image of herself. Her acceptance of diverse responsibilities may be related to her feeling of being overwhelmed. It appears, too, that many of her rewards are external, beyond her control. Her parent-like role is rewarded when her students grow up and move away, and she awaits their return to voice their

appreciation. While she attends to her students' emotional problems, they ultimately have to solve their own. In spite of our many conversations together, Sarah's
internal satisfactions with her work seemed elusive.

Kate

Kate teaches in a tiny makeshift classroom at the end of the hall, cluttered with
books, chairs, her desk, and a computer. The one window at the back was barely visible, as piles of materials were stacked on the windowsill. A group of her sev-
enth-grade students sat in a circle as Kate read a story. This was her 30th year of
teaching.

> I just gave a short story the other night to this class and if they read it and
> enjoyed reading it, they would have come back to me and told me that they
> really liked the story.

> They need to hear my voice with inflection in it and they need to connect
> with it. I call it bonding. You cannot do it before someone takes you there.
> They won't taste other things unless you lead them to it. All my children
> would be reading these teenage love books if they could choose what to
> read.

Kate described how she carefully selects the stories they read together, tries to
imagine what students would be connected to, and which books would enhance
their experiences. When she is successful in her choice, the students would build a
trusting relationship with each other and with her. In reading the stories together,
they would come to share a common experience and eventually speak a common
language. And, in their memories, they would always have the image of talking
about a much-loved book with Kate—in her tiny room at the end of the hall.

> So far this year their favorite book has been *Lottery Rose,* about an abused
> child, and they still talk about it. You have to understand that most of these
> children have never read a whole book until I get them. They look forward
> to other books I am giving them now, because they wonder, is it going to be
> as good as *Lottery Rose*? The boy in the story turns out to be a winner. He
> learns to communicate with people, which he could not even do before.
> That kind of a theme got them stimulated to reading.

> And you really have to touch those feelings in them. They are so numbed
> by television, and it is on such an adult level, either violence or sex. For
> them to tune into people's real feelings, it does not happen very often.
> They are thrilled with what is going on in these movies, but they do not feel
> the feelings. But to touch them, that does not happen often, and it hap-
> pened with this book. They were touched.

Kate's best preteaching experiences at the university were with "real" teachers during practice teaching. In our conversation, she went back to long ago when she was a student.

> In the beginning of the sophomore year we went into the classrooms and worked all the way to our junior year observing teachers. By the time we got into student teaching we were not overwhelmed by the classrooms, or were not terrified. We knew what we were getting into. I do not know how many methods courses you give a student, but it really does not have a value until you actually get into a classroom.

> I remember the students. There were 30 in the classroom. The children all seemed to be using what they were doing; they were trying to accomplish something. They were grouped and there was a lot of interplay. And that was something I enjoyed doing. That was an impression! More impressions I do not remember. It must have been pleasant, because I continued on. It was something to look forward to, teaching. I could not wait to teach.

As a college student, Kate's images of teaching were positive and based upon close observations of teachers relating to students. She began to construct images of herself as a teacher from her impressions of classroom life. Thus, her images were reality-bound, originating from experiences, from the practice itself.

Kate related how she could not wait to get into teaching. Why had she been so attracted to teaching? Her reply helps explain why she was able to change the way she viewed herself and to focus on her central role as educator.

> I always loved drama, and I always think that teachers are kind of mini actors. I just do not mean that a teacher must be an actress, present dramatic presentations. What drama really is is a little bit of life; it is taking ideas and making things happen with them. I do not know another way of saying it. That is what I believe. In drama of course there is conflict and you get plenty of conflict in teaching.

Over the years, Kate came to a deeper understanding of the bond that developed with students. In reading together she both learns from them and leads them to a larger world. However, as we shall see, to arrive at this realization she needed to make a conscious effort to change some of her ways.

> There was a time in my life when I played the many roles of a teacher. I was the confessor, the mother, the problem solver, friend—the person they turned to when they have a serious problem. Some teachers still try to do that. I have moved away from that and I have to tell you I did that purposely. Children will absorb you and it is very hard to pull back and to work back with ideas. It is very hard to be a social worker, a psychologist, and an educator at the same time. I did it and it was draining.

> I made the decision that I was trying to get a different point of view: to not go to the person, but to start with the literature and then it became personal. When you start getting personal with a child, it is very hard to get back to being an educator. But if you start with an idea in literature and those things involve their personal problems, a lot of them can be solved by themselves; not with the teacher lifting up, but solving themselves through literature. To me that was more important.

Kate also elaborated on some of the ways she tries to start with an idea in literature to help her students learn to reach beyond themselves. Through literature, she hopes they will develop their own strategies to solve their problems and find their own meanings.

> On Monday two children from M. School died in a fire. One was in kindergarten and the other in first grade. I knew them. It was tragic and there were quite a few teachers affected by it. They really had a hard time handling it. That is a tragedy and a problem you cannot hide away or run from. But you cannot constantly involve yourself in the problem, you need to reach out for something else. We need to learn to grow from the problems. They need somebody to listen to them. Our priority is to educate them and to help them look for solutions. Literature can get them to a different kind of plateau in life. For example, after reading *Lottery Rose,* if a student has a problem of being abused, he knows that a child can survive that kind of problem. Through the story, he knows that he can turn to others for help. He can find his way, which the child did in this story; there are rays of hope out there. Saying it in a book is more real to me.

Kate decided to change when she found her role as a problem solver too draining and she began to question her role as an educator in these situations. She turned to literature to see how it might help lead students out of their problems, to help them reach out and not get overwhelmed. This thought came to her one day as she was counseling a child and urging her to reach out beyond her problems. "I knew then I was giving this advice to myself," she told me.

Earlier, in her studies, the groundwork for these insights had been laid. She realized, "You cannot reach out, or lead, unless someone previously has taken you there."

> One of my small talents is painting. I did art work when I was young, and even though I loved to paint and I loved to do drawings, I never bonded with art until I got the right kind of a teacher who led me in there. I had him in a class and he made me feel that there was something to paint that was worthwhile. He made it alive.

What teaching might become was the topic of our last interview. Kate talked about some of her concerns and her visions for schooling.

The bad part of teaching is that there is so much junk involved besides the drama. If it would just be drama, it would be a wonderful profession to be in. Reading for so many years was based on skills, and we did that for a long time. Many of our children turned out to be proficient readers by using merely skills, but if you asked me whether of not that is truly educating a child, I would say no. Children have to be connected to literature. They have to enjoy it and it must take them beyond themselves. What is happening to our educational system is that students are not allowed to create anymore. I would love to see students become independent readers, independent learners. I would like to see children getting together to work together. I would love to see children grab books because they are thrilled by a subject.

Maria

Maria was interviewed on one of the hottest spring days; the temperature in the school was close to 95 degrees. Maria taught in a small room that was created by walling off a section of the hall near the windows. The day was too hot for the computers to be used, so the 20 children from first and second grade worked in two groups. The very quiet ones slowly looked through magazines for pictures of objects that they could use for their personal dictionaries. Her responsibility as an English as a second language (ESL) teacher was to provide ways for the children to acquire English.

Maria believed that there are pressures on these children that go beyond the usual urban pressures.

> I grew up in Chicago, but it was different then. I went to a school near here. When I started school, I did not know English and came to be afraid of the school, the teacher, and even of the other children. When I came to the school door in the morning, the sounds overwhelmed me. I spent the days being as quiet as I could so no one would notice me and ask me any questions. Even with that, I was terrified. I don't remember events, or teachers or specific children. I just remember the fear.

The children in her classroom were not afraid. They were quiet, but their stillness seemed to be result from the effect of the heat, not from distress. The children who searched through magazines had an intensity that emanated from involvement in a task. They talked in low sounds to each other about the pictures they chose and about the way to say the names of the pictures.

> When I started teaching here, we had only a few children who did not know English. Now each classroom has 10 or 15 children who need help. They need understanding. They need to be taught things that the other

children already know. I can feel the fear again when they start in my group and I spend as much time on getting the children to relax as I do on English. Once they see me as a person who knows what and how they feel, we can actually begin learning English.

The group of children sat with the teacher around the table. She talked about the tiny furniture spread out before them. On the table, she also placed what looked like a blueprint or floor plan of an apartment. The squares and rectangles were labeled for rooms of the apartment. Maria said things like: "I put the sofa in the living room"; "I put the tub in the bathroom." In spite of the distracting heat, the children watched her closely and listened to her words. Then the teacher asked the children to perform certain activities that she had been doing. They began to respond with confidence to the directions as the teacher explained them. Maria noticed this, too, and chose one of the children to be "the teacher."

I used to spend my time with the alphabet and the sounds of the letters. I went to some ESL workshops and they told us that the children need to develop some oral language that they can use to analyze for the sounds. There are so many teachers who don't understand that. They keep asking me to teach reading so the children won't "get so far behind." I think I spend a lot of time just talking to the other teachers trying to help them understand. I even ask them to come down here to see the class so they will have an idea how little they [the students] can do with English. I think I need to get some more information .... I almost said ammunition.

Some of the children began to pack up their things and prepare to leave the group. At about the same time, other youngsters appeared at the door and looked around for empty places. It seemed that this class was a "pull-out" program and the children were scheduled for brief periods during the day as they came from their mainstream classrooms for ESL. When we talked about this later, Maria explained:

I am trying to get a firmer schedule. That's one reason I want the teachers to come and see us "at work." They are concerned that the children will "fall behind" in their classrooms. I understand their concern, but would like them to really see how little English the children understand. My husband keeps telling me just to do my job and not worry so much about the children and the other teachers. But I see my job as not just providing ESL lessons, but also helping the children and the teachers to understand language and language learning.

Maria spoke often of the lives of the children and the needs that she recognized in them. It was clear to us that much of her empathy arose from her own experiences and her desire to do whatever she could to help these children.

Creating and Discovering Teacher Images

Margaret, Irene, Sarah, Kate, and Maria shared their present images of themselves as well as much of how the imaging process had been going on in their lives. They do not represent types, yet they do serve to illustrate patterns of images and processes of imaging in teachers' lives. To understand the nature and implications of teacher imaging, it is useful to consider some of the main sources of the images and the factors related to their construction. We can only begin to speculate on some possible origins, but believe that the following three areas are worth consideration. We have named these constructed images, ideal images, and given images.

Constructed Images

Most teachers construct images about their teaching through reflecting upon their experiences with students. These images are created during their career and directly relate to their practice. The process of imaging and the practice of teaching develop together. Images emerge from the practice itself, and inform and even guide it. When the image informs practice and is viewed as useful, the teacher includes it in her repertoire. Similarly, "given images" (from tradition, society, and media) may undergo modification, or elaboration and deeper understanding, as teachers examine the consonance between the images of teaching and their teaching practice. "Ideal images," the third type, are individual hopes and expectations and that are usually unattainable. As visions of what can be, they are useful to teacher development.

Images are especially constructed when teachers begin to reflect upon and become more aware of the nature of the relationships and interactions taking place in their classrooms. The constructed images originate from "both sides"—from the interchange between students and teacher, and from consciously engaging in conversation. In brief, image building takes place during social interactions; they emerge from the mutual act of teaching and learning.

Creating and capturing images about teaching can be viewed as essentially an autobiographical narrative. Teachers comprehend their work by telling stories about it. The images they create are the basis for these stories. Moreover, both teachers and students become storytellers. Shared experiences lead to conversations about them, and hence a shared describing and naming of what has been lived. In addition, in naming their experiences of creating and telling their story, teaches and students embrace and name the world (cf. *The Holy Bible,* 1966, Genesis). The most profound images of teaching, and hence the most powerful stories, are created in "I and Thou" types of encounters, of meeting in the middle, of forming a meaningful bond with students (Buber, 1947/1961).

Students are socialized into roles and images teachers expect of them, but also mutually share in the construction and creation of the images of teaching and learning. The importance of student imaging can be illustrated by considering what can happen when teachers need to step out of their classrooms. The "controlling" teacher carries with her the sanctions of behavior and often feels the need to appoint a student monitor. The teacher who has established a bond with her students leaves behind an image of a relationship, a commitment, a sharing of norms. Students, thus, do not feel abandoned or free to "go out of control." They have internalized an image of the relationship between their teacher and themselves that guides their behavior. To us, Dewey's (1897/1959) words seem particularly relevant as we think about constructed images:

> I believe that the only true education comes through the stimulation of the child's powers by the demands of the social situation in which he finds himself. Through these demands he is stimulated to act as a member of a unity, to emerge from his original narrowness of action and feeling, and to conceive of himself from the standpoint of the welfare of the group to which he belongs. (p. 20)

Ideal Images

Images emerge, too, when teachers examine their own beliefs, values, and ideals about teaching and learning. But unlike the situation in which they construct images through interactions, teachers look mainly inward to more idealistic or ideal models. "I believe teaching should be like this, no matter what this particular class or school is like" is an example of this kind of imaging. Another may be "Schools ought to be places for the development of the intellect; unfortunately these types of children are not capable of that sort of intellectual rigor."

Images about teaching may originate from early and significant models of relationships—parent and child, pupil and teacher (Bowlby, 1988). Socialization into particular images of self-identity and self-esteem takes place during these early relationships. Career models and images of adult roles begin to be formulated during this time and tend to continue into adulthood. These often are idealistic types of images and models, and more realistic ones await entry and socialization into the work setting (Lortie, 1975). Most teachers remember the teachers they had when they were students, and these often serve as role models or ideal images (for better or for worse) for their teaching.

Similar types of images—symbols, icons, and mandala objects that tap a community consciousness (see Bruner, 1986; Campbell, 1990; Jung, 1972)—could also shed some light on teacher imaging. For example, iconographic imaging (especially those from worship or ceremony settings) may have had an especially profound impact on certain children and, hence, are instructive for understanding particular kinds of teacher–student relationships. A study of the image of teacher as icon surely would enlighten our understanding of why some students overly idealize their teachers, and why some teachers place themselves upon altars or pedestals.

Given Images

The expectations of teaching by society, tradition, parents, and the school system, tend to result in teachers accepting (either actively of passively) the culture-bound images of teaching. We call these given images. The office of teaching, the institutional role, shapes the images held by the teacher. Baby-sitter, caretaker, monitor, record keeper, parent, disciplinarian, trainer, moral model, expert, authority, subject specialist, tester, grader, and cafeteria supervisor are some examples of roles that teachers assume because of institutional requirements, tradition, and cultural mores. Given images are often accepted by teachers as their destiny or as legitimate requirements of their role.

What is curious about the teaching profession is that teaching has so little role differentiation. Teachers are responsible for professional, paraprofessional, clerical, and even housekeeping duties. Even when teachers work mainly outside of the classroom, much of their work is clerical, and managerial rather than central to instruction. Few teachers are employed in schools as researchers, instructional leaders, or curriculum developers. Moreover, even when principals create opportunities for teachers to define a new role, too many teachers return to given roles, not maintaining an image of themselves as instructional leaders. We question, what hold do given images have upon teachers' professional identity?

The three types discussed here overlap and it is probably true that teachers hold images of each kind. As teachers examine the images of their work, a consideration of their origins may illuminate why some images speak to them and inform their practice, while others are mainly a burden and constrict teaching potential. Our belief is that once teachers begin to actively create their own images of their work, they will discover their unique images, the ones that reveal something of their presence, their person. Perhaps then they will begin to help create more professional opportunities for themselves in their schools.

Interpreting Teacher Images

What meanings and possible interpretations can be discerned from the many images portrayed by our teachers? We have identified eight groupings of interpretations that serve to highlight essential aspects of teacher images and illustrate how relationships among teachers and students interact to create powerful images. The discussion that follows portrays teachers as interpreting what happens in their classroom and as constructing meanings about the teaching–learning relationships taking place. What these teachers have in common is their ability to learn from their work, to be open to a new level of understanding of what they do, and, when necessary, to be willing to change. In so doing they become experienced teachers. We believe that constructing images of teaching is fundamentally an act of interpretation and, thus, a valuable guide for effective and satisfying teaching. Tracy (1987) believes that good interpretations are

> Those that enrich our experience, allow for understanding, aid delibera-
> tion, and judgement, and increase the possibilities of meaningful action.
> To understand at all is to interpret. To act well is to interpret a situation de-
> manding some action and to interpret a correct strategy for that action. To
> be "experienced" is to have become a good interpreter. (p. 9)

We are reminded of Irene struggling to change old images of her work, of trying to give up the confining models of teaching she had been following. She
learned from her students and her colleagues and created new images and interpretations of herself: a teacher who is more free—not so bothered with demanding the students' attention and who now is able to share decision making with her
students. Her new perspective has given her a deeper understanding of her teaching. It has liberated her.

Kate's learning was equally dramatic. While always a very independent teacher
who was familiar with sharing leadership, she came to a new awareness of her relationship with students. From being overwhelmed with students' emotional problems, she has learned to engage her students in literature where they are invited to
develop strategies for self-examination and problem solving. When she looked at
herself as problem solver, confessor, mother, she felt absorbed and thought that she
was avoiding her teacher role. Now she sees herself as educator, one who leads students to examine their lives through literature and to reach beyond themselves.

Teacher as Presence

Teachers with a central image, a clear and vivid focus of what they do, seem to
have in common a sense of their own personality, point of view, of their individuality. They have a style of teaching. They have a presence. The teachers have sifted
through the multiple images that could be held and have centered on those that most
aptly speak to their uniqueness and the way they relate to students. They have examined their life experiences and realize that their teaching reflects their character.
The unforgettable teacher is one whose presence is felt by her students; her countenance is imprinted on their memories.

Vaclav Havel (1989), writing to his wife Olga while he was in prison, talked about
the absence of her presence. His reflections upon the meaning of human existence
and about human personality speak eloquently to the image of teacher as presence.

> You mention that almost every day you speak about me and with someone
> and thus I am, in some small way, present at home … and that leads me to a
> theme I sometimes ponder, the question of what human existence really is,
> viewed in space and time. Human personality is a particular view of the
> world, an image of the world, an aspect of the world's Being. It is as if it
> were a light constantly reilluminating the world; a crystal in which the
> world is constantly being reflected. We therefore imagine the other person
> not merely as someone we know from the past … but we know him and ex-

perience him as an integral part of our own present and future and our own potentialities ... a dimension of our own existence. (pp. 138–142)

Kate's experience in art and drama helps her define her view of herself and her teaching style. Her reflection about how she relates to students not only led to changes in her teaching, but also gave her insights on her own personal development. She is more aware of her feelings toward students and the limitations of trying to solve their problems. She has come to the realization that problems can lead to growth and that struggles can be liberating. Just as she learned to find deeper meaning and worth in her art studies, she is now helping students find meaning in the books they read. Kate engages her students in the world of ideas and her presence is felt among them.

Teacher as Elder

Most teachers noted that a major reason for becoming a teacher was to share their knowledge, to hand down what they had learned. This grouping of images we have called "teacher as scholar, as expert, and as elder." High school teachers, especially, view their main role as "subject-matter" specialists (they are teachers of math, English, biology, history, etc.).

The larger reality of this grouping of images is that the teacher has "been there." This is teacher as adult and grandparent (and, similarly, as mentor and model). She has a sense of continuity in life, is aware of the changes, growth, and development; the journey humans take; and the cultural values they hold. She has experienced the joys and pains of life and shares her insights of the lived life with her students. Moreover, she has experienced the traditions, the ways of the culture, and is a party to the wisdom of the community (folklore and legends handed down). As elder, the teacher embodies not only the accumulated knowledge of the community, but the moral dimension as well. She not only wants to share these, but also invites the young to contribute to this wisdom.

Teacher as Child

Nearly all teachers interviewed stated that they entered teaching because they wanted to work with children, with young people. Many told us that they feel young in working with children, that they enjoy the sense of wonder children have, and that they, too, experience a sense of adventure, of the new, and even of awe in their teaching.

DuBois (1989) recalls how Rabindranath Tagore, in discussing the characteristics of the true educator, focuses on the need to be open and awake to children, and to become like children:

Clearly, education comes out of ("is the gift of") joy resulting from the association with the teacher's mind which is avid for learning. It is not merely that teacher's experience in the field, but rather his openness to life, his wakefulness. In this, he is like a child. Tagore believed that true teachers were "born," not made. He says here that "the born teacher is the man in whom the primal child responds readily to the call of children." Due to his childlike quality the teacher can be a friend to children and is considered one "of their own species." (pp. 179-180)

Teachers who view themselves as childlike identified with and affirmed their students. The teachers remember what it was like when they were children, and thus are able to enter into communion with their students.

Teacher as Therapist

Many of the teachers we interviewed see themselves as providing emotional support for their students. A frequent position, especially among primary school teachers, is that teaching had to be concerned with both the cognitive and emotional development of students. How to help students with their emotional problems, however, posed a dilemma for teachers. Balancing their major role of educating with that of therapist or counselor was a frequent challenge.

After much reflection, Kate decided to move away from the role of "the confessor, the mother, the problem solver." She felt absorbed by the many personal problems students brought to her and now feels more comfortable in helping students through literature. Sarah, on the other hand, sees one of her essential responsibilities as helping students deal with their emotional problems. Her belief is that once student feelings are dealt with it is possible to work on academics. Sarah admitted, however, that this is tiring, especially with the busy schedule she is expected to follow.

Writing about the emotional component of teaching and learning, Salzberger-Wittenberg, Henry, and Osbourne (1983) note the importance of helping children understand their feelings and discuss how children elicit emotional responses from teachers.

> The effect a student or group of students has on us may be a valuable indication of the kind of feelings they want us to have. These may be ones of being idealized and admired and all sorts of positive aspects of a relationship, but more often what is deposited in us are the feelings the other one cannot bear or cannot bear on his own, such as helplessness, confusion, panic, guilt, despair or depression. He may need another person to help with them. (p. 59)

In trying to come to terms with how they might deal with students' personal problems, teachers need to be aware of the kinds of feelings that students elicit from them. We comprehend that such reflections would help teachers better understand their own feelings toward students and assist them in creating positive relationships in their classrooms.

Teacher as Parent

This grouping of images overlaps with the one just discussed. Teacher as parent is a prevalent image and open to many interpretations. Some teachers readily portray themselves as second parents to their students. Others shy away from such images and even deny any type of resemblance with their style of teaching. The many interpretations of teacher as parent make this grouping a particularly fruitful one for analysis. We can recall some of the multiple images of parents—from nurturing, caring, sharing, giving, and guiding; to controlling, dominating, abandoning, rejecting, and abusing—in order to begin to understand the possible interpretations of this image for teachers.

We must also consider that how children relate to their teachers is largely influenced by the kind of relationship they have with their parents. Bowlby's (1988) attachment theory enlightens our understanding of parent–child relationships and has implications for teacher–student relationships.

> The pattern of attachment consistent with healthy development is that of secure attachment, in which the individual is confident that his parent (or parent-figure) will be available, responsive, and helpful should he encounter adverse or frightening situations. With this assurance, he feels bold in his explorations of the world and also competent in dealing with it. (p. 167)

Salzberger-Wittenberg et al. (1983) directly address the parenting issue faced by teachers.

> The task of the teacher may be thought of as resembling the parental function: that is, to act as a temporary container for the excessive anxiety of his students at points of stress. It will mean that he will experience in himself some of the mental pain connected with learning, and yet set an example of maintaining curiosity in the face of chaos, love of truth in the face of terror of the unknown, and hope in the face of despair. (p. 59)

The authors believe that teachers are important in helping students think through and organize their thoughts and feelings and hence help them come to terms with them:

> The pupil's ideas and thoughts are aided by a teacher who assists him in ordering them, particularly at such times when the learner becomes overwhelmed by too much undigested knowledge. The teacher's capacity to be reflective and thoughtful about data rather than producing ready answers enables the learner to internalize a thinking person. He in turn will produce new conjunctions of thoughts and meaning which may set off in the teacher a new combination of thinking about his subject. (pp. 60–61)

Teacher as Animator

This grouping encompasses images of teacher as catalyst and as activator. A basic feature here is intrinsic motivation—that originating internally from the interests of the student. The teacher's role is one of activating this interest. Dewey (1897/1959) puts this aptly: "I believe that interests are the signs and symptoms of growing power. I believe that they represent dawning capacities. Accordingly, the constant and careful observation of interests is of the utmost importance for the educator" (p. 29).

Margaret, Irene, and Kate have learned to observe and nurture the interests of their students. Over the years, they have found ways to cultivate the "dawning capacities" of their children. In bonding with their classes, they activate the potential for growth. Margaret demonstrated how she helps her students become part of the story and Kate reflected about building trust among her students and helping them relate to the books they read together.

A variant of this grouping is the teacher as actor, as dramatist. Some teachers understand themselves as engaged in a drama with their students, as mutually participating in a play. Kate explicitly stated this when she noted that she saw teaching as drama, as bringing "a little bit of life" to the classroom, of "taking ideas and making things happen with them." This is possible when one finds utmost value in what one does. In such valuing, a bond is activated and a drama unfolds.

Teacher as Companion

The essence of this type of relationship is one of mutual benefit for teacher and student. When teachers try to see students from the students' perspective, they begin to enter the relationship in a more meaningful and intimate way. A similar viewing must take place among students. Rather than an "I–It" type of relationship, teacher and student enter an "I–Thou" type of relationship (Buber, 1947/1961). The teaching–learning relationship becomes one of a dialogue, an encounter, not merely one of playing out institutional or traditional roles.

Kate most clearly represents this grouping, though all the teachers studied, to some extent, are companions to their students. Sarah's image of being a "second parent" to students, indeed, reflects a kind of companionship. And if the parent and child roles are symbiotic in nature, the companionship is one of mutual benefit. However, when the parent role is one of controlling or maintaining dependency, it is quite different from the companionship concept discussed here.

For example, Kate explicitly stated that she read to her students in order to create a bond between them and the story. She recalled her own art teacher as an example of the bonding she has in mind. The bond is to an idea, to a craft, a talent, a story, and a desire for something worthwhile and meaningful. Her students bond within the context of literature—a literature she selects (that begins with them and takes them to a larger world). She learned that the "bond" implied in becoming involved with students' personal problems may befit a therapist or social worker, but it did not meet her idea of an educator. Kate is a companion to her students in a world of ideas, a world of literature. Together they share their views of the book being discussed. They become companions in exploring literature and the diverse meanings it holds for them.

Teacher as Storyteller

Teachers do not merely act out a prescribed role, but create roles and opportunities for learning among their students. Working together, students and teachers share experiences and even tell the story of what happens when they are together in the classroom. They create special names for what they have shared, thought, and felt together. They capture a way of life. When they record what they do, we all benefit from their insights (Coles, 1989; Richardson, 1964; Wigginton, 1985).

Kate, Margaret, and Irene are more actively engaged in storytelling with their students. Margaret elicits students' interests and experiences so that she can help them become "part of the story." Literature and experiences are linked in Margaret's classroom. Similarly, Irene believes that the best stories come when students feel comfortable in playing with ideas, writing journals, and reading each other's writings. Kate selects stories that speak to the life experiences of her students. She reads aloud to them so they can hear her voice and get into the story. She asks them to try to connect the stories they have read, so that they can find the images they hold and these serve as a foundation for storytelling.

Conclusion and Further Reflection

When teachers begin to construct images of their work, core meanings of teaching–learning relationships manifest themselves. That is, teachers begin to see their work as one of learning, being, comprehending, and affirming what students do. They begin to be aware of themselves as healing, creating the setting, and bonding with their students. Some, too, tell the story of what they or their students have created. Throughout this chapter, we have mentioned implications of teacher images and imaging. We have noted the areas where this focus would prove helpful and places where the information might be applied. We now bring these to an explicit level and describe how this information might be used.

1. In conversations with teachers, we ("we" as researchers, teacher educators, colleagues, or fellow students) can offer the opportunity for them to reflect on their sense of themselves. This means that we can listen to and nurture the "emerging" images to bring those images to the level of consciousness where they can continue to inform the teachers' practice in the classroom.
2. We can assist teachers in integrating their images of themselves with possible teaching behaviors. We can focus on choices available and how those choices fit or do not fit with the images of the self that already exist. Thus, consonance

will develop between those images and what the teachers do in the classroom. We can also focus on the negotiating process necessary for change of behaviors. The self-image may have to change in order to accommodate changing practices in the classroom.

3. We can help new teachers to anticipate the differing images of teaching they will meet in their positions as the "new kids." The culture of the schools in which they work will either support or deny the new teachers' images of teacher and teaching.

4. In staff development programs, we can make reflecting upon teacher images a part of assessment of the school environment, as a place to nurture the teacher as educator.

5. We can emphasize for teachers that their work with students is enhanced by their increasing sense of themselves. We believe that it will help them to recognize that same need in their students and help their students to create positive and helpful images of themselves as learners—learner as creator, interpreter, companion, or storyteller.

All the teachers interviewed had images of their work that reflected some aspect of the cultural-social context. A key message was that the essential role of school as a place for education is being corrupted (Goodlad, 1979). Sarah finds that American culture does not revere teachers as other societies do. We recall her voice of warning: "In order to function and to blossom you need recognition and praise." While she finds satisfaction in her work, she wonders how many young people will enter teaching, given the low status afforded the profession. Kate similarly is concerned that the school system does not cultivate creativity and has lost sight of its essential purpose of educating children. Even the strongest teachers, the ones who actively construct images of their work, are heavily influenced by the often uncaring and negative environment in which they teach. Positive teacher images compete with cultural images that far too often do not nurture the teacher as educator.

In constructing and reflecting upon images of our teaching selves, we are able to get in touch with our feelings, values, and character. We begin to realize which images of our teaching enhance our feelings of self-worth and expand our roles as teachers, and which ones limit, confine, and even cripple us. We learn to look into the mirror of our inner selves and find ways to know and to love our work, our students, ourselves. Constructing images and interpreting significant aspects of teaching can help us find meaning in our work. The challenge is to find images that liberate us and take us to a deeper awareness of ourselves, of others, and of the world. We believe that conscious focus on images and their influence will help free both the teachers and society from imposed images and the damage these imposed images may cause. Our hope is that someday we can all say as Irene did, "And now, because I feel freer as a teacher I understand more of what I am doing. Now I can let things go and let the children kind of pick up where they would like to work from."

NOTES

1. Data for this study were collected over a period of 5 years, from 1984 to 1990. Both authors worked in staff-development programs with five inner-city Chicago public schools over an extended period of time and thus were able to become familiar with the culture of the schools as well as to build trusting relationships with teachers. This greatly facilitated the discussions with teachers. Notes taken during and after these discussions were analyzed for the images they contained. Structured interviews did not characterize this part of the study. Rather, the discussions were an outgrowth of the working relationships established with the teachers by the authors.

   During the second and later part of the study, a sample of teachers was extensively interviewed on three different occasions. Broad questions relating to the school reforms being implemented in Chicago, career history of the teacher, new ideas they wanted to work on in their classrooms, and how they viewed their work and their teaching, guided these interviews. With the teachers' consent, the interviews were recorded and transcribed to facilitate analysis.

   M. School is an inner-city, predominantly Hispanic, school in Chicago. Margaret, Irene, Sarah, and Kate are from M. School; all were interviewed by Joe Fischer. Maria is from another inner-city school in Chicago; she was interviewed by Anne Kiefer.

   In addition, the authors teach in the field-based master's of education program at National-Louis University, in which an intact group of teachers works together with a core instructor for 2 years. This program results in considerable bonding between students and professors, permitting candid and in-depth dialogues and reflection about teaching. These experiences provided an additional rich source of information for the study.

REFERENCES

Bowlby, J. (1988). *A secure base.* New York: Basic Books.

Bruner, J. (1986). *Actual minds, possible worlds.* Cambridge, MA: Harvard University Press.

Buber, M. (1961). *Between man and man.* Boston: Beacon Press. (Original work published 1947)

Campbell, J. (1990). *The hero's journey: Joseph Campbell on his life and work.* San Francisco: Harper & Row.

Coles, R. (1989). *The call of stories.* Boston: Houghton Mifflin.

Dewey, J. (1897/1959). *My pedagogic creed.* In M. S. Dworkin (Ed.), *Dewey on education: Selections* (pp. 19-32). New York: Teachers College Press.

DuBois, F. (1989). *The true teacher: Rabindranath Tagore and Martin Buber.* Frankfurtam Main: Arnold Kopcke-Duttler.

Goodlad, J. (1979). *What schools are for.* Bloomington, IN: Phi Delta Kappa.

Havel, V. (1989). *Letters to Olga.* New York: Holt.

The Holy Bible, King James Version. (1966). Philadelphia: National.

Jung, C. G. (1972). *Mandala symbolism.* Princeton, NJ: Princeton University Press.

Lortie, D. (1975). *School teacher: A sociological study.* Chicago: University of Chicago Press.

Richardson, E. (1964). *In the early world: Discovering art through crafts.* New York: Pantheon.

Salzberger-Wittenberg, I., Henry, X., & Osbourne, X. (1983). *The emotional experience of learning and teaching.* London: Routledge & Kegan Paul.

Tracy, D. (1987). *Plurality and ambiguity: Hermeneutics, religion, hope.* San Francisco: Harper and Row.

Wigginton, E. (1985). *Sometimes a shining moment: The foxfire experience, twenty years teaching in a high school classroom.* Garden City, NJ: Doubleday.

6

Beyond the Classroom: Progressive Activist Teachers and Images of Experience, Meaning, Purpose, and Identity

Edward R. Mikel
Stan Hiserman

No classroom is an island. Teachers soon become painfully aware of how factors beyond the classroom limit what they can accomplish with their students. Overcrowded classes, tracking, crumbling social services, social inequality, and the isolation of teachers themselves all undermine effective education .... Reform-minded teachers must complement their efforts inside their classrooms with alliances to transform the schools, districts, and communities they work in.
—Bigelow, Christensen, Karp, Miner, and Peterson (1994, p. 161)

Although most do not receive great public attention or acclaim, many teachers have heeded such a call to progressive action beyond their classrooms. They have participated in the struggle for social justice, democracy, and core multicultural values in schools, districts, communities, and regional and national education.

Progressive activist teachers surely realize that life in their classrooms does not stand apart from, insulated from, life in the larger society.[1] The social world is highly interrelated, as systems theory and common reflection tell us. How we live in one realm both shapes and is shaped by how we live in every and all realms, the mutual shaping occurring along both direct and indirect paths, tangible and intangible (Wheatley, 1992).

Thus, teachers do become activists outside their classrooms for tough-minded strategic reasons. Most important, they take action for the purpose of re-creating social life and experience in whatever locations they find themselves in the faith that local influences toward better schools and society may radiate outward with singular or collective effect.

The strategic political purpose of activism is clearly set forth in the quotation beginning this chapter. The words are found in an anthology compiled by *Rethinking Schools,* a self-described "activist publication."[2] This journal has become a nationally prominent forum for analysis and strategy on educational and social-change issues, clarifying the hope and the struggle for more just, democratic, and intentionally multicultural schools, communities, and society. In this endeavor, *Rethinking Schools* stands alongside other national centers for progressive educational reform.[3]

Activist teachers engage heartily in the political struggle. They plan and work hard in many ways and in many arenas for policy, institutional, and school-level change. They take great joy in the successes and deep disappointment in the defeats. Above all, they are resolved to stay the course: to persist in creating and carrying out effective projects for reform. The images that lie at the heart of this commitment, however, as expressed in teachers' own words, constitute much more than a calculus of strategic gain and loss. They are images more broadly concerned with experience and meaning, purpose, and identity, images of a life more open, more whole, and more integrated for teachers and students alike. They are images affirming that existing material conditions, institutional relationships, and everyday practices may be transformed from the present norms of distance and denial, exclusiveness, and inequality. They are images pointing to a fundamentally changed state of personal and social being within the associations of a democratic, just, and inclusive community. Responsive engagement across boundaries of social difference is understood to be the source of enlivening experience and underpins commitment to a good life for all.

The Inquiry and Participants

In the following pages, we offer a connected portrait of four progressive activist teachers. Our aim was to draw from the teachers' words images that put into high relief what has proven vital to them about activist teaching. We focused directly and extensively on their personal histories and experiences articulated in lengthy audiotaped, but informal "interview conversations" with us. We did not use a protocol of carefully composed questions; instead, we engaged the teachers in spontaneous talk around topics we posed to them as well as topics they raised on their own.

The teachers did the greatest amount of talking, but we occasionally would describe for them a related event from our own experience or state how we were hearing something significant they were telling us at that moment. Our intention was to ask them about what it has meant for them to engage in critical teaching in the classroom (where their "focal experience" lies) and strategic action beyond the classroom, what they have encountered in doing so, what they have learned about effective strategy and its possible long-term effects, how they construe the present nature of society and its prospects, and what they desire for themselves and see as their future.

In reading over each teacher's words—and conferring with them later about what we recorded—we have seen common themes behind their personal images, themes that thread consistently through the fabric of all their lives and commitments. Although individual images are personal and particular in their content, they express the sort of coalesced meaning that bears significantly on the whole of an individual life as well as on other lives taking a similar course. The thematic significance of core images is well described by Connelly and Clandinin (1988):

> An image reaches into the past, gathering up experiential threads meaningfully connected to the present. And it reaches intentionally into the future and creates new meaningfully connected threads as situations are experienced and new situations anticipated from the perspective of the image. (p. 60)

The orientation of this study was more "individualist" than "collectivist," although an absolute separation of the personal and social dimensions is untenable. In its individualist orientation, our study more nearly resembles the emphasis of a recent interview study of 1960s social and political radicals (Chepesiuk, 1995) than that of another recent study (Casey, 1993) that explores the life histories of women engaged in progressive activist teaching and projects beyond the schools. In the latter work, each of the participants situates herself within a "specific historical network of human relationships" (representing the Catholic, Marxist, or African-American tradition) imbued with the "feminist ethos" of care and connectedness. Their transformative activities—pedagogical, institutional, and political—arise within, taking direction and support from the "grounded relationships" of the collectivity. Our account of four progressive activist teachers endeavors to find what animates their individual lives and work, what, in other words, is the "moving spirit" that keeps them going over the long course against heavily institutionalized social resistance.

The four teachers who are the principal participants in this inquiry are hardly typical teachers, if by "typical" is meant those who are reasonably like that total population working in United States public and private elementary and secondary schools. Nor do we claim that the four are necessarily representative of all teachers who could meet our notion of progressive activists. There is substantial ethnic, racial, gender, age, and regional diversity among the four, but, most important, together they have given us images of their lives and experiences that are sharply revealing of common themes around meaning, purpose, and identity.[4]

The Four Teachers

Matt has reached his mid-life years. He was quite active in the American anti-war movement of the late 1960s and early 1970s. He came to teaching during that time and has spent a total of a decade and a half teaching in secondary schools in various cities. The most important time for him was 5 years teaching and directing a community alternative youth high school located in the Latino community of a large midwestern city. By all indices, this was an "inner-urban" school, serving youth of color who essentially had no other school option. It was operated by a community social service agency. That teaching in the school was a critical experience for Matt is made no less significant by the fact that at the end of his fifth year, he and all but one other teacher on the staff were fired or forced to resign by a newly hired director who returned the school to a traditional GED preparation.

Matt and his teaching colleagues were able to achieve a progressive democratic form of education that, in his words, affected a "qualitative leap in my own consciousness" and "altered my life."

> What [teaching at Community Youth High School (pseudonym)] did for me personally as a teacher—I had been teaching for a while and involved in the anti-war movement—it wasn't so much about teaching as it was about my life as a whole. It was like taking my politics, what I thought about learning, education, teaching, and other areas of my life, and not separating them into pieces. We moved beyond the questions of: Should a school be democratic? Should it be participatory? Is race an issue we must engage? Is culture a critical issue? We moved beyond just continuing to ask these sorts of questions to making the answers a reality.

Doris helped start the Rochester (NY) Educational Alternative, a free high school begun in the late 1960s. At age 20 she went to Mexico to study with Paulo Freire at Centro Intercultural de Documentation in Cuernavaca. The next spring she migrated to the Pacific Northwest where she fell in love and has remained. She finished her bachelor's of arts degree by contract study with Empire State College of New York, became a licensed massage practitioner for 10 years, completed a second B. A. with teaching certification, and later a master's degree in educational counseling, to which she added an administrative credential. For the last 7 years, she has worked as a school counselor in elementary and high school settings in a large urban school system.

> In my life, I've lost friends to the AIDS epidemic starting in the 1980s, sat with friends as they died from cancer, and know many who struggle with chronic fatigue or other life-changing illness. I see all of these as environmentally induced diseases, from years of stress and living in pollution. Urban stress is increasing, and in schools more and more responsibility is placed on teachers and support people, while funding is shrinking. Politi-

cal reality and the reality of environmental pollution go hand in hand at this moment in our history. All this has caused me to think deeper about the meaning of my work in education. What are we trying to do with children in sending them to school every day? What are educators about when we go to school in the morning?

Dana and Carlton have recently been teaching an academically advanced ninth grade world literature class in an east coast urban high school that largely serves students of color from working-class homes in communities struggling with myriad social and economic issues. What distinguishes this program is that an effort is made to ensure that each classroom reflects the whole school's characteristics in race, ability, and gender. In effect, the three de facto academic tracks (which are racially and socioeconomically distinguishable) have been collapsed into one comprehensive grouping.

Dana is a young teacher with only a few years in the profession. Rosemont High School (a pseudonym) is the second place she has taught. In her first year she taught traditionally tracked senior literature courses, but has since committed herself to the untracked ninth grade program. Along with colleagues, Dana is pressing hard to have de-tracked, high-quality classes as officially sanctioned offerings at the school. This effort has brought these teachers squarely into the politics of school, district, and community reform. Dana commented on what their challenge has been:

> We've been using literature as a vehicle to kind of open the kids up to other experiences and also have them see their own experiences reflected in literature .... It's an awful lot of writing, it's a lot of reading .... It's very rigorous .... It's very intense work that the kids do and it leads to some very ... intense, deep conversations in the classroom. What I'm always amazed by, I think, are the responses from the students ... they really say brilliant things and it comes from anywhere, any person who's in the room.

> I don't think that I understood when I was hired what I was walking into and I certainly have no regrets about it, but there was nothing in my training or background that had really prepared me for this work. It was collaborating with the former chair of the English Department and really using her as mentor and just gaining experience by being in the classroom where I kind of developed strategies and ways of teaching to such a diverse group of kids.

> To this day, I can't see myself teaching any other way .... I would say that it's absolutely changed the way I see the world.

Carlton taught at the State University of New York, Albany, as adjunct lecturer in the African American Studies Department and, after that, for 6 years at Rosemont

High School. After starting out teaching 9th- through 12th-grade language arts courses, encompassing all levels from low-remedial through advanced placement, the department chair approached him about teaching "de-tracked" 9th-grade world literature. At first he declined, but the more he thought about it, the clearer it became for him that de-tracking was the only way to ensure real education for all students. For him, it was

> … knowing that whenever we have a tracking system, kids of color, and in (Rosemont), black kids mostly, will be in the lower tracks and knowing that too many people who look like I do get crappy educations.

> At Rosemont I taught in world literature, which is sort of, well, my claim to fame, I guess. And the world literature course which we attempted to de-track, I think we did it successfully. De-tracking language arts for ninth graders meant that all ninth graders will take language arts at rigorous levels.

> What I'm doing now is working for the Education Trust. One week a month I work with the Achievement Council in California. In California, it's strictly at this point about standards—trying to help urban schools teach to standards so that we can bring kids up to higher levels. And, for the Education Trust, it's sort of a national push towards de-tracking language arts.

Changed Consciousness

What most moves and shapes the lives of these progressive teacher activists is having a quality of experience that is so extraordinary in meaning and moment that it becomes a touchstone for their lives. They seek to return to it in fuller, deeper, and more conscious ways in virtually everything they do, though it is centrally focused in the immediacy of teaching and learning. It is an energizing experience that arises from crossing social boundaries that are typically made into reinforced barriers by the prevailing hegemony of social and cultural privilege. In these crossings, it is possible to engage in lively learning relationships involving teachers and students considered and stigmatized as "other." These teachers told us that despite the fact that little in their academic training prepared them for this experience, they would never consider "going back."

Matt spoke of working with young people considered "outcasts" and drawing out of a collaboration with them an educational program that embodied all the progressive ideals that are typically left at the level of rhetoric or fatally compromised in practice.

> So, the Community Youth High School could be seen as serving in the eyes of others the "worst of the worst." Together, teachers and students and

other staff created this amazing educational experience, based on our mutual core progressive and radical educational and political ideas. It showed me that the school we imagined could be done. We actually lived it! It formed a qualitative leap in my own consciousness. It convinced me that it could actually be done.

Doris described the influence of Paulo Freire, Jonathan Kozol, and Joanna Macy on her life, convincing her of the power of imagining a better future, of seeking straightforward but visionary responses to the critical problems of contemporary society, and of understanding the origins of despair as well as the sources of empowerment to accomplish change with those who we might not believe share our common destiny.

> The three greatest influences on my career have been the winter I was at CIDOC in Cuernavaca, Mexico, when I was 20, and studied with Paulo Freire [author of *Pedagogy of the Oppressed*]; he told me, "As you denounce the old world, you must announce the new one," and I guess I've been working on that ever since.

> Then I got connected with Jonathan Kozol when he was on a book tour for *Illiterate America,* and I was charged by the way he researched and articulately suggested big, sensible solutions—like that the United States could do a one-time literacy campaign in this country as they did in Cuba—it helped me think in terms of doing really major things to address problems.

> A third influence that really helped me was studying deep ecology work with Joanna Macy. I did a week of training with her about despair and empowerment. It was important because it gave me grounding to see myself as a person of change, allowed to grieve and challenged to get on with creative solutions.

> I've also been completely challenged and changed by students I've worked with—who are homeless, or have learning or behavior difficulties in school so they're not making it in their classrooms, or whose families have been killed in wars on other continents, and now here they are, beginning to make a new life in [my city], in my school, in my office, in my heart.

For Dana, the lively learning relationships she has been able to maintain with her students have changed her and her students' awareness of themselves, of what education really is and it has enriched their feeling of connectedness to the world around them. They have also gained new perspectives on the lives and experiences of others with whom they had not, until recently, seriously communicated or shared mutual appreciation. She emphasized the students ... it's their contribution, their participation, and just who they are in the classroom that motivates me. First and foremost ... it's like I'm always waiting to hear what they say next .... You know, usually at the beginning of the year, I get responses from students that are kind of off the top of their heads, that are regurgitations of what they've heard at home or from society at large. To see them stop and rethink it is pretty amazing. They ... show up like just extraordinary people and ... wow, ... I don't know how to pin it down. Except that who they are in the classroom is just really enlivening and invigorating and I learn .... And I think that if that ever stopped, I'd have to get out of the system ....

[In addition] ... my colleagues, ... people who are very supportive, and being engaged in conversations with them about the course and what it's produced is definitely motivating. I think colleague support is critical .... I'd go into Carlton's room and he'd come into my room, and we talked. We ... were constantly in conversations about what was happening in our rooms, looking for ways to deal with things, looking for strategies ....

Carlton is affected by the importance of providing high-quality public education, especially for disenfranchised youth and by the energy he gets participating in learning of students who are typically written off by the dominant sector of U.S. society.

What keeps me going ... I don't think public education, ... I don't think we're cats; we don't have nine lives. I don't know what's going to happen next, but if we don't do something, especially when we know what we should do, then we're in trouble. When I look out into the classroom and I see those who are disaffected are children of color, ... that's the energy. I believe that I have to teach by faith ... I might not believe it, but I have to do this until it finally breaks through. Seeing kids who were not considered writers really become writers, that's the energy.

Activist Politics of Making Change

These teacher activists have sought to re-create their local spheres of teaching and to change conditions of the school, district, and community contexts bearing decisively on them. The importance of such political activity in the service of altered and renewed classroom relationships is without question for these teachers. A spirit of resistance and transformation must be kept kindled in progressive classrooms and brought into the locales of which they are part.

Matt spoke of recreating the relationships and everyday practices that make up the local community of the school. In them reside the possibilities of human learning.

At the Community Youth High School, we wanted to create a setting where state or external mandates did not drive what we did in our curriculum and teaching. We took seriously the idea that we were an alternative school and tried to do it the way we really wanted to together with the students. The school was always very politically involved, as was the agency that ran it, as well the community they both served.

... Over the 5 years, we built a curriculum that was bilingual dual language and became mostly Latino-centric in parallel to an Afrocentric approach. We took the ideas of the students seriously, tried to find relevant literature, used process approaches to reading and writing (stressing skills in context), and focused on the community, too .... What we did reached a level I have not seen since. Students won scholarships, were showcased at a national writing conference, created projects, and built bridges with rival gang neighborhoods and schools.

Doris also spoke of creating new forms of community within schools and their neighborhoods, around relationships that are "sustainable."

This is where I am now: I want to be part of education that is livable, that is sustainable in the full sense. Creating [a greater number of] smaller schools [that are] smaller communities would seem a good step. I know I could work in an independent school, but with funding realities, a lot of children don't have access to them, so I keep working in the public system. But it can be pretty exhausting. At my present school, I try to create an atmosphere of safety around me, an atmosphere of openness and truthfulness about what's going on. [As a counselor] I always try to work with teachers, talk with them and support them in what they are doing, talk straightforwardly with students, tell them their options.

Dana and her colleagues are committed to the perpetual struggle for equity in school programs and to convincing others in their community to join them at multiple levels on which the efficacy of their methods of teaching and learning are contested.

... There have been many who are opposed to this methodology. They feel that one of two things will happen. Either the bright kids ... will somehow be left unchallenged or the kids who have struggled in school will somehow not rise to the challenge and what I've found is that neither happened, ... but it has created a lot of conflict and tension in the district.

... I would say the battle lines were drawn around race. That, really, it isn't just an academic question; it is a racial issue. People have concerns and notions about what certain kids are capable of and they won't necessarily want their sons or daughters in the same room with them. I would say second to that, it's not on par with that, are the economic issues. Without question.

And so, by battle I would mean that if the Board of Ed. in any district were moving toward this kind of teaching or this kind of course in their district, they would certainly have many parents speak out in opposition, and really, very vocally ....

You know one of the most important things, I would say, is that the community has to be informed about the course, about the philosophy and it should be informed through research. What would be said in any district, I think will vary, but I'm certain that issues about race and class and even gender open up. It kind of exposed ... the community for what it was—that it wasn't this racially integrated, harmonious place.

... There's been a good deal of effort over the years to kind of shut down the course or ignore it, kind of pretend that it's not really happening .... What a teacher might expect is conflict between himself or herself and their peers, their administrations, the community, the Board of Ed. They will have support and they will also have very strong opposition. So they have to really gear up and be confirmed in their belief about doing this.

Carlton continued Dana's discussion of the impact of pursuing the de-tracked program, underscoring the damaging effects he felt, and his subsequent decision to move on from this struggle.

I don't think any of us who were teaching it were prepared for the way it took off, so on that level it changed a lot of how my life fit into place on a daily basis .... It changed the whole way I teach and the way I see education and it also I think threw us out in places where teachers have to go.

We were either the ills of the town or the best thing since sliced bread, depending on whom you spoke to. I think that had reverberations for me, which is probably the reason I'm no longer there. We were in a position that things started to happen for us—they came so quickly and we made the video (Fine, Annand, Sherman, & Jordan, 1998); we have the contract for the book—so that I think it created jealousies, so that ... changed my relationship with colleagues.

The Prospects of Progressive Activism in the Larger Society

At one level, our teachers expect that the "sky might fall upon" or the "ground cave in beneath" their current projects and that they will have to move on. They do not count on society transforming itself or even on being insulated from the corrosive forces of the status quo that constantly undermine their work. However, they have a sort of faith that progressive good work can always find a place for itself locally. The larger purpose of local projects can gain influence in the wider world through strategic connections among projects or through the occasional and unpredictable contact of people, information, or artifacts from local initiatives. Taking any local action for progressive values can set the stage or foundation for possible future projects that continue the struggle for justice and enhancement of individual lives.

Matt described how the success of the Community Youth School in reforming itself educationally and democratically eventually brought it into conflict with its sponsoring organization. It was then that the school was diverted to the prevailing "corporate rationale" that generally holds formal organizations of contemporary society in its institutional grip.

> In the third year we went on strike against the current director's plan to cut support for our young mothers program—a highly successful program valued by everyone at the school—and took most of the rest of the agency with us. We attracted rather wide support from the community, especially members of other agencies. We won the strike, the director left (although he pursued his case in court for some time after), and we had a very successful following year.

> Then there was a turnover on the board. A new director was hired who projected himself as a Latino activist from California, but he soon implemented a "profitability" structure in the agency, a philosophy incompatible with the high school. Eventually, he just went after us. All the democratic norms were shoved aside. He refused to renew our contacts and pushed us out. Subsequently, the program was turned into a traditional GED program.

> At this point, the staff was tired from the struggle that had gone on. We needed time and energy to continue our work on the program. It was hardly finished. And we didn't see that the new director was willing to yield his institutional power. We had no union. We had no signed contracts. He dissolved the cooperative, democratic mechanisms.

Doris spoke of her abiding "dreams" for a different kind of school. She could easily imagine what this would look like based on her previous, although largely frustrated and unfinished, efforts to come to terms with the critical issues brought to public schools by those who should be served, but are typically manipulated or exploited.

> As a school counselor I have worked with a lot of students I call "active learners"—experiential learners, children who need a lot of movement,

have different attention priorities, or for whatever reason, don't fit well in the "uniform" classroom. I would love to work full time in a school program designed for them—with lots of opportunities for music, drumming, play, theater, self-expression, self-discipline through the martial arts, you name it—Internet pen-pals with youth in other states or countries, community service projects, gardening, recycling, connections with mentors, apprenticeships in local businesses. Kids who are labeled learning or behavior "disabled," ADD or ADHD—whatever the case—can be given medication, placed in highly structured classrooms, given numerous "interventions" to help them succeed. Or what I'd like to do is offer an environment where their high energy is an asset, where there are places and ways for them to be positively active, in the context of building community.

Dana sees the potential of a powerful positive influence on public education and society at large if the perspective through which she now sees herself, her students, education, and the world was more prevalent in other learning communities.

I think that if a program like this was implemented nationwide, it would force a change in the way we educate kids, in the way we look at education, in the way we look at kids, in the way we look at ourselves as educators .... I think, for myself that it has so much to do with my perspective .... I think that if I, as a teacher, don't hold them as capable people, then it won't work. It's really essential.

Carlton does not underestimate power of the political forces that threaten efforts to de-track curriculum and instruction. Nonetheless, he still feels hopeful because of the community's willingness to speak out on behalf of students for whom the status quo consistently yields unsatisfactory results. For him, a pivotal moment occurred when his community had to come face to face with the issue of equity. It could no longer stay behind a veil of disregard or indifference. The community came to understand the issue of de-tracking all the ninth-grade literature classes as being about the most fundamental matters of race and class. Whatever the other results from the Rosemont project may be, there is no turning back from having opened the eyes of the community to the possibility of better ways of teaching and learning and the expectation that all students will meet rigorous standards of achievement.

The best days outweigh the bad days ... and so I'm convinced that the impact is that we have kids that will sort of demand the best in education and know that there is a lot more. So I think there is that impact on the school itself. I think there was an incredible impact on the community because even people who were against the course, generally, when their kids came through the course, they were able to see that it was an incredible, incredible experience.

I think it also mobilized the town. I mean if you could have seen some of those meetings about this course where the Board of Ed. meeting moved from a normal small room into an auditorium. So it really then was no longer just about education, it really became a story about race and class. And who really gets the best education and who doesn't get a good education and so if for that alone, it just pulled the rug off and allowed a place that loved to talk about diversity to see what it really meant to put those words into action, so I think it changed the town. I think it will never be the same again.

Identity, Commitment, and Hope

Finally, certain other images expressed by the teachers reveal an evolving personal identity. Within this identity the deepest and most enduring feeling of being alive and well lies in the unerring commitment to the future of those accorded least in the present scheme of things. This is not a narrow partisan commitment, as it holds that the best future for the whole human species rests on the social destiny of all of its members. Such an identity is developed through continually moving into new or changed perspectives while, at the same time, re-creating relationships and institutional patterns in specific locales. Commitment is to citizenship for society in re-formation: a responsibility not only to interrupt the current norms, practices, and relationships, but also to help initiate modalities through which human lives always can be moving toward new richness and value.

Matt talked about the "faith" in an inevitable future of further good work, by himself and by others, which he took from the aborted Community Youth High School project:

> In any institutional setting, you must have room to become progressive and alternative. You have to be able to resist those possible dictates that will violate your principles and try to compromise enough to meet them without letting them drive what you do. Or you can go the other way because the dictates are tied to money and regulations and power, and let yourself give in to them.

> There will probably always be tensions over power and control and money, but can they be held in check enough institutionally to allow the progressive practice and values to sustain themselves? I believe they can, at least for significant periods, if we resist the temptation of conventional models. The satisfaction of doing the good work is so strong that it keeps you going even when the situation at hand crumbles. I have faith from that experience that it must and can be re-created and we look until we find other suitable places to try. Specific projects may end, but the larger possibility doesn't, and things will again coalesce as we keep working and looking.

Doris commented on her next venture, a project called the Turning Institute, which could provide impetus and support for programs and individuals. In that way, a progressive future may come through personal and institutional means.

> The purpose of the Turning Institute is to provide support for people who are at turning points in their lives. They could be adults, teachers, health care providers, and families experiencing disease or death among them—anyone at the crossroads of change. Children are at the crossroads of change dozens of times a day ....

> I'd love to start an after-school program for active learners or children with learning or behavioral challenges, through the Turning Institute some day. One thing the Turning Institute can do as a first step is to provide scholarships for students who are active learners to participate in existing programs that work for them and help them (and their parents or guardians) get linked up with opportunities. For example, I worked in a summer school program a couple of summers ago [which Doris helped design and secure funding to operate] with a really active young man who loves dancing. Once he has the dance in his feet, it's his; he can take it anywhere. That's sustainable.

Dana explained how change can happen and the benefits of change as awareness grows about its possibilities:

> I was much more limited, I think, in my perspective of human beings, in human nature when I first began; although I was open to the possibility of anything happening, I couldn't have articulated that and I didn't know what it would have looked like if I actually worked in a space where ... everybody was represented in terms of Rosemont's demographics.

> You know it all comes together. It's like you have to orchestrate so many things at once and at times it's a lot of work. It's a lot of work, but it's also incredibly rewarding and ... for me it becomes more of a way of life .... It simply has become how I approach matters in my life in general .... I would say the kids have given me that, just by virtue of their contributions in the classroom, what they've said, what they've written [have] opened up so many other possibilities for me.

Carlton emphasized the importance of helping students to find personal relevance in literature and to make connections with each other. He said that teachers' academic training does not prepare them to teach in this way and teachers must learn these approaches on the job. Moreover, he believed that teachers must continue their personal professional growth and never stop reading and learning.

Seein' the life and really creating a space where kids can talk. I think that's where the real democracy comes in—not keeping things the way they are in the status quo and this idea that we are trying to create or continue society so that if they work hard enough, if they study long enough they're going to get it—that's just not true. And so part of the course is to be honest sometimes and say what is it really that's keeping some folks in their place and privileging some even when it's not meritocratic; I mean they don't necessarily deserve this, but it seems like things are going in their favor.

So, I think part of it is really ... the expectation is interrupting what education does. It kind of reproduces this stupor, this idea that you come in, and go the way you came in and we're trying to interrupt that ... you have to connect in ways probably that you've never connected.

Part of what we're supposed to do is to create relationships .... I think I'm at point in my life that if you're going to do the work, you're going to *do* it. There's no half-stepping, so to speak. You can't just talk diversity and multicultural literature, because it sounds like the words that people cringe from, but if you're really doing it, it changes you entirely. It causes problems, but it's worth it.

Final Thoughts

Activist teachers, we believe, realize that either classrooms or surrounding contexts can be altered functionally and yet remain essentially unchanged—in themselves or in how they may influence one another. Different rhetoric in policy or mandates, redefined roles, new or additional resources may come on the scene, but the nature of human contact, of quality of experience, or the depth of awareness can stay unaffected. The reverse, however, is also true: Functional change can lead to meaningful new forms of association, contact, and experience. Moreover, any social sphere is, in itself, capable of re created relationships that provide for rich and uncommon experience. The aim, truly, is to struggle for a different mode of shared life in all spheres, including but certainly going beyond whatever may link them together functionally and strategically.

What makes these teachers different from others? They have chosen to cross social and cultural boundaries that delimit everyday practice in its beliefs, attitudes, and contact with others. They have re-created relationships with students, colleagues, and communities so as reach the uncommon experience of lively engagement that animates the "moving spirit" of progressive activism. Many others have approached situations that promised such a quality of experience, but have ultimately avoided pursuing them fully enough, either in action or in appreciation, for their meaning. Activist teachers have come to know and value most highly the experience of authentic contact and mutual relationships, especially around shared, open, and rigorous learning. They are willing to take on the risks of changing present institutions on local and broader scales, facing certain resistance and the likelihood of overt conflict. To live with such hope and commitment is a matter of integrity, for these teachers cannot imagine anything other than a social life offering relationships of deep connection and authentic experience.

NOTES

1. We use "progressive" to refer to teachers who situate themselves squarely in the intersection of two traditions Dennis Carlson (1997) describes as chiefly the legacy of John Dewey's formulation of democracy and education. These are the traditions of "democratic pragmatism" and "social reconstructionism." Within the orientation of democratic pragmatism, teachers are committed to engaging the full participation of all students and to centering their teaching and curriculum on the range of interests and learning dispositions all students bring to the classroom community. In this sense, Alfie Kohn (1999) has recently described progressive education in the following way:

    Progressive education takes as its point of departure that kids should be taken seriously. Because learning is regarded as an active process, learners are given an active role. Their questions help to shape the curriculum, and their capacity for thinking critically is honored even as it is honed .... Facts and skills are important but not ends in themselves. Rather, they are more likely to be organized around broad themes, connected to real issues, and seen as part of the process of coming to understand ideas from the inside out. A [progressive] classroom is a place where a community of learners—as opposed to a collection of discrete individuals—engages in discovery and invention, reflection and problem-solving. (p. 4)

    Progressive teachers also incorporate the imperative of the tradition of social reconstructionism: to guide young people's education toward the ends of social justice and democratic equality within the spheres of formal schooling and the larger society. Toward this purpose, teachers such as those who are members of the Portland (OR) Area Rethinking Schools group (PARS) promote K–12 education reform grounded in equity, social justice, and quality education. They take an activist approach, dividing their collective work between policy/political strategy and curriculum development. As described by Bill Bigelow (cited in Childs, 1999), PARS is a "network of teachers who meet to figure out what it means to teach for social justice, to figure out the relationship between lively curriculum and participatory teaching .... And we organize for the right to pursue that kind of teaching" (p. 9). Although the particular balance of the two orientations may vary from time to time and activity to activity across the whole of a teacher's practice, a fulcrum point substantially acknowledging the mandate of both is achieved in all instances.

2. The urban education journal *Rethinking Schools* is published by Rethinking Schools, Ltd., 1001 E. Keefe Ave., Milwaukee, WI 53212. On-line: www.rethinkingschools.org

3. Among these centers are National Coalition of Education Activists (Rhinebeck, NY), National Coalition of Advocates for Students ((Boston, MA), Network of Educators

of the Americas (Washington, DC), FairTest (Cambridge, MA), Cross-City Campaign for Urban School Reform, Institute for Democracy in Education (Ohio University, Athens, OH), and Teaching Tolerance (Southern Poverty Law Center, Montgomery, AL).

4. Although we did not have the space to include their words, we talked briefly with three other teacher activists in preparing this writing: Chris, Robby, and Sylvie. As they discussed their lives and projects, they used images that were very close to those of our four teacher participants in strongly conveying the themes of critical consciousness, fundamentally changed social relationships, and identity around long-term progressive commitment. These three also expressed the spirit of richer, fuller, and more integrated experience that arises from just and inclusive social life and that keeps them dedicated to a future of progressive activism. We thank them for their contributions that deepened our understanding of this study.

REFERENCES

Bigelow, B., Christensen, L., Karp, S., Miner, B., & Peterson, B. (Eds.). (1994). Rethinking our classrooms: Teaching for equity and justice [Special issue of *Rethinking Schools*]. Milwaukee, WI: Rethinking Schools.

Carlson, D. (1997). *Making progress: Education and culture in new times.* New York: Teachers College Press.

Casey, K. (1993). *I answer with my life: Life histories of women teachers working for social change.* New York: Routledge & Kegan Paul.

Chepesiuk, R. (1995). *Sixties radicals, then and now: Candid conversations with those who shaped the era.* Jefferson, NC: McFarland.

Childs, S. J. (1999). Networking, organizing, and resisting. *Rethinking Schools, 14*(1), 9.

Connelly, F. M., & Clandinin, D. J. (1988). *Teachers as curriculum planners: Narratives of experience.* New York: Teachers College Press.

Fine, M., Annand, B. T., Sherman, D., & Jordan, C. (Eds.). (1998). *OFF TRACK: Classroom privilege for all* [Video]. New York: Teachers College Press.

Kohn, A. (1999). Forward … into the past. *Rethinking Schools, 14*(1), 4.

Wheatley, M. (1992). *Leadership and the new science.* San Francisco: Berrett-Koehler.

Images in Textbooks, Literature, Television, and Film

7

"The Ideal Teacher": Images in Early 20th-Century Teacher Education Textbooks

Pamela Bolotin Joseph

I f you had been a student in an American teacher education class or a school-teacher attempting to buy a book on self-improvement during the first several decades of the 20th century, most likely you would have been given a textbook that told you how to become *The Ideal Teacher* (Palmer, 1908/1910), *The Excellent Teacher* (Avent, 1931), or to succeed at *Getting Ahead as a Teacher* (Duke, 1923) or *Developing a Teacher Personality That Wins* (Sandford, 1938). Even if your textbook had a more negative approach *Problems of the Teaching Profession* (Almack & Lang, 1925) or *Clarifying the Teacher's Problems* (Gist, 1932)—you would have read about the authors' conception of a teacher paragon, an exemplary or ideal teacher.[1] If you had doubts about the qualities you would need, checklists of ideal traits could explicitly guide you[2] (Charters & Waples, 1929; Overn, 1935; Sandford, 1938). The textbook writers would not just explain about classroom management, school organization, or curriculum; they would implore you to become an archetype of this virtuous profession. Paragons of teaching would be described with flourishing style or pedantic rhetoric, entreating or commanding you to make yourself into the image esteemed by the authors.[3]

I chose to study teacher education textbooks before 1940 for several reasons. Initially, I kept noticing dusty but beguiling volumes at university libraries when I was looking for more recent works about the teaching profession. I amused myself with wonderful and appalling bits of trivia for my department's bulletin board (e.g., tips on good grooming for teachers circa 1920), but increasingly I became fascinated with the book titles, the authors' sympathetic as well as cruel advice, and the charming but peculiar use of metaphors to describe teachers.[4] I began to think that there was a story in those antiquated texts that might be worth telling.

The idea of studying teacher education textbooks also appealed to me because I frequently use old and current school textbooks in my teaching to learn about how children have been instructed. These books certainly reveal the writers' worldviews and the social, economic, and moral values they affirmed. I believe that textbooks for teachers similarly can convey authors' beliefs and values and can explain something about how teachers were acculturated into their profession and what expectations were held for them throughout their careers.

In this chapter, I will seek answers to these questions: How did textbook writers portray the characteristics of the excellent schoolteacher? What images did teacher educators create and sanction in order to illustrate ideal traits? How did textbooks "school" young people into the profession of teaching and counsel experienced educators to teach and to behave in schools and their communities? I will also explore several other issues that are germane to this study: the existence of teacher paragon archetypes, the authors' use of language and metaphors expressing American cultural values, the dichotomy between their concern about teacher stereotypes and the authors' own negative representations, and the resulting conundrum for teachers who might have wanted to take such advice to heart.

The Noble Teacher

In the textbooks of teacher education, one image of the schoolteacher paragon had a continuous and dramatic presence: teacher as selfless altruist, dedicated soldier, patriot, saint, or redeemer. A striking commonality of this literature was the theme of the intrinsic rewards of teaching. "There is a free-will devotion which he puts into his work that draws its own peculiar form of compensation," wrote A. C. Perry in 1912; "teaching, like virtue, is its own reward" (p. 54). Textbook writers repeatedly proclaimed this sentiment: "The excellent teacher is forgetful of self. He thinks of others' comfort first. He is willing to labor on, spend, and be spent, even to be forgotten for the sake of *others*. While others are practicing 'Safety first' for themselves, his motto is 'Safety last' for himself" (Avent, 1931, p. 128). Another author fervently noted, "She is so unselfish that any thought of reward or personal consideration is usually far from her mind" (Milner, 1912, p. 17). Self-sacrifice, the textbook writers apparently believed, gave teachers a gallant nobility.

The authors endeavored to depict teachers as professionals, but clearly the notion of professionalism evoked a selfless ideal. The criterion of a profession (in contrast to a trade) wrote Almack and Lang (1925) is that "monetary consideration is secondary. Unselfishness is one of its prime principles. Altruism is the prevailing spirit" (p. 59). Pulliam (1930) commented upon "the disposition on the part of the professional man to place the service he renders to the public above the pay that he gets for it" (p. 371). "This is not to say that professional men are martyrs," added Edwin Lee (1938), "but they want, also, those personal satisfactions which are higher than and not represented in economic reward" (p. 67). Perry (1912) went so far as to write that money actually tainted the professional by not allowing him to perform to the fullest. Perry wrote that "the physician frequently gives his most devoted service when he has lost all thought of his fee. So does the teacher best serve the pupils before him when his service in unrelated in his mind to his salary check" (p. 54).

Nevertheless, there were compensations for schoolteachers, even if not financial in nature. Frequently, the writers explained that teachers found reward simply by working with young people. Students were tonics; they could magically rejuvenate teachers: "Good teachers stay young through the very contagion of youth" (Bagley & Keith, 1932, p. 2); "Truly, to live is to grow. It is the teacher's privilege to deal with youth, and youth enjoys life" (Marsh, 1928, p. 2); or "the greatest social satisfaction of the teacher comes in his contact with youth. His own spirit draws refreshment from the spring of youth" (Snyder & Alexander, 1932, p. 58).

The teaching of youth was thought to provide stimulation that would invigorate teachers. "The teacher has the pleasure of watching pupils' mental growth. Is not this a precious reward?" (McFee, 1918, p. 246); "There is something in the contact with childhood, something in the miracle of human growth which soon interests the newest recruit at teaching" (Palmer, 1914, p. v). So, too, the teaching process enlivens the teacher. "Another reason for the fascination of teaching doubtless lies in the new problems that it continually presents. There is a never-ending variety in the human material with which the teacher deals, and this means a never-ending variety in the problems that must be solved" (Bagley & Keith, 1932, p. 2).

The texts also declared the nobility of teaching as service because of what teachers could do for young people. "There is no higher opportunity than that which comes to a teacher. She has an opportunity to give to many children many opportunities that a mother gives a few children" (Winship, 1919, p. 17). "To make even one pupil better may be a greater service to humanity than to amass a fortune; and you may make thousands better" (Wright, 1920, p. 4). Several authors embellished the argument that creation of better individuals would improve humanity. They gloried in teachers consciously working for humanity, for a better world (Lee, 1938, p. 11; McFee, 1918, p. 249).

Not content to imagine teachers serving humanity, a few textbook authors actually compared teachers to holy men. Teaching, declared Averill (1939), "is a way of life comparable with the way of the preacher and prophet" (p. 136). Palmer (1914) advised teachers to realize that teaching has a "redemptive character." He added, "the scientific man and the artist are redeemers too, in their several modes. No less than we they would save mankind from a low order of living" (p. 19). In addition, comparing teachers with the wise men, Avent (1931) announced, "The excellent teacher has much higher ideals than people in general; otherwise he could not be excellent" (p. 284).

Only a few authors appeared to see the dangers of such grand idealism. Palmer (1914) maintained that people should enter teaching because they want to teach: "The notion of benefitting somebody comes afterwards" (p. 15). Averill (1939) cautioned teachers that their desire to help humanity "must bow to patience; one generation cannot change humanity" (p. 19). Vehemently critical of the image of "self-sacrifice and nobility of the profession" (Simon, 1938, p. 34), Simon believed it actually was harmful to the teaching process. Furthermore, Simon urged teachers not to consider their pupils first in forming their rationale for personal interests and activities: "The teacher, who visits a picture gallery or reads a book because he thinks he ought to do it for the sake of the little ones, might almost as well not do it at all. Your first duty is to yourself. Children instinctively react to vitality and will get its full benefit soon enough" (p. 42).

Explaining to teaching candidates that they may not always feel rewarded, Milner (1912) warned that students often do not appreciate or realize the teacher's contribution: "Let anyone who enters upon the teaching profession in the hope of these rewards pause before it is too late to turn aside. Two things are as sure as death—the thoughtlessness of youth and its supreme selfishness" (p. 16). Milner noted that, occasionally, teachers will receive a little consideration "just often enough to renew your courage." But, she mused, "this is as it should be. Youth is and ought to be egoistic" (p. 16).

Overall, the ideal of the noble, selfless teacher permeated these texts and captured the writers' zeal. Less prominent, and certainly less passionately deliberated, were the effects of such benevolent nobility upon the teaching profession. Raised often as an afterthought, in a hesitant or apologetic manner, some of the authors explained that the profession needed higher status, security, and even more money. A few urged teachers to form professional associations and demand better compensation (Almack & Lang, 1925, p. 64; Simon, 1938, p. 57), but militant unionism had no advocates. Most writers believed that teachers should overcome or ignore difficulties by living within their means, not caring about status, and delighting in the dignity of the profession. As Averill (1939) expounded:

> There is a security in one's task that transcends mere economic security, indispensable as the latter is. It is a security that comes from the awareness of social respect and esteem for conscientious and generous service rendered. In the fullness of satisfaction created by such wholesome mental attitude as this toward one's task, there is no room for conflict. (p. 10)

In these textbooks, authors reiterated that the noble teacher does not worry about reward; such concerns could only damage the profession and, perhaps, even do harm to the mental health of teachers. Over again, the authors insisted that the problem of lack of reward and status did not lie in society or social values, but with the teachers themselves. When teachers became even more professional, nobler, more selfless, then society would honor and reward them properly.

The Scholar

Having some characteristics in common with the archetype of the noble teacher, principally the intrinsic rewards of working with youth, was a more dynamic paragon—the intellectual schoolteacher. This educator was described as an open-minded scholar, a leader, a scientist, or an artist. This teacher paragon existed as a role model to students—of scholarship and analytical thinking. Such vibrant images pervaded many teacher education texts either substantively or superficially; in some cases such teacher paragons epitomized the authors' goals for teaching, whereas in others the authors paid lip-service to these images, but gave otherwise contradictory counsel.

Qualities of the Intellectual Paragon

How did textbook authors describe the intellectual schoolteacher? In *The Ideal Teacher,* Palmer (1908/1910) stipulated that a teacher paragon must possess four characteristics: (a) the capability of living with little reward, (b) the ability and passion to create scholars, (c) an accumulation of knowledge, and (d) an active, open mind. To Palmer, the teaching profession, whether one was a college professor or a classroom teacher, was noble and self-sacrificing—and yet powerful, dynamic, and fluid. "A finished teacher is a contradiction in terms," Palmer (1908/1910) proclaimed; "our reach will forever exceed our grasp. We can always be more stimulating, imaginative" (p. 29). Palmer's ideal was succinctly captured by Snyder and Alexander (1932) when they wrote, "There must be a thinking teacher before there can be a thinking child" (p. 56).

Several authors expressed Palmer's sentiments when they described the teacher using a plant metaphor—as a "live tree that grows at every branch, not a petrified tree" (Marsh, 1928, p. 6; Winship, 1919, p. 64). Milner (1912) urged schoolteachers to make books "close personal friends" and to read different books because "in a growing garden the same flowers do not blossom day after day" (p. 13). Scholarship could bring delight to the teacher who grew intellectually along with the students (McFee, 1918, pp. 16, 245).

Poor teaching occurs, explained Grant (1927) when the teacher does not grow, because of "mental crystallization, the inability to act on new ideas" (p. 243). Further, "Twenty years after normal-school graduation some teachers are teaching reading in the same way that they did the first year. They secure what *they* call good results, and fight nothing but change" (Grant, 1927, pp. 245–246). As Milner (1912) suggested, devotion to one's work alone does not make the excellent teacher:

> A man once asked a teacher if she had read a certain book, mentioning one of excellent merit which was then attracting wide attention. "No," she replied, "I haven't had time for 20 years to read anything but primers and first readers, and the nature book which I have to teach." If this woman

were a good teacher in spite of this narrow, contracted, pitiful condition, what a great teacher she might have been if she could have but climbed the hill-side ever so little a way. (pp. 33–34)

This crystallization was described by authors when they depicted teachers' use of the textbook in the classroom: "Many pupils have been advised to 'see what the book says,' until they have become dependent on the text. They have acquired the habit of believing all that is printed. Many teachers have taught the text and nothing but the text" (Grant, 1922, p. 129). Teachers' overdependence on the textbook limited both schoolteacher and pupil. Furthermore, because textbooks and teachers did not encourage critical thinking, wrote Zirbes and Taba (1937), "young people are denied the most invigorating parts of the thinking process" (p. 103).

Authors critical of schoolteachers for their lack of scholarly capacities and broad-mindedness implied that inflexible personalities and poor academic preparation kept teachers from being intellectuals. Teachers were told to rid themselves of their intellectual rigidity. The authors who portrayed excellent teachers as intellectuals insisted that unless schoolteachers were scholars, professional growth was impossible.

Obligations to Students

The ideal teacher as scholar did not by itself complete the vision of this paragon; the teacher also had to lead students toward their own intellectual development. Rather than extolling the academician who merely could impart knowledge, most textbook writers sympathetic to Palmer's paragon understood scholarship as the catalyst for teaching. The teacher as intellectual would learn along with the student. This was a powerful image of transformation and the antithesis of the metaphor of tradition edition in which the teacher pours knowledge into a passive vessel. Colgrove (1911) romantically expressed this thought by writing, "The true teacher at work is a liberator" (p. 390).

As intellectuals, teachers clearly had a social mission. The textbook authors wrote about a democratic vision in which students would become more informed, critical, cooperative, and yet independent citizens (Bagley, 1932, p. 3; Strayer & Engelhard, 1920, p. 377; Zirbes & Taba, 1937, pp. 115–116). The teacher paragon could understand that by making it possible for children to think critically, the independence and democratic vision of future generations would be insured because the "wellspring of democracy is the independent intelligence of its several members" (Valentine, 1931, p. 32).

A few texts reflected George Counts' (1932) galvanizing speech to the Progressive Education Association in which he insisted that it was necessary for teachers to "disturb the social order." According to Lee (1938),

To a very large extent, the ability of any citizen to take part intelligently in his government depends upon the kind of education he has received. To teach his pupils to think clearly, to criticize fearlessly and to judge intelligently—this is the great, the almost matchless privilege of the teacher in a democracy. (pp. 18–19)

Several writers discussed teachers' obligation not only to the students but also to society, including future generations. Wrote Watson (1937), "The chief responsibility of the teacher is to improve the quality of life in the coming generation" (p. 155). Only by enabling students to obtain "social insight to replace the blind prejudices which now so often rule" can the teacher so improve society (p. 155).

The schoolteacher, as scholar and intellectual, guided students to discover "truth"—the greatest wisdom of the ages. Colgrove (1911) explained, "The child, like the primitive man, is the slave of ignorance, of fear, and of nature. It is the purpose of teaching to set him free" (p. 391). The emancipation of students meant the banishment of ignorance and prejudice and their recognition and acceptance of the most humanizing and ennobling ideas of civilization.

The Teacher's Presence

Textbook writers who concluded that teachers' missions was to develop students' critical thinking abilities or characters urged that teachers must convey their strong presence—the essence of their personalities and values—in order to transfer their own beliefs and behavior to their students (Colgrove, 1911, p. 391; Grant, 1927, p. 295; Snyder & Alexander, 1932, p. 4). Authors who conceived of the scholar teacher advocated neither child-centered education nor the teacher's role as facilitator.

Several textbook authors assumed that the ability to influence students was more important than the teacher's own intellectual capacities. "He may not be a great scholar," wrote Wright (1920), but the teacher still could make his students "wise and good men" (p. 45). So, too, could students be shaped by the teacher's presence as a human being—"his attitude toward life, his way of thinking, his friendships, his prejudices" (Simon, 1938, p. 40).

However, role-modeling fine qualities did not satisfy many of the textbook authors. Rather, they preached that the teacher should demonstrate leadership by influencing the child educationally and morally (Hines, 1926, p. 169; Winship, 1919, p. 142). Even those teacher educators who were appalled by dogmatic instructional methods responded to critics of child-centered education (who feared that nontraditional education would create a totally unguided classroom) by insisting that the teacher can provide guidance and still help develop students intellectually (Zirbes & Taba, 1937, p. 108).

A minority of the textbook authors who feared the strong presence of the educator suggested that an overpowering teacher personality could prevent the empowerment of students. The harm to children could be seen when the teacher left the school or students passed on to another grade.

> When that time comes, it is usually clear enough that the "strong Personal-
> ity" of the teacher has actually weakened the pupils. They have become so
> thoroughly dependent on this stimulus that they are unable to stand alone.
> The interest that they displayed in their lessons turns out to be only a bor-
> rowed interest. (Bagley & Keith, 1932, p. 339)

However, as in case of the teacher portrayed as selfless paragon, authors generally
offered little criticism of the archetype. Forceful, magnetic personalities were envisioned for teachers, but possible consequences for students were seldom contemplated.

Scientists and Artists

How could teachers help students to reach their full potentials? Many of the textbook authors turned to scientific knowledge of child development and pedagogy
and to the educator's artistry for the answer. Some recommended that teachers
study not just subjects but the interests and capabilities of the students themselves
(Davis, 1930, p. 105; Grant, 1922, pp. 124, 129). The teacher also must look ahead
and "chart the correct course" for the child (Milner, 1912, p. 228) or "knowing just
where she is bound intellectually, the teacher can make adequate provisions for
proper teaching equipment" (Holley, 1922, p. 59).

An intellectual teacher not only studied child development, but also approached
education scientifically. Perhaps no author stated that idea as clearly as Freeland
(1925): "The teacher who advances in the profession use his classroom as a laboratory. Each day holds the possibility of a new discovery" (p. 7). Similarly, Melby
(1937) declared that the teacher "must become a full-fledged practitioner in educational science. He is more comparable to the physician than to the nurse" (p. 128).

Several textbooks introduced dual concepts of the teacher as scientist and as artist. "There is, in fact, a close kinship between the scientific discoverer, even in education, and the creative artist" (Valentine, 1931, p. 34). Excellent teachers develop
their expertise through the laboratory of the classroom; what they achieve is an artistic expression of craft through "controlled experimentation" (Grant, 1927, pp.
246–247). "The true teacher is a combination of artist, scientist, and skilled crafts-
man," wrote Lee (1938); "… like all artistic pursuits, the teacher's task is a creative
one" (p. 38).

The scholar teacher as an artist, a creative force, appeared often in the teacher education literature (Avent, 1931, p. 34; Grant, 1927, p. 244; Holley, 1922, p. 5; Valentine, 1931, p. 27). The admirers of this paragon maintained that the teaching
profession afforded creativity and individuality in the approach to the teacher and
response to each student—a stark contrast to workers in other occupations. In this
regard, Averill (1939) commented,

> The teacher-operative is about the only artisan left in the modern world
> who still maintains the same relationship to her craft that the guild workers

enjoyed centuries ago. The machine has not destroyed the unity of the relationship. The teacher continues still to work upon the totality of the raw
material placed at her disposal, and continues thus in a position to experience the fullest pleasure and satisfaction at every stage and in every process. (p. 6)

Or as Valentine (1931) ironically remarked, "No factory manager would employ a
staff of artist-minded workers to turn out his product. Standardization would be impossible. They would 'gum up' the machinery" (p. 40). Similarly, Sandford (1938)
warned that "present tendencies in education fail to create inspiration among teachers"—the mechanistic school day would drain the energies of teachers; individuals
with "initiative" could not survive the routine of the school system (p. 51).

Proponents of the paragon of teacher as artist feared that the modern school
would not allow for creativity—that science could not be in harmony with art
when it brought only standardization. The molding and the vitalizing of students
would be impossible because schools and classrooms modeled after factories
would crush the teachers' artistic gifts and not allow them to evolve their own talents and intuition to realize their goals for students. Authors who imagined various versions of the teacher as artist believed in their vision of the teacher's
potential power, but had less faith that American schools would sanction the existence of this paragon.

The Controller and the Controlled

In this study, only a minority of textbook writers unequivocally envisioned
teacher paragons as scholars who would cultivate their students' intelligence. Having little or no realization of the intellectual possibilities of the teaching profession
for teacher or student, many of the authors portrayed the image of teacher as a controller—the maker of order. Numerous texts emphasized order and organizing, control and discipline, authority and power. Examples of such sentiments include:
"Order is heaven's first law, and it is scarcely more essential to the peace and harmony there, than it is to the happiness and success of a school" (McFee 1918, p. 13);
"There is, however, no exception to the principle that within the schoolroom the authority of the teacher is absolute" (Perry, 1912, p. 35); "The teacher is the hub of the
educational wheel, for he controls the immediate environment of the pupils"
(Overn, 1935, p. 7); and "The last step in the transformation of the student into the
teacher is the acquirement of power to bring things to pass. The teacher is not all instructor; he is organizer, ruler, and trainer" (Colgrove, 1911, p. 65).

Even if they acknowledged the idea of teachers as scholars, the textbook authors
generally did not acknowledge how difficult it could be to be a stimulator when one
must also be a controller. Few noted, as did Donovan (1938), the tension between
the teacher's roles as disciplinarian and catalyst:

> The schoolma'am must constantly be two persons of opposite tendencies. She must be the one who sees and represses undesirable traits and unsuitable behavior; at the same time she must also be the one who stimulates the thinking and draws forth the expression from her pupils which means successful classroom procedure. (p. 16)

Realistically, the ideal teacher as an intellectual might not have been a successful teacher if the measurement of success was keeping a job by continually enjoying the blessings of the administration and the community. In his *The Sociology of Teacher,* Waller (1932) concluded that "the ability to discipline is the usual test" for teacher advancement. A teacher must "fit in" and have "a degree of dexterity in manipulating the social environment" (p. 30). In order to be successful, teachers had to control their classrooms and positively manipulate their own images within the community.

The expectations of those who hired teachers (administrators and boards of education) thus would influence teachers' goals for themselves. The attainment of order would preempt any other purpose for teaching: "No teacher can expect to succeed until she is able to govern her school. The first thing that patrons expect of their teacher is to 'keep order,' and the second thing they expect of her is to teach. If she can't do the first, she can't do the second" (Grant, 1922, p. 95). Regardless of whether these teacher educators seemed genuinely excited about the teaching process and the development of children, they counseled teaching candidates to be authority figures: "It is better to be inflexible than to be always undecided" (Wright, 1920, p. 39), or "being a drill-sergeant is also better than being a dishrag" (Simon, 1938, pp. 83–84).

If fear of censure from school officials or citizens of the community was not enough to dissuade teachers from keeping unruly classrooms, textbook writers also insinuated that teachers who could not control their classrooms were incompetent, neurotic, or foolish. Furthermore, they cautioned that control of the classroom must emanate from self-control.

> The teacher who is not complete master of herself will certainly fail to master others. If she finds she cannot exercise this self-control, she should seek other employment. (McFee, 1918, p. 13)

> The good teacher knows that temper begets temper, that noise begets noise, and that order begets order. She knows that the teacher who would control her pupils must first control herself. (Grant, 1922, p. 96)

> Many of the serious problems that the teacher faces in her everyday work originate from her own personality. Three of the greatest maxims a teacher can practice are those announced hundreds of years ago: "Know thyself. Control thyself. Deny thyself." (Lewis, 1926, p. 324)[5]

The textbook writers played on teachers' and teaching candidates' anxiety about losing control, threatening them with nightmares of chaos in the classroom and the ruin of their standing in their schools or communities. Teachers had to know that to survive in the classroom they must dominate children.

Donovan (1938) lamented that the need to create classroom order eventually would alter the personality of the teacher: "All successful teachers acquire a dominating personality. Some conceal its outward manifestations better than others, that is all" (p. 18). Waller (1932) also surmised that teachers' personalities have been influenced by the expectation that they must maintain order. He explained that "teachers fear two things above all others: the loss of control over their classes, and the loss of their jobs"—these fears, in Waller's analysis, become "the central features of the personality" (p. 156).

Images of control also were fostered through descriptions of teachers' function in the order of the school and their place in the organization of the community. Prospective teachers were reminded that achieving authority in the classroom was somewhat symbolic; real power would be held or granted by administrators and community members. Within a system of subordination to administrators and public opinion, teachers were shown their place (Sandford, 1938, p. 103; Walsh, 1926, p. 214). Thus, depictions of teachers in orderly classrooms were juxtaposed with images of teachers' place in the order of the school system. The textbook authors created a tension between authority and submission; the image of the teacher as controller thus became connected with that of the teacher as the controlled.

The implication that teachers must be submissive to the authority of others—and thus deny their own interests or opinions—became more explicit when the textbook writers discussed the relationship of the teacher to the community. What did it mean to live as a teacher in the early decades of the 20th century? Particularly in nonurban areas, textbook authors explained that being a teacher meant existing in a fishbowl: "The teacher, because he is widely known, is a convenient topic for conversation. Only the checking influence of numerous friends will keep those reports (that hint at questionable habits, tastes or judgment) down and prevent their gaining both weight and momentum as they go" (Van Nice, 1929, p. 92). According to Simon (1938), "A teacher's life is, in a small town, practically public property: almost everyone regards himself as a duly constituted censor of a teacher's behavior—not to mention his professional skill" (p. 44).

Schoolteachers had to scrutinize their own behavior more than most other people not only because they were well known in the community, but also because teachers had to live according to a special code of conduct. As Davis (1930) advised, "The teacher ought to know that it is the standard which the community sets for teachers that counts, not the standard which it may set for itself" (p. 59). Or, explained Knudsen and McAfee (1936), "Parents expect teachers to exemplify behaviors more worthy of emulation by youth than that of the parents themselves" (p. 10). Furthermore,

Teachers in general are bound by a stricter moral code than other professional persons, ministers of the gospel alone excepted. Thus it follows that they are considered unethical if they violate the standards set by the community for conduct of the teacher, even though there be no real infraction of the broader moral code. (Jordan, 1930, p. 258)

Social scientists writing at this time concluded that educators had a nearly unique position among occupations. Because teachers were thought to be able to influence the young, communities exerted strict control over schoolteachers. Parents and other community members feared that teachers could influence young people to adopt socially unacceptable opinions about economics or politics.

Several researchers in the 1930s concluded that the teaching profession endured scrutiny and repression from many sources. Elsbree (1939) noticed that parents and organizations had shifted their emphasis of control of teachers from social reactions and church attendance to the teachers' political viewpoints (pp. 540, 542). Beale (1936) wrote: "In most communities this tradition means that the teacher shall not in thought or action violate the local mores and shall stand a more rigid test in the least common denominator of the dominant religious faiths than that required of most citizens" (p. 624). Beale also blamed repression of teachers on administrators' intentional or oblivious behaviors and on "social forces for which no individual is responsible" (p. 13).

Most textbook writers confirmed the existence of social and political restrictions upon teachers, but had varying responses to repressions. Their responses ranged from approval of placing teachers on a moral pedestal to despair over the effect of repression on teachers' personalities.

The authors who approved of the peculiar moral code for teachers and the limitations upon social and political freedom created rationalizations for agreeing with the situation. First of all "the excellent teacher" would not "disregard local sensibilities; he adheres to the social code and complies with social conventions" (Avent, 1931, p. 246). An excellent teacher would not be interested in entertainment of which the community disapproved; therefore, some authors self-righteously wondered, why should a teacher paragon criticize limitations on freedom (Pulliam, 1930, p. 437)?

Some authors went so far as to suggest that such repression is a badge of honor, the sign of the community's respect for the teaching profession; the community did not care what amusements entertained the bank clerk and the stenographer (Knudsen & McAfee, 1936, p. 9). Other writers claimed that although the standards were difficult to live up to, the teacher who lived in an exemplary fashion (morally and socially) would reap the reward of a "favorable reputation" (Marsh, 1928, p. 155).

Recognizing the strict social controls on schoolteachers, textbook authors gave advice about how to deal with communities' restrictions. Such advice can be summarized briefly: If you don't like the restrictions, don't take the job (Davis, 1930, p. 59; Weber, 1937, p. 34); "make do," but look for a new position for next year (Gist, 1932, p. 306); or just sacrifice your own inclinations and don't offend the community (Carpenter & Rufi, 1931, p. 229; Jordan, 1930, p. 258; Snyder & Alexander, 1932, p. 58). Almack and Lang (1925) suggested that first the teacher should follow the "behavioral modes" of her new community, but later she had a chance to express her individuality after winning the community's confidence (p. 295). Other writers saw the possibility of the teacher influencing the community's standards through education and by setting a good example—not by criticizing the community (Carpenter & Rufi, 1931, p. 204).

Successful teachers were described as "people pleasers." In their personal and professional lives, they had to modify their attitudes, values, and behavior to those of the community. Teachers thus would become smoothly adaptable, never calling attention to themselves (Avent, 1931, p. 197) except when someone noticed their dependability and helpfulness, such as their availability to the community as Sunday school teachers.[6] Neither could teachers call attention to themselves by letting community members or students know their political affiliations nor dare to become involved with political campaigns (Davis, 1930, p. 53; Marsh, 1928, p. 166).

Several textbooks that contained advice on pleasing a community gave counsel urging concessions that would restrict the teacher from friendship and intimacy. For example, teachers were warned to avoid intimate relationships not only because a love interest would attract attention to themselves, but because an intimate friendship demands loyalty; "intimacy is dangerous—to enter into intimate friendships is to assume the enemies of those people" (Van Nice, 1929, pp. 62, 104). "Excellent teachers" and "tactful teachers" surrendered their own humanity for the sake of obliging the community.

A few textbook authors worried about the effect of such submission on the personality or the character of the teacher. For example, Valentine (1931) feared that the inhibited person could not be a creative, artistic teacher (p. 283). Simon (1938) had foreseen that social repressions would create a "timidity and conservatism" in teachers:

> In small towns, particularly the teacher thus becomes not a courageous, independent thinker and an adventuresome person, as the leader of children ought to be, but a timid soul censored by a board and spied upon by everyone. Consideration of his every action is prefaced by those two hamstringing words, "Dare I?" "Dare I wear these clothes?" "Dare I go to this restaurant?" "Dare I be seen soon again with this young man or woman?" "Dare I vote thus?" "Dare I say this?" and finally, "Dare I think so-and-so?" (p. 46)

Yet, Simon (1938) did not forthrightly take the position that the teacher must fight most repression. Rather, his advice was to "lie low" and first establish a good reputation. He recommended that the teacher should concede to more trivial impositions such as standards of dress (issues of "personal convenience") in order to "fight his real battles" (p. 47). Simon reminded the teacher "not to flaunt his disrespect for the conventions of his community in regard to symbols," but to care about more substantive issues (which he did not specifically enumerate) involving "principles much more far-reaching than your personal convenience" (p. 47).

In book after book, the textbook authors—including admirers of the scholar paragon and even those who advocated for greater teacher professionalism and activism—rendered images of the teacher as controller and controlled. They routinely advised teachers to give up their individuality, to adopt a dehumanizing conformity to local or popular customs. At best, these books taught teachers "how to play the game" in order to obtain a teaching position and keep it. At worst, they tried to persuade teachers to be submissive to an extent that only the most repressive societies could imagine.

Ideal schoolteachers had to withstand close scrutiny and exhibit flawless behavior in all aspects of their lives. They had to demonstrate their ability to control not only the children but also themselves. What teacher education textbooks had in common was their advocacy of conformity to dominant community standards and their authors' perception of the coercion manifest in the community's relationship to the schoolteacher.

Teacher Images and Metaphors of American Culture

Textbook authors continually used language and metaphors that reflected the then-contemporary American culture. As befitting the times, the texts were replete with images from the military and World War I, factories and business, and, finally, the social and economic upheaval of the Great Depression.

Textbooks written shortly after World War I portrayed ideal teachers through specific references to elements of the conflict among nations and to American war experiences. In demonstrating that the exemplary teacher must not be authoritarian, Winship (1919) proclaimed, "The sudden collapse of the Kaiser was at the same time the collapse of Germany, the collapse of autocracy everywhere, the collapse of bossism in school and out" (p. 47). Another author insisted that the ideal teacher must be a moral educator by admonishing, "If all teachers in all nations would only give proper emphasis to moral training, we would not have to worry over making the world safe for democracy" (Grant, 1922, p. 220).

Others writing in this time period conceptualized metaphors of teaching through images of war and soldiering. In *Education as a Life Work: An Introduction to Teaching,* Jordan (1930) asserted that teaching was not just women's work and tried to persuade males to enter the teaching profession by recruiting:

> A man who is looking for an opportunity for service, who wants to do a really big thing in life, a thing which calls for men of red blood, of tremendous vitality ... to go into the world with those ideals and skills which will make them fit to maintain the glory of our country and to insure its perpetual prosperity. This is a real "MAN'S JOB." (p. 28)

Lee (1938), in *Teaching as a Man's Job,* thought that schools ought to place signs outside their doors that read "American Education Needs Men" (p. 11). Moreover, the same author compared the heroic "unknown teacher" to the Unknown Soldier (p. 10). Such metaphors of teaching obviously carried the message that to teach is patriotic, that men might no longer serve their country on the battlefield—but they could serve in the classroom.[7]

During the period of time examined in this study, however, the most prominent images of teachers related to American culture were formulated from the realm of business and industry. Teachers should "give a personal touch to customers" explained Milner (1912, p. 68), in reference to teachers' relationships with parents. "Education is a business enterprise," commented Walsh (1926, p. 213). Hines (1926) deduced that hiring a teacher was "in a limited sense a purely business transaction" (p. 19). Striving for "trained and informed intelligence" in order to save civilization, Bagley and Keith (1932) also described teachers using the metaphor of industry: "The teacher is actually and essentially a producer" (p. 3). Metaphors connoting management, productivity, sales, and customers in the business world routinely were applied to teaching in the literature of teacher education.[8]

In particular, textbooks contained various references to products: education was a product, a child was product, and so, too, was the teacher. "The public is not completely pleased with the schools and their products," wrote Palmer (1914, p. vi); "Parents can neutralize all the classroom product" (Dearborn, 1925, p. 27); "The world demands a better product," proclaimed an author arguing for better teacher training (Hines, 1926, p. 3); or "We are striving to make the teacher a finished product," wrote a successful administrator in a chapter of advice to teachers (Duke, 1923, p. 24).

Not only was the school compared to business; writers also described schools mechanistically, fostering images of machines and automation; for example, "The school may be conceived as a factory" (Overn, 1935, p. 14). Furthermore, in order to run industry economically, one must get rid of waste or inefficiency; authors made similar statements about teachers and students. Because of the problem of teacher selection "the causes for waste are perhaps more evident in teaching than in other professions" (Hines, 1926, p. 80). Or "The teacher realizes that she has a responsibility to society in training childhood for the highest possible degree of efficiency" (Gist, 1932, p. 6).[9]

Limits of the applicability of the metaphor of industry applied to teaching also were noticed by some authors. Milner (1912) demonstrated her skepticism about education in America: "If, in the grinding process, a few grains of humanity escape, there are compulsory education laws and vigorous able-bodied truant officers to gather up the grains and return them to the mill" (p. 224). Others criticized the effect of schooling as an industrial machine upon teachers saying that "the classroom teachers feel lost in a machine-like organization" (Lewis, 1926, p. 13) and "little confidence has in the main been placed in teachers and their ability to direct their own activities" (Melby, 1937, p. 119). Although the opponents of the industry metaphor defended their positions eloquently, textbook writers comfortable with such imagery applied to teaching far outnumbered the critics.

The third pattern of language and metaphors alluded to the great economic and political changes (the Russian Revolution and the Great Depression) that influenced American thought and culture. Strayer and Engelhard (1920) warned, "If the school does not give the best and most extensive training possible to the intellectually capable, those children will rise as leaders of social and economic groups which may be expected to be antagonistic to a social order whose advantages were denied them" (p. 377). Sandford (1938) urged educators to free themselves from old ways of thinking: "The willingness of most of our people to give drastic experiments in other fields a fair trial shows that they think almost everything better than the old order" (p. 48). Whether apprehensive or fearful, such writers encouraged teachers to possess more insight about the future.

Therefore, some authors urged that teachers think of themselves as leaders responsible for changing humanity, focusing on "social engineering" (Davis, 1930, p. 66; Snyder & Alexander, 1932, p. 4) or "race betterment" (Gist, 1932, p. 6).[10] The economic and political crises of the 1930s also prompted authors to urge teachers to bring about better conditions by creating better citizens. But how could teachers improve society? Various paths were suggested. Teachers could influence "the social order of the next generation" by exposing children to ideas and habits that would eventually determine if society would become "competitive or cooperative" (Snyder & Alexander, 1932, p. 4).[11] Or schoolteachers must appreciate "the importance and dignity of their function in human society by building "character and morale in children" (Averill, 1939, p. 15).

How might we interpret the language and metaphors that the authors used in presenting their arguments and describing the archetypes? Nearly all of the textbook writers apparently wanted their portrayals of paragons to have meaning in the vernacular. By using the words and issues of their times, they may have hoped to have their books appear timely or to set their advice in a context their audiences would understand. It may not be even too cynical to suggest that the writers constructed images not only because the imagery seemed significant to them, but also because they hoped to enhance the popularity of their books by the use of jargon.

These textbooks must be understood, however, as more than simple vernacularism. Instead, they can be seen as revealing some of the essential questions and tensions in America life of that era regarding the relationship individual to society. In this study, it is evident that the vast majority of these textbooks displayed a wholehearted acceptance of American social and economic beliefs in the modern industrial era. Moreover, the writers wanted educators to live by accepted values and teach them to their pupils. Only rarely did authors protest the possible consequence for teachers and students of American society's preoccupation with conformity and consumerism.

Resisting Stereotype and Caricature

Throughout these texts, American social values also were apparent in discussions about stereotypes of the teaching profession. The authors contrasted their impressions of ideal teachers with obnoxious images that exhibited a variety of unattractive characteristics. Teacher educators insisted that the ideal teacher should recognize and resist the deplorable stereotypes and caricatures of the profession that so provoked the authors' scorn.

Paradoxically, teacher educators dared to encourage people to enter the profession despite their communication of extremely negative stereotypes. The textbooks revealed juxtapositions of reassurance with trepidation. A person should be "proud to be a teacher," expounded an author, who nevertheless commented that "there is often a disposition on the part of ... some teachers to dread to be thought of as a teacher" (Winship, 1919, pp. 17, 18). Why should people dread to become teachers? One might look no farther for the answer than to the textbooks themselves that presented numerous caricatures and contemptuous comments about schoolteachers:

> There is no need of calling attention to the artificial attitude of a certain type of kindergarten teachers, to their affected tone of voice, their lovey-dovey manner, the smile that is lip service only. (Milner, 1912, p. 47)

> Most of the disparaging jokes about teaching picture a meticulous prig, who is out of sympathy and completely out of touch with living men and women. (Pulliam, 1930, p. 435)

> Though she may be 30 pounds overweight, popular conception sees in her a hard thinness of personality; although she has the curves of a houri, she remains a sexless human slab. Her blouses may be entirely without collars but she wears a neckpiece that chokes her. (Donovan, 1938, p. 14)

Textbooks for teachers thus portrayed schoolteachers as inhuman, unattractive, asexual prudes.

The authors rendered these caricatures in their texts supported by a variety of rationales. In warning teachers to repudiate repugnant stereotypes, the writers used negative images to support their superficial recommendations or cure-alls. Sandford (1938) concentrated on the narrowness of teachers' interests:

> For the enrichment of our own personalities, we need to broaden our range of interests. Our tendency to talk shop, in season and out, betrays us. Our paucity of interests outside of our work is apparent whenever we are in a social group that does not appreciate shoptalk. To have some of our statements successfully challenged will help us to escape the offensive air of finality so common to those who work with their inferiors. (pp. 107–108)

For his part, Van Nice (1929) called attention to teachers' traditionally poor grooming:

> Many a teacher has remained low in the esteem of people because he or she failed to recognize the importance of personal habits of neatness and

cleanliness. The race has long suffered from the consequences of untidiness, carelessness, and indifference. Whenever they appear, they bring their heritage of annoyance and contempt. (p. 51)

Such passages reflected the contempt these textbook writers felt for schoolteachers. Petty suggestions about socialization and grooming essentially conveyed teachers' deficiencies and gave the message that they must raise themselves to imitate the conversation and clothing of nonteachers.

Other authors suggested that teachers must become more attuned to their own interests and personalities in order to defy stereotypes in more than a superficial manner. Such changes in themselves included less preoccupation with "administrative detail" and seeking more intellectual stimulus (Davis, 1930, p. 336; Simon, 1938, p. 41). Teachers were admonished to critically examine the caricatures and change themselves accordingly (Davis, 1930, p. 305). The authors implied that if candidates became stereotypical schoolteachers, they had only themselves to blame; after reading the textbook, the pitfalls of becoming a caricature—replete with obnoxious habits of thought and behavior—had been brought to their attention.

The authors had another purpose for writing about negative stereotypes: They wanted to introduce the problems of the teaching profession in order for people to contemplate realistically their vocational choice and to prepare themselves to deal with difficulties. They instructed prospective teachers to understand that no matter what their demeanor, the daily existence of teaching in schools as well as the expectations of communities and American society created stereotypes.

Textbooks that raised the specter of unattractive caricatures frequently blamed the nature of the profession itself for molding teachers into the stereotype. Averill (1939) contended that after years in the classroom, teachers "may lose their youthful outlook and grow stale and uninteresting long before their time" (p. 16). He attributed schoolteachers' "narrow, cranky and harsh attitudes" to "accumulating physical strain and fatigue that go with years of teaching" under unhealthy conditions, for example, in unventilated classrooms (p. 16).

Some authors tempered the idea of the schoolteacher caricature with the notion that any profession may encourage certain behaviors or characteristics among people who practice it (Donovan, 1938, p. 13; Marsh, 1928, p. v). Conversely, Donovan questioned if such caricatured behaviors actually existed or if the popular image, the American cartoon of the "schoolma'am," prevented people from responding to the teacher as a human being; Donovan wrote, "She is to the community not an individual but a teacher" (p. 14).

Others wrote that schoolteachers faced special circumstances that made them different because of the unusual characteristics of their work. "In his relation to others in the community, the teacher occupies a position different from that of any other worker," commented Walsh (1926);

This difference is most marked in the case of teachers in the elementary school, especially in the lower grades. The teacher's actual work is with the children and these have little to do with adult interests. Thus the teacher, by his very work, is often set apart from the actual affairs of life and from the activities that are occupying the minds of other adults. (p. 271)

Waller (1932) similarly stated that the teacher lived somewhat apart from the community because of the nature of the child-focused vocation. The isolation for the teacher was increased, Waller observed, because of constant mobility of teachers that prevented their sustained interaction with community members (p. 49).

However, both Waller (1932) and Simon (1938) implicated communities for encouraging the stereotype—for desiring schoolteachers who could impart little of their humanity. Communities hired and maintained positions for mundane personalities, Simon cautioned: "So you may fall into the easy temptation of the blameless, colorless, safe existence which most communities buy from their teachers with a sense of security" (p. 40). Using parallel reasoning, Waller explained, "The community can never know the teacher because it insists upon regarding him as something more than a god and something less than a man. In short, the teacher is psychologically isolated from the community because he must live within the teacher stereotype" (p. 49).

From the standpoint of the sociologist, Waller beheld what teacher educators inspiring young people to enter the profession could not see or would not admit: a circuitous state-of-affairs that would prohibit teachers from overcoming caricature. Despite teachers' own interests and inclinations, they would be pigeonholed by the community and perceived in a stereotypical manner. Schoolteachers constricted by cultural images of teachers—as absurd prudes or pedagogues—would have had little chance of social interaction with community members in order to repudiate such likely misconceptions.

Contemplating the Ideal Teacher

The predominant images of ideal teachers in teacher education literature in the early 20th century demonstrated textbook authors' distinct and sometimes contradictory convictions about teaching and the roles of schoolteachers. Powerful images of teachers transforming students and society contrasted with conceptions of apprehensive employees warned against engaging in any activity that would make them visible to the community. Within the pages of these textbooks are found illustrations of teachers as honored professionals countervailed by offensive descriptions of schoolteachers as priggish caricatures. Moreover, the textbooks reflected their writers' various intentions: to recruit teaching candidates by eulogizing the possibilities and the nobility of teaching, to prepare new teachers to cope with low status and even ridicule of the profession in the eyes of the public, or to use these books as excuses for publishing patronizing "self-help" books for a large occupational audience.

Notwithstanding, I am convinced that despite their disparate and, at times, contradicting positions, these textbooks shared a fundamental commonality: the depiction of the teaching profession's singularity. The authors articulated the notion that working and living as a teacher was not comparable to the experience of other human beings (except for the clergy). The demand for sainthood in both the teacher's impetus and personality, the exorbitant hopes for the teacher's attainment for children and society, the stringent codes of conduct that had to satisfy dominant community groups, and the necessity of withstanding repulsive stereotypes made schoolteaching an extraordinary occupation. In order to be an ideal teacher, it was not enough to work as a skilled and talented professional. Teacher paragons could not have been merely excellent teachers; they had to have been sublime.

NOTES

1. I looked at textbooks written for teachers and those becoming teachers, books whose introductions or prefaces contained these sentiments: "The teacher who reads the different chapters should obtain a new insight into the problems of her profession and the place and importance of her work" (Almack & Lang, 1925, pp. vi–vii) or "This volume is dedicated to good teachers and to students who will become good teachers" (Knudsen & McAfee, 1936, preface). I also looked at books about supervision and administration because they illustrated images of teachers and their authors urged teachers to read them.

2. Various teacher education texts referred to a checklist devised by Charters and Waples (1929) that listed 26 traits from A (adaptability) to T (thrift). Textbook authors also developed their own charts. Their categories include such items as academic preparation, the ability to manage the classroom, the teacher's moral influence on children, and the teacher's taste in clothing. These checklists were widely used to evaluate classroom teachers.

3. With few exceptions, the textbook authors were teacher educators. Many of them worked in state universities and normal schools and, less frequently, in prestigious universities. Numerous writers held positions in administration or supervision; rarely did any of them work as classroom teachers. A few authors were retired from their professions in education but desired to share their experiences and wisdom, thus, as one publisher's introduction explained, "devoting themselves to educational guidance and giving inspirational talks at all kinds of meetings" (Sandford, 1938, Publisher's Introduction). The vast majority of the authors were men. For this study, I also used a few classic works by sociologists who wrote about the teaching profession during this time period.

4. Since writing this chapter for the first edition of *Images of Schoolteachers,* I have looked over many teacher education textbooks from 1940 through the mid-1970s. (It appears that university libraries have not kept large collections of these texts after those years.) One obvious difference between the books from mid-century and those referred to in this chapter is that encyclopedic foundations texts replaced the earlier advice books and the practice ended for authors to write in first person and to earnestly express personal beliefs.

5. Although I have attempted to provide examples of ideal teacher characteristics that speak to both male and female teachers, advice about self-control appears to be aimed at female readers. Furthermore, knowing that many authors refer to the teacher as

"he," I examined advice about self-control in the male-oriented texts and found a switch to the plural; for example, Avent (1931) wrote, "*they* often take out their bad feelings on their pupils. *They* have no shame for show of temper" (p. 217, italics added).

6. Teaching Sunday school, however, could be hazardous to one's job security. Various authors warned that Sunday school teaching could lead to controversy because if a teacher taught in a certain church, the members of other denominations might turn against the teacher for not teaching Sunday school for their church.

7. I found no indication that the authors carried the comparison of soldiering and teaching to the extreme that the classroom is a battlefield—a public image of schooling that appears in the mid-20th century. Their intention seemed merely to point out the schoolteaching is a service-oriented and vital profession, perhaps suggestive of the hymn, "Onward Christian Soldiers."

8. An extreme example of admiration for business is found in *Teaching as a Profession: Its Ethical Standards* by M. J. Walsh (1926). The writer criticized educators and praised business people. He insisted that "In a rapidly changing social order in which other vocations, both business and professional, have caught something of the unselfish spirit of service and have realized the economic value of business integrity, teaching has lagged behind" in developing standards of conduct (p. v).

9. The phenomenon of describing schools in terms of efficient factories was by no means unique to teacher education literature. In the early decades of the 20th century, many plans and studies for American schools dealt with such concepts as scientific management, cost efficiency, standardization, and so forth. Perhaps there is no better source of describing the business/factory mentality in American schools than Raymond E. Callahan's (1962) *Education and the Cult of Efficiency: A Study of the Social Forces that Have Shaped the Administration of the Public Schools.*

10. "Social engineering" was a term used by many educators of this time period, especially by advocates of vocational education in junior highs and high schools. The concept referred to tracking students into career paths early in their lives and thereby providing an "appropriate" education for them. In this way, it was supposed that students would find their education useful and not be bothered with irrelevant subject matter, for example, the classical studies that would continue to be offered to more elite students. Racial betterment was an expression that implied building students' character, but primarily revealed educators' beliefs about the superiority of White and (usually) Anglo-Saxon heritage. Joel Spring's (1997) book, *The American School 1642–1996,* offers an outstanding discussion of this thinking and its historical context.

11. The metaphors of social vision and change correspond to a dynamic educational milieu in which educators and philosophers imagined the schools and teachers leading a new generation to a more equitable and democratic American society. A classic description of these ideas can be found in Merle Curti's (1935/1971) *The Social Ideas of American Educators.*

REFERENCES

Almack, J. C., & Lang, A. R. (1925). *Problems of the teaching profession.* Boston: Houghton Mifflin.

Avent, J. E. (1931). *The excellent teacher.* Knoxville, TN: Author.

Averill, L. A. (1939). *Mental hygiene for the classroom teacher.* New York: Pitman.

Bagley, W. C., & Keith, J. A. H. (1932). *An introduction to teaching.* New York: Macmillan.

Beale, H. K. (1936). *Are American teachers free? An analysis of restraints upon the freedom of teaching in American schools.* New York: Scribner's.

Callahan, R. E. (1962). *Education and the cult of efficiency: A study of the social forces that have shaped the administration of the public schools.* Chicago: University of Chicago Press.

Carpenter, W. W., & Rufi, J. (1931). *The teacher and secondary-school administration from the point of view of the classroom teacher.* Boston: Ginn.

Charters, W. W., & Waples, D. (1929). *The Commonwealth teacher-training study.* Chicago: University of Chicago Press.

Colgrove, C. P. (1911). *The teacher and the school.* New York: Scribner's.

Counts, G. (1932). *Dare the school build a new social order?* New York: John Day.

Curti, M. (1935/1971). *The social ideas of American educators.* Totowa, NJ: Littlefield, Adams.

Davis, S. E. (1930). *The teacher's relationships.* New York: Macmillan.

Dearborn, N. H. (1925). *An introduction to teaching.* New York: Appleton.

Donovan, F. R. (1938). *The schoolma'am.* New York: Frederick A. Stokes.

Duke, C. W. (1923). *Getting ahead as a teacher.* Harrisburg, PA: Handy Book.

Elsbree, W. S. (1939). *The American teacher: Evolution of a profession in a democracy.* New York: American Book.

Freeland, G. E. (1925). *The improvement of teaching.* New York: Macmillan.

Gist, A. S. (1932). *Clarifying the teacher's problems.* New York: Scribner's.

Grant, E. B. (1927). Principles and characteristics of good teaching. In M. B. Hillegas & T. H. Briggs (Eds.), *The classroom teacher* (pp. 243–296). Chicago: The Classroom Teacher.

Grant, J. R. (1922). *Acquiring skill in teaching.* New York: Silver, Burdett.

Hines, H. C. (1926). *Finding the right teaching position.* New York: Scribner's.

Holley, C. E. (1922). *The teacher's technique.* New York: Century.

Jordan, R. H. (1930). *Education as a life work: An introduction into education.* New York: Century.

Knudsen, C. W., & McAfee, L. O. (1936). *An introduction to teaching.* Garden City, NY: Doubleday.

Lee, E. A. (1938). *Teaching as a man's job.* Homewood, IL: Phi Delta Kappa.

Lewis, E. E. (1926). *Personnel problems of the teaching staff.* New York: Century.

Marsh, J. F. (1928). *The teacher outside the school.* Yonkers, NY: World Book.

McFee, I. N. (1918). *The teacher, the school, and the community.* New York: American Book.

Melby, E. O. (1937). The teacher and the school system. In W. H. Kilpatrick (Ed.), *The teacher and society* (pp. 119–142). New York: Appleton-Century.

Milner, F. (1912). *The teacher.* Chicago: Scott, Foresman.

Overn, A. V. (1935). *The teacher in modern education: A guide to professional problems and administrative responsibilities.* New York: Appleton-Century.

Palmer, G. H. (1908/1910). *The ideal teacher.* Boston: Houghton Mifflin.

Palmer, G. H. (1914). *Trades and professions.* Boston: Houghton Mifflin.

Perry, A. C., Jr. (1912). *The status of the teacher.* Boston: Houghton Mifflin.

Pulliam, R. (1930). *Extra-instructional activities of the teacher.* Garden City, NY: Doubleday.

Sandford, C. M. (1938). *Developing teacher personality that wins.* Evanston, IL: Row & Peterson.

Simon, H. W. (1938). *Preface to teaching.* New York: Oxford University Press.

Snyder, A., & Alexander, T. (1932). Teaching as a profession: Guidance suggestions for students. *Teachers College Bulletin, 23*(3), 1–69.

Spring, J. (1997). *The American school 1642–1996* (4th ed.). New York: McGraw-Hill.

Strayer, G. D., & Engelhard, N. L. (1920). *The classroom teacher.* New York: American Book.

Valentine, P. F. (1931). *The art of the teacher: An essay in humanism.* New York: Appleton.

Van Nice, C. R. (1929). *Tact and the teacher.* Lawrence, KS: Plainview Publications.

Waller, W. (1932). *The sociology of teaching.* New York: Wiley.

Walsh, M. J. (1926). *Teaching as a profession: Its ethical standards.* New York: Holt.

Watson, G. (1937). The economic status of the teacher. In W. H. Kilpatrick (Ed.), *The teacher and society* (pp. 143–173). New York: Appleton-Century.

Weber, S. E. (1937). *Cooperative administration and supervision of the teaching personnel.* New York: Thomas Nelson & Son.

Winship, A. E. (1919). *Danger signals for teacher.* Chicago: Forbes.

Wright, H. P. (1920). *The young man and teaching.* New York: Macmillan.

Zirbes, L., & Taba, H. (1937). The teacher at work. In W. H. Kilpatrick (Ed.), *The teacher and society* (pp. 93–118). New York: Appleton-Century.

8

The Sentimental Image
of the Rural Teacher

Mary Phillips Manke

A deep and sentimental nostalgia for certain images of our national past is a recurring theme in American popular culture. Remembered or imagined settings are forever desired, forever recalled—yet hidden beneath a coat of sugary icing, concealing their reality.[1] It is easy to call up some of these images: the warm kitchen of a prosperous farmhouse, filled with loving care and the rich aroma of apple pie; the summer days of a traditional country boyhood, quintessentially carefree and rebellious; the whole-hearted patriotism of a small-town Fourth of July, glowing with pride and community solidarity; a legislature or constitutional convention of the early republic, where wise and thoughtful representatives sat solemnly to weigh the needs of their neighbors and make rational decisions for the good of all. Another such recollected setting is the one-room country school, home to happy, well-behaved children and ideal teacher.

Before going on to discuss our nostalgic memory of these schools more fully, it is important to recognize how the coating of sentiment that lies over these images not only obscures the negative aspects of their reality, but also makes it difficult for us to see what about them was real and desirable, and thus might be revived or revisited to enhance our modern lives. For example, the life of the rural farmhouse was based on a level of physical work by both men and women that few would choose to undertake today and was frequently pervaded by the sadness caused by the early deaths of adults and children. Yet unity and continuity of family was often maintained in that setting through those formidable obstacles. The boys we remember playing through the summer often worked harder than most adults do now and grew up with little education or knowledge of the world outside their neighborhoods.

Still, they probably did claim freedom from adult restraints during some part of their childhood, an opportunity that the fears and pressures of the modern world deny to most children today.

Those happy July Fourths were founded on an unquestioned faith in our national rightness—a luxury we cannot afford in these times. The unified communities that celebrated those holidays were likely to exclude from their membership those who were perceived to be "different" in religion, ethnicity, or values. Yet those communities did know how to celebrate their shared values and how to build bonds of care and concern among neighbors. Similarly, the remembered legislators were far from representative of those for whom they made decisions, were often narrow and exclusive in their views; they did, however, embody a belief in the obligation of service to the community that is far from pervasive among well-educated and successful members of today's society.[2]

As these images appear, bathed in a golden aura of nostalgia and sentiment, we too often fail to discern in them what was not good in our national past, what we want to leave behind us. Equally, because our cynical modern intelligences warn us that nothing lighted by that golden glow can be real, we are unable to find in these images of the past the benefits they might have for our present and future. This is particularly true of our image of the country school.

The popular American view of the history of schools has been characterized by nostalgia for the teachers, the classrooms, the students, and the curricula of the imagined rural past. The continuing popularity of images created by Norman Rockwell and of reprints of the *McGuffey Readers* indicates this nostalgia.[3] In a remembered "golden age" of American education, many believe, learning and teaching were successful enterprises conducted in country and small-town schools by dedicated, competent, and morally superior teachers who maintained discipline and passed on important knowledge to well-behaved and willing students. These beliefs have led to a persistent demand for a return to the education of the past. If the past was perfect, how could we not want to return to it?

Sources and Overview

This study began as an attempt to reconcile conflicting images of the early 20th-century rural school. Popular culture made me aware of a nostalgia for the schools of the past, for versions of the rural school presented by Norman Rockwell and the *McGuffey Reader.* In contrast, however, I had read early 20th-century fiction that seemed to counter these romantic images and, moreover, I knew that educational historians often presented a view of these schools that seemed substantially negative.[4]

In an effort to gain better understanding of the nostalgic images, I began to read the then-contemporary novels about schools and teachers as well as some memoirs written by teachers from the period.[5] Relying on the realistic nature of such fiction and memoir, I made notes of each incident that had to do with schooling and began to see particular themes emerging from my reading. Later, looking for confirmation of the images I had found in fiction and memoir, I sought out texts intended to prepare teachers for service in rural schools and searched for material in those texts on the themes I had found in literature.[6]

These varied sources led me to two general conclusions. First, the image of rural teachers and rural schools presented in them is far more diverse than the common nostalgic and sentimental vision of rural schools. Most of the same problems troubling schools today were part of daily life in the rural schools of the past. Not only do many of the novels and reminiscences include passages revealing what was difficult and daunting about the teacher's life in the rural school, but the advice given in the texts, while phrased very positively, is evidently aimed at helping the teacher surmount these difficulties.

Second, it is remarkable the extent to which many of these writers, whether novelists, teachers, or textbook writers (usually instructors at normal schools), held as a positive value what the more modern thinker or scholar would call sentimentality. Not only is the rural teacher often sentimentalized—that is, painted with a rather sickly wash of one-sided praise and positive thinking—but the textbooks actually recommend the reading of such schoolroom novels as a way to improve the teacher's mind and show her what she should try to achieve. All of the three kinds of sources, most likely, have shaped our memory of the rural school. We thus see it through a lens of sentimentality. The golden glow veils the less attractive features that call into question our romanticized notions.

The Image of the Rural Teacher

I will consider four aspects of the image of the rural teacher: (a) her character, (b) her concerns about discipline, order, and student behavior, (c) the curriculum and teaching methods she used, and (d) her preparation to teach. These are only discussed separately for the sake of convenience. Clearly, the teacher's nature and her educational beliefs were linked tightly to issues of her own classroom management, subject matter, and instructional methods, especially when the teacher herself was likely to have received most of her education in a school much like the one where she ultimately taught.

The Character of the Teacher

The very use of the word "character" to describe what we might now call personality has its own set of connotations. Personality may simply refer to a set of individual qualities, innate or acquired through one's life experiences. Character is something to be created, worked on, developed, judged. It is good or bad, strong or weak, not simply (and less judgmentally) introverted or extroverted, friendly or quiet, as personality might be. The lengthy descriptions of the teacher's character found in the texts they were to use suggest that building a strong character for themselves was a vital task for which teachers were responsible.

Lowth (1936), who had been the principal of the rural teacher training school at Janesville, Wisconsin, suggested that teachers score themselves on various aspects of their character (e.g., a list of 25 personal attributes). Consequently, a teacher might give herself 100 on honesty (the highest grade), but only 60 on initiative. She might be worth 95 in sympathy, but only 65 in accuracy (Lowth, 1936, p. 43). After this self-appraisal, a teacher should work to improve her score.

Slacks (1938), who was a professor of rural education at Iowa State Teachers College, gave a list of qualities necessary for the rural teacher that are representative of those provided in nearly all the texts here encountered. He called for the teacher to be healthy (with health considered to be the result of good personal hygiene), be enthusiastic, be alert, be consistent, be self-controlled, be fair, be good-natured, have a well-modulated voice, possess a sense of humor, be hardworking, be orderly, be honest and sincere, be energetic, and have sympathy and patience.

Some of the most telling statements about the desired character of the rural teacher are found in the texts intended for their use. For example, Kirkpatrick (1917) declared,

> The teacher who has drunk deeply from sorrow's cup, and is rich in experience that has left him not hardened and embittered against the world, but softened and sweetened with a charity that looks for goodness in all men and all women has a preparation for a life work that has for its accomplishment the building of a citizenship based upon the love of man for man. (p. 135)

Woofter (1917) insisted upon teachers' dedication: "Teaching is a great profession. Human life is the greatest thing in the world, and he [sic] who is called to the training and development of human life has the greatest calling in the world. Only those who can so appreciate the greatness of teaching should enter the profession" (p. 25).[7]

Teacher educators demanded that teachers have lofty characteristics and aspirations. Furthermore, their textbooks recommended that teachers could find role models in sentimental novels, with protagonists possessing all the desired traits worthy of emulation.[8] Teachers were told to read novels about rural teachers, not to glean suggestions for teaching from the descriptions of schooling that they contain, but rather, to see portrayals of exemplary personality and character.

For instance, Lowth (1936, pp. 52-53), in *Everyday Problems of the Country Teacher,* explained that one such novel "exemplifies the everlasting truth that the teacher's personality is by far the largest factor in the work of the school," while another "sets forth some of those great and inevitable truths of our human relationships which all teachers need to know. The young instructor made good. Discover how he won out." In fact, Owen Wister's (1917) *The Virginian,* appearing on virtually every recommended list in teacher education texts for rural teachers, has as its heroine a lovely young teacher whose teaching is never described at all. Moreover, the teaching position only acts as a hindrance to the development of her romance with the Virginia-born cowhand of the title. Reading this novel was advocated strictly as a guide to character development, particularly of that "womanly sweetness" and steadfastness of purpose that characterized the heroine.

The teachers described in the novels based on reminiscences and in memoirs, by contrast, were painted as quite ordinary persons, with characters no more or less "developed" than those of other people. Laura Ingalls Wilder (1943/1971), in her self-portrait in *These Happy Golden Years,* is no paragon, but a young and inexperienced woman trying to survive her first teaching job from day to day. Though *Glengarry School Days* (Conner, 1902) includes the portrait of one teacher who was well educated and of admirable character, of the other two masters described, one is friendly and pleasant, but not remarkable, while the other is weak and cruel, even sadistic.

Mary Ellen Chase (1939), in her memoir *A Goodly Fellowship,* tells us that she approached her first teaching job, as a young woman of 18 or 19, so frightened that if possible she would "then and there have run for cover, leaving the Buck's Harbor School to whatever fate awaited it" (p. 37). She referred to the "mental and physical agility [rather] than mere knowledge" that the school required of her (p. 39). The difficulty of accomplishing the prescribed program for all the classes in the available time, together with her own "weakness" in arithmetic, left her little time to think about her character, though she noted an improvement in her ability to be well organized and to keep her mind on what she was doing.

Reminiscences do not appear to corroborate the images in texts for rural teachers. For example, the rural teachers interviewed by Christensen (1986) told about many aspects of their life and work in the schools, but nowhere did they speak of their character or its development as important to their work. They liked teaching or they did not, they loved children or they did not, they found the conditions difficult or they did not, but if they rated themselves on a scale of 1 to 100 and tried to improve their characters, they do not remember doing so as important to their teaching.

Discipline, Order, and Student Behavior

A second aspect of the image of the teacher relates to the issues of discipline or student behavior. The nostalgic popular image of rural teachers includes a sanguine representation of students who—unlike today's children—are well behaved and eager to learn. Perhaps some of the boys were a bit rambunctious at times, but serious difficulties with discipline were not part of the picture. However, the reminiscences in this study unsentimentally portray teachers as having to focus on maintaining discipline. Far from presiding, gently but firmly, over quiet and well-behaved students whose cooperation could be taken for granted, they are often shown as using harsh methods to control their classes.

In a vivid example from Wilder's (1933/1971) *Farmer Boy,* an incident from the childhood of Wilder's husband, Almanzo Wilder, is described. Almanzo was only 6 or 8 years old when a kind and weak-looking master taught the local school. All went well until the winter term, when there was little farm work to do and the oldest boys came to school for the first time. "These big boys were 16 or 17 years old and came to school only in the middle of the winter term. They came to thrash the teacher and break up the school; they boasted that no teacher could finish the winter term at that school, and no teacher ever had" (p. 46). The last master to teach at the school had, in fact, been hurt so badly by the boys that he had later died. Little Almanzo was very much afraid of what would happen to the gentle schoolmaster in the inevitable conflict. He was surprised—as the big boys were—to learn that the master kept a blacksnake whip in his desk drawer and was ready to use it to drive his attackers out of the school.

Dangerous students and teachers' use of brutal methods to defend themselves were not unique circumstances. Connor (1902) described the Glengarry School under three masters. The first, Archibald Munro, was respected by all, and was "the only master who had ever been able to control, without at least one appeal to the trustees, the stormy tempers of the young giants that used to come to school during the winter months" (p. 14). Munro was replaced by a new master who favored inflexible enforcement of numerous rules. He whipped so many of the smaller boys that the older boys left the school, considering it beneath their dignity to "carry [the master] out" (p. 118). A confrontation finally occurred when a little boy refused to put out his hand to be beaten and the master believed his "whole authority" was at stake. "I cannot have boys refusing to obey me in this school,'" he insisted, and treated the boy so brutally that the oldest of the remaining boys attacked him, knocked him to the floor, and were prepared to tie him up when they were interrupted by an adult (p. 118).

Mary Ellen Chase (1939), later a novelist and an English professor at Smith College, was required by her father to teach school for a year following her first year of college. He left her on the steps of the schoolhouse where she was to teach with "no aid but a stout razor strap" (p. 36). She was afraid, so afraid that she raged at "certain boys of 16 or older who otherwise might have been at sea," flourished the strap, and had no more difficulty that term. Later she described a school in Montana and spoke admiringly of the principal, "She could use a wide leather strap across the knees of unruly boys, who sat calmly in the chair without the least outcry" (p. 186).

In other cases, gentler methods of gaining the cooperation of students came into play. When Laura Ingalls Wilder (1943/1971) went at the age of 16 to teach at her own school, she had trouble controlling the oldest boy and thought longingly of giving him the whipping he needed. She was too small to do it, however, and had to find other ways to deal with him. When she asked her parents for advice, her father said, "Everybody's born free, like it says in the *Declaration of Independence.* You can lead a horse to water but you can't make him drink, and good or bad, nobody but Clarence can ever boss Clarence. You better just manage." Her mother advised her, "It's attention he wants, that's why he cuts up .... It's all in that word 'manage'" (p. 54). So Laura shortened Clarence's assignments, commiserated with him on how hard it is to catch up once you are behind, and ignored his challenges. Soon he did the work and improved his behavior.

However, Wilder also recounted less successful stories. In *Little Town on the Prairie,* Laura recounts a childhood memory of when a young schoolteacher arrived in the school saying, "You must not look on me as a taskmistress, but a friend" (Wilder, 1941/1971, p. 132). The young woman believed that there was no need to punish and that she and the students could work together through love, not fear. But the students grew increasingly unruly, and in anger she began to make students stand in the corner and sent some home from school. Only a visit by members of the school board enabled her to regain control. Wilder (1943/1971) also described her own apprehension about being nice to students when she herself was the teacher; she feared she would incur the wrath of her school superintendent if she allowed her students to warm themselves at the stove in her cold prairie school (p. 80).

The textbooks contained many references to discipline and suggestions for controlling students' behavior. Lowth (1936) took a different view of the role of discipline in the rural school. "There is something radically wrong with the teacher's spirit, aims, and plans, if she needs to give much attention to order. In an orderly school the children are busy of their own volition" (pp. 187–188). He then characterized "disorderly teachers" as those who are "loud-talking" and "irascible," and attributed disorder among pupils to lack of "proper treatment and training." He held that it is "rare indeed to find a pupil who persists in disorderly practices simply out of a spirit of meanness," suggested that most problems with pupils can be solved by giving them appropriate assignments, and described deprivation of privileges and "a private interview" as "drastic treatment" that will rarely be needed (p. 189).

Nonetheless, Lowth contradictorily contended that issues of punishment and discipline would be important for the teacher. He described the circumstances in which the teacher may be forced to punish a student, but ruled out as inappropriate such disciplinary tactics as threatening and nagging, sarcasm and ridicule, humiliation, and physical punishment. Thus the sentimental view of the firm and friendly teacher working with cooperative pupils was placed next to—but not reconciled with—the image of a teacher dealing with students who were found "lying, cheating, [using] profane language on the playground, marring furniture and outbuildings, [or giving] impertinent responses" (p. 193).

Woofter (1917), dean of the School of Education at the University of Georgia, began his chapter on discipline with the statement: "Discipline is the feature of the school which first puts the young teacher on trial" (p. 105). He proceeded to define the purpose of discipline as the production of "the harmony of life." Yet the chapter provides a wide range of suggestions to assist the teacher in controlling the behavior of students, including, in its final pages, the statement that "corporal punishment should not be entirely forbidden" (p. 131). Though it is to be used as a next-to-last resort, expulsion being the only harsher penalty, some "offenders" will require it, at least up to the age of puberty.

What were the rules that teachers were enforcing with these methods of discipline? Some examples include: "No whispering permitted in school, and no fidgeting. Everyone must be perfectly still and keep his eyes fixed on his lessons" (Wilder, 1933/1971, p. 8). And "no speaking in school unless you raise your hand for permission to speak; written excuses must be presented for absence or tardiness; no sound should be heard in the school" (Connor, 1902, p. 83).

Silence, immobility, and order were presented in these sources as essential to schooling, even though teachers might have to use strong disciplinary methods to achieve them. Woofter (1917) wrote that school government formerly was repressive. For example, If a pupil was caught drawing pictures, he might expect to have his ears boxed. "Absolutely still" was the order (p. 112). He rejoiced in the more enlightened attitudes of 1917, but nevertheless delineated a formidable list of rules for good behavior that should become children's habits. The students were to be prompt and regular in their attendance—"no lagging nor straggling"—and to be working busily at all times. They were to produce only neat and orderly work and to keep silent—to avoid "whispering and other unnecessary communication." There should be proper times for interruptions, and pupils should be trained to wait for those times (pp. 111–114). Later, he mentioned such offenses as "whispering, note-writing, leaving the room too often, and noisy walking" as reasons for punishment (p. 126).

Learning, like behavior, was considered a matter of discipline, and students who had not mastered their lessons were described as subject to whipping, shaming, and other penalties. Almanzo Wilder was very fond of the gentle master with the blacksnake whip in his desk because he "never whipped little boys who forgot how to spell a word" (Wilder, 1933/1971, p. 5). By implication, other masters did. Laura Ingalls Wilder's (1943/1971) difficulties with a recalcitrant pupil were not based on active misbehavior, but involved his failure to learn the lessons she assigned him. As mentioned previously, she would have whipped him if she had been big enough. In these books, failure to learn was caused by laziness or idleness—both defects of character.

The image of the firm teacher, presiding over well-behaved and cooperative children, is not supported by these sources. Teachers varied in their approach to discipline and found in their schools both children whose behavior enabled the orderly running of the school and those whose behavior made order difficult to maintain. Neither the disciplinary techniques they used nor the influence of their characters produced the well-disciplined and effective classrooms that the sentimental or nostalgic image of the rural teacher would imply.

Instructional Methods and Curriculum

The teachers' views of learning and discipline were, of course, tightly connected to the instructional methods they used, and those to the curriculum that was taught. An important determinant of these methods was the structure of their schools. Since most of those described in these sources were one-room schools, and since children of the same age might have attended school for quite different numbers of years, and perhaps mastered quite different skills or amounts of knowledge, it was customary to place the children at an appropriate point in the graded curriculum and allow them to proceed from there.

When Mary Ellen Chase (1939) taught at her first school in Maine, she was responsible for 49 children, ranging in age from 5 to 16, as well as up to six "babies" between the ages of 2 and 4, who enjoyed watching the school's "furious educational progress" (p. 44). These she sorted into a total of 29 groups for arithmetic, reading, geography, history, and spelling. Grammar was taught to the whole school. She learned to hear one group reading while another group was doing arithmetic at the chalkboard and the rest of the students were studying in their seats. Her day consisted of hearing all the arithmetic and reading groups by mid-morning, then hearing four geography groups before lunch, and teaching grammar after lunch. Afterward, she heard four history classes and she finished the day with spelling. Chase commented that there was no time for music or art—which one easily can believe (p. 40).

At the school attended by Wiggin's (1903) Rebecca, "There were classes of a sort, although nobody, broadly speaking, studied the same book with anybody else, or arrived at the same proficiency in any one branch of learning" (p. 45). Rebecca was placed in the sixth reader, but was "threttened [sic]" with being put in the baby primer class in arithmetic because she could not say the sevens table (p. 39).

In these circumstances, rote and drill were the basic methods used by teachers. The pupil sat at her desk and read her lesson, either silently or aloud, through a buzz of other voices reading their own lessons aloud. Or she might use a slate to write out a lesson in spelling or arithmetic. When she was called up for the teacher to "hear" her lesson, she was expected to recite it verbatim, or to solve correctly the problems given in the arithmetic lesson. The established goal was to do these things perfectly and then to do them again for another lesson.

The consequence of these methods was that content that could not be memorized was not taught or learned. It was the teacher's task to set the lessons to be memorized and then to hear them to determine whether they had been learned. Geography was the locating of features and the "bounding" of states and countries, not the understanding of the world's cultures and economies. History was the memorization of events and biographies, not the exploration of historical processes. Reading was the correct oral reading of passages; comprehension was assumed to follow. Arithmetic was the successive mastery of more difficult kinds of problems by working examples and memorizing algorithms.

Teachers' efforts at enlivening the learning process are described in these sources. However, although there seemed to be a need to add enjoyment or relieve boredom, there is little indication of a felt need to expand the scope of the curriculum. Both *Glengarry School Days* (Conner, 1902) and *Little Town on the Prairie* (Wilder, 1941/1971) contain colorful accounts of spelling bees that produced great excitement. In the latter book, some of the adults in the community joined in the competition. Competitive problem solving in arithmetic is also mentioned in Barber's (1938) memoir. Two of the teachers described held an annual public examination of the school, with prizes for the best performers (Connor, 1902; Wiggin, 1903).

Some of the teachers allotted time to activities they and their students considered more pleasurable than routine studies. These often took place on Friday afternoons and were seen as a reward for hard work and good behavior. A teacher might play the violin (Connor, 1902, p. 261) or tell stories of shipwreck and pirates (Chase, 1939, p. 19). Such diversions clearly were not part of the ordinary work of the school.

Qualifications of Teachers

A final, though somewhat equivocal, aspect of our image of teachers of the past is that they were quite competent, passing down significant knowledge to students. We would like to think of them as well-educated professionals, leading their charges perhaps more effectively than teachers of today. Yet the teachers described in these sources are young and have had little advanced education.

"Anyhow, she knows how to teach. She has a certificate" (Wilder, 1941/1971, p. 125). This was the comment of an older child about a new teacher. The certificate, however, had been obtained by passing a test on the content of the graded school curriculum, which in many cases the new teacher had just completed herself. No added knowledge, either in the content areas or in pedagogy, was required. When Laura Ingalls Wilder was finishing school, she went to town on Saturday and took a test for certification. Her score would be the only determinant of her qualifications (Wilder, 1943/1971, p. 148). By this time, however, she had already taught a term in a country school. She felt perfectly qualified to do this, as she had always been a good student and had progressed further than any of the children (some of whom were older than she was) she was asked to teach.

In Stratton-Porter's (1918) *A Daughter of the Land,* two sisters persuaded their brother to teach at a school where neither of them wanted to work. The girls each had completed a summer at normal school, where they reviewed the content of their years of schooling, but the brother had received no training at all. Nevertheless, the county superintendent gave him a certificate to teach for 1 year (p. 98), only on the basis of passing a county examination required of pupils ages 10 and older when they finished the county schools. Mary Ellen Chase (1939) was also unprepared when she went to teach in a village school in Maine. It was her father's view that a girl should teach school for a year or two before entering college or after her first or second year of college. Chase had always been a poor student in mathematics and did not herself know all the things that she had to teach. Her first year of teaching found her "weeping at night over bank discount and compound proportion" (1939, p. 43).

It was during the period described in these novels that teacher training began to be available and increasingly required, and that its length gradually was increased. For example, not until 1934 were 2 years of training required in Wisconsin (Christensen, 1986). Before that time, however, at least some brief periods of training began to be required for the better teaching jobs. For example, in Stratton-Porter's Indiana at the turn of the century, a girl who wished to teach in a desirable school for the next school year had to spend 8 weeks of the summer at the normal school in the city (Stratton-Porter, 1918, p. 25).

There is a some evidence that novices who trained in these normal schools received some theories about learning and teaching. For instance, in the novel *A Daughter of the*

Land (Stratton-Porter, 1918), one of the sisters said that she learned some theory during the 8-week summer session of normal school that she had just attended. However, a more likely training ground for new teachers was their own schooling experiences. Thirty years after she began her teaching career, Mary Ellen Chase recommended that a young teacher's best plan was to emulate her own instructors. Her common sense, initiative, and enthusiasm would then help her in solving any problems that might arise (Chase, 1939, p. 59). Laura Ingalls Wilder (1943/1971) also relied on her knowledge of being a student. When she opened her first school, she "thought it best to maintain the routine of the town school and have each person come forward to recite." She solemnly intoned, "Third Reading Group, come forward" (p. 18), and watched one little girl make her way to the front of the room.

A fitting summary of the state of teacher qualifications was offered by Mabel Carney (1912), who was director of the Country School Department at Illinois State Normal University: "It is true, as frequently maintained, that country teachers are young and inexperienced and poorly prepared for their work. But it is also true that as a group they are filled with a great sincerity" (p. 195).

Discussion

As I revised this chapter at the beginning of the 21st century, the issue of returning power over schools from the educational experts and bureaucrats of the "one best system" to parents and communities was undergoing active debate. In the face of standardization movements on the state and national levels, there are many recent efforts to involve parents and community members in the governance of schools, as well as calls for voucher systems, charter schools, and individual parent choice of schools inside and outside the public sector. M. W. Kirst (1995) suggested that local control of schools continues to be seen as positive and in the tradition of American individualism. Though school reformers often have wanted to remove the operation of schools from local control, citizens, especially in rural areas, have resisted this change and longed for the locally controlled schools of the past. This desire informs current resistance to national and state standards.

Both sides of the debate warrant examination. While it is crucial to investigate the notion of standardization as a panacea for schools, it is also important to take a careful look—not a romantic but a realistic, critical one—at what the small community schools and teachers of the past were really like.

The representations of teachers in the sources I read are far from the nostalgic images of rural teachers in one-room schoolhouses. Rather than being competent, dedicated, and morally superior people who maintained discipline and passed on important knowledge to well-behaved and eager students, teachers appear to have been poorly prepared in both academic and pedagogical training. They struggled with disobedient students for the control of the school, used strictly rote methods, and taught a limited and fact-bound curriculum. The historical reality of the rural school and the rural teacher was summarized by Mary Ellen Chase (1939):

[The schools] were hewn out of respectability and governed by necessity. No one thought of them as either good or bad, and without doubt they possessed qualities of both .... The rural school has gone never to return, at least in its original state. It has become an outworn institution, to be regarded by those who knew it more with sentiment than respect. (pp. 5, 52)

Moreover, the sentimental image of the schoolteacher's character found in textbooks written for teachers is revealed as a product of the romanticism that shaped the views of professors of education and some earlier novelists, but certainly not the teachers' viewpoints. Those rural schoolteachers worked hard under difficult conditions; they never thought of themselves as paragons of virtue.

The nostalgic image of community involvement and control also warrants a more realistic interpretation. Tyack (1974), in his discussion of rural schools, observed that this tight connection between school and community had both advantages and disadvantages. In a cohesive community, the school reaped the benefits of cohesiveness. Teachers, parents, and community members could work well together for what they all perceived as the welfare of the children and of the community as a whole. However, if the community was at odds within itself, all would suffer, as the school became a battleground on which community dissension was played out.

Why, then, does this nostalgic view of the rural educational past persist? If there are two perspectives on history, one that sees its course as a progress toward a future golden age and one that traces its decline from a golden age of the past, the first has been central to American ideology. Always Americans have claimed to be moving from less to more, from worse to better, fulfilling our country's manifest destiny. As de Tocqueville pointed out in 1840, Americans believe that in our nation human perfectibility is being enacted. However, this ideology leads to frequent frustration. What is one to believe when the looked-for perfection does not appear, when somehow the golden age does not arrive?

Perhaps it is in these moments of frustration and fear that we seek the golden age in our past, hiding in a cloud of sentiment the indications that it never existed at all. As we are more and more often bombarded with criticisms of our schools, teachers, and students, we may feel more and more strongly the need to believe that once, if only in the past, our schools approached the ideal we set for them. If that ideal was once achieved, perhaps it can be regained. If it never has been, then what we ask of schools and teachers may be forever out of reach.

The task of searching the history of rural schools for what was good about them is beyond the scope of this chapter. Yet elements of the portraits of schools presented in these texts call for our consideration. The rural schools they describe were, as Mary Ellen Chase (1939) pointed out, very much part of the communities they served. The community and the parents were responsible to the school, and the school and teacher to them. The schools reflected what parents and teachers believed was right, rather than the views of educational experts, corporate leaders, or national politicians.

The rural school system with its community control recalls the liberty held to be part of the American heritage. If this study reveals that community autonomy produced an inferior educational system, then it is to some advantage that we have remembered what was "beautiful and good" about the rural school and forgotten what was problematic.

NOTES

1. Marion Kirkpatrick (1917), author of *The Rural School From Within,* describes President William McKinley (1896–1901) traveling by train through rural America. He noticed two boys herding cows and warming their feet where the cows had lain. He pointed out the scene to his cabinet members, and they agreed that the days of their rural youth had been their happiest. They gave three cheers in memory of the joys of rural life.
2. These ideas are discussed at length in Bellah et al. (1985). *Habits of the Heart: Individualism and Commitment in American Life.*
3. Peter Schrag (1965), in *Voices in the Classroom,* wrote of how "proudly" Iowa citizens maintained their small schools for the education of just a few students. He described their "fear of remote control, suspicion of new courses and teachers, and anxiety about excessive exposure to the modern world" (p. 38).
4. A different notion is expressed by Larry Cuban (1984) in *How Teachers Taught: Constancy and Change in American Classrooms 1890–1980.* He notes that some rural schoolteachers used innovative child-centered activities more often than their urban counterparts.
5. Limiting myself to works published in the 20th century, I read the following: *Rebecca of Sunnybrook Farm* (1903) by Kate Douglas Wiggin (now thought of as a "children's classic," but was originally written for a general audience); *A Daughter of the Land* (1918) by Gene Stratton-Porter (a novel seldom read in contemporary times); *Glenngarry School Days* (1902) by Ralph Connor (another novel now little read); *Farmer Boy* (1933/1971), *Little Town on the Prairie* (1941/1971), and *These Happy Golden Years* (1943/1971) by Laura Ingalls Wilder (each contains considerable material on rural schools; these "Little House" books have enjoyed continuing popularity as children's books since they were published in the 1930s and 1940s); *A Goodly Fellowship* (1939) by Mary Ellen Chase; *The Schoolhouse at Prairie View* (1938) by Marshall A. Barber (a full-length memoir); *The Rural School from Within* (1917), by Marion G Kirkpatrick (another full-length memoir); *The Schoolma'am* (1938) by F. R. Donovan (a reminiscence and book about schoolteaching); *Cloverdale: A Salute to One-Room Schoolteachers* by H. B. Christensen (1986; a collection of briefer reminiscences).
6. The textbooks I read were written in the early 1900s. Their dual purposes were to serve as texts for the short courses offered at normal schools for the preparation of rural teachers and to be ready references on educational questions for those same teachers when they had returned to the isolated work of their rural schools. Of these I read: *Country Life and the Country School* (1912) by M. Carney; *Rural Life and the Rural School* (1915) by J. Kennedy; *The Rural Teacher and His Work* (1917) by H. W. Foght; *Teaching in Rural Schools* (1917) by T. J. Woofter; *Everyday Problems of the Country Teacher* (1936) by F. J. Lowth; *The Rural Teacher's Work* (1938) by J. R. Slack.
7. It is interesting to note the use of masculine pronouns to refer to members of a profession predominantly female, then and now.

8. Many of these novels are no longer to be found in libraries. Some of those included in several lists are: Elizabeth Enslow, *The Schoolhouse in the Foothills*; Bess Streeter Aldrich, *A Lantern in Her Hand*; Owne Wister, *The Virginian*; Dan Stephens, *Phelps and His Teachers*; Edward Eggleston, *The Hoosier Schoolmaster*; W. H. Smith, *The Evolution of Dodd*; and Angelina Wray, *Jean Mitchell's School,* as well as Kate Douglas Wiggin, *Rebecca of Sunnybrook Farm* and Ralph Connor, *Glengarry School Days* (from the list of novels used to illustrate this study).

REFERENCES

Barber, M. A. (1938). *The schoolhouse at Prairie View.* Lawrence: University of Kansas Press.

Bellah, R. N., Madsen, R., Sullivan, W. M., Swidler, A., & Tipton, S. M. (1985). *Habits of the heart: Indivualism and commitment in American life.* New York: Harper & Row.

Carney, M. (1912). *Country life and the country school.* Chicago: Row & Peterson.

Chase, M. E. (1939). *A goodly fellowship.* New York: Macmillan.

Christensen, H. B. (1986). *Cloverdale: A salute to one-room schoolteachers.* Winona, MN: Apollo Books.

Connor, R. (1902). *Glengarry school days.* New York: Fleming A. Revell.

Cuban, L. (1984). *How teachers taught: Constancy and change in American classrooms 1890–1980.* New York: Longman.

de Tocqueville, A. (1956). *Democracy in America* (R. D. Heffner, Ed.). New York: New American Library. (Original work published 1835–1840)

Donovan, F. R. (1938). *The schoolma'am.* New York: Frederick A. Stokes.

Foght, H. W. (1917). *The rural teacher and his work.* New York: Macmillan.

Kennedy, J. (1915). *Rural life and the rural school.* New York: American Book.

Kirkpatrick, M. G. (1917). *The rural school from within.* Philadelphia: Lippincott.

Kirst, M. W. (1995). Who's in charge? Federal, state and local control. In D. Ravitch & M. Vinovskis (Eds.), *Learning from the past: What history teaches us about school reform* (pp. 25–26). Baltimore: Johns Hopkins University Press.

Lowth, F. J. (1936). *Everyday problems of the country teacher.* New York: Macmillan.

Schrag, P. (1965). *Voices in the classroom.* Boston: Beacon Press.

Slacks, J. R. (1938). *The rural teacher's work.* Boston: Ginn.

Stratton-Porter, G. (1918). *Daughter of the land.* New York: Grosset & Dunlap.

Tyack, D. (1974). *The one best system: A history of American urban education.* Cambridge, MA: Harvard University Press.

Wiggin, K. D. (1903). *Rebecca of Sunnybrook Farm.* New York: Houghton Mifflin.

Wilder, L. I. (1971). *Farmer boy.* New York: Harper & Row. (Original work published 1933)

Wilder, L. I. (1971). *Little town on the prairie.* New York: Harper & Row. (Original work published 1941)

Wilder, L. I. (1971). *These happy golden years.* New York: Harper & Row. (Original work published 1943)

Wister, O. (1917). *The Virginian.* New York: Macmillan.

Woofter, T. J. (1917). *Teaching in rural schools.* Boston: Houghton Mifflin.

9

And the Oscar Goes to …
Teachers as Supporting Actors
in Fiction for Young Adults

Gail E. Burnaford

Yesterday, I viewed the film *Music of the Heart.* It is about a violin teacher in East Harlem who persists in believing that music education is good for children—for all children. She builds a program for young, mostly minority students who wind up in Carnegie Hall, playing to a packed house and supported by celebrity violinists such as Itzak Perlman and Isaac Stern. The teacher is clearly a hero in the eyes of parents, children, and even her own building administrator.

There seem to a parade of such heroes in films about teachers, including *Dangerous Minds, Dead Poets Society,* and *Conrack.* (See Ayers, chap. 11, and Lowe, chap. 12, this volume.) As I thought about *Music of the Heart,* the latest in the larger-than-life teachers on film stories, I searched my memory for teacher-heroes of that dimension in literature for young adult or adolescent readers. I struggled for awhile and finally came to the conclusion that a book based on a teacher hero would probably not make it in the world of young adult fiction. That is because the heroes in this genre are the youth themselves. They play the major roles and the teachers are the supporting actors. There are teachers who do extraordinary acts and who genuinely change the playing field of the plot. However, the notion of "hero" is recast when we move from the big screen to a work of literature. I explore this phenomenon in this chapter and try to determine what is unique about the act of reading that shifts focus and influences upon the imagery surrounding teachers.

Reading Texts: In the Eye of the Beholder

Joel Taxel (1995), scholar and writer in the field of children's and adolescent fiction, notes that there is a "social power" that is inherent in works stemming from a culture. This power is represented in movies, literature, art, and in all other aspects of culture. The identification of the holder of power in these cultural artifacts is crucial in order for certain groups to achieve and maintain their control. Taxel (1995) explains that "literature is a product of convention that is rooted in, if not determined by, the dominant belief systems and ideologies of the times in which it was created" (p. 159). In the teacher-hero movies, power and authority ultimately reside in the lone teacher mavericks who resist the system and succeed. And yet even these teachers are not too far from the dominant culture. They are, for the most part, middle-class, reasonably privileged, middle-aged White people. So, where are these heroes in literature for young readers? They are there, but they do not seem quite as heroic as their counterparts on the big screen. In fact, teachers in fiction can be downright strange.

Herbert J. Gans (1974), in his analysis of popular culture, suggests that a society's art and entertainment do not develop in a vacuum, but, in fact, tend to grow directly out of a society's values and the characteristics of its members. A society's literature is, truly, its shared history. It is a public representation of cultural norms. If this premise is accurate, then we must look closely at portraits of teachers that fall outside the realm of familiar recollection and easy categorization, those portrayals that wake us up and make us think by showing us a world of teaching with a twist. Such representations point the way to the challenges that face us in our contemporary society. They are, despite their strangeness, a part of our shared history.

The world of text is very different from the worlds of film or real life because of what literary theorists have called the transaction between reader and the written word (Dias, 1992; Rosenblatt, 1978). A transaction occurs as a reader reads, between the reader and the text; meaning does not exist in one or the other, but rather in the transaction that happens between them (Beach, 1993). Literature offers a different mode of apprehension than film; the reader plays a very different role in meaning making than that of the moviegoer. Whereas filmmakers seek to appeal to a large mass audience that ideally crosses age boundaries; books seek out the individual who becomes a player, a thinker, an interpreter, a hero, and a user of texts (Applebee, 1989).

Stanley Fish (1980) notes that when works of literature are analyzed, the reader is often forgotten, left behind, or ignored, while the literary critic becomes enmeshed in the text itself. Instead, Fish (1980) suggests that the reader is an "actively mediating presence" in the analysis—one whose sensitivity and experience should not be neglected (p. 23). Therefore, who the reader is becomes crucial to understanding the imagery in the text. The fact that this transaction occurs shapes the kind of imagery we find in written texts as opposed to the visual texts found in films. The fact that the reader may be a young adult or adolescent challenges the idea of just who is permitted to be the hero.

The convention in young adult and adolescent literature is that young people are the central characters in their fiction and that the central concerns of this genre are those of adolescence (Langer, 1992; Probst, 1988). G. Robert Carlsen's (1980) research has investigated the reading interests and patterns of adolescents. "Generally, the concerns of the great middle-aged section of the population have little appeal," Carlsen (1980, p. 42) notes. Teachers, in the eyes of most adolescents, fall into that "middle-aged section of the population" that Carlsen describes; they are simply not that interesting to young readers—unless, as characters, they are strange or eccentric and when they have supporting roles to the youthful protagonists. Only then will we have a teacher story that adolescents will read.

Paul Zindel (1990), writer of adolescent fiction, describes a teacher he had in school who remains memorable, not just because of her strangeness, but also because of her influence on him. She fits the standard in that she is the supporting actor for youth itself, but she deserves billing because she is "different."

> Miss Burger was the only one in school who didn't think I was a misfit. And she was the only high school teacher I had ever heard of who had a doctorate in Shakespearean studies. She was so brilliant, but I was the only one in her class who wasn't bored and didn't throw M&Ms or pennies at her when she read *Macbeth*. She told me things about myself I'll never forget—the kinds of things that changed my life. Until, finally, she had a nervous breakdown and they took her away. (Zindel, 1990, pp. 228–229)

M. E. Kerr's (1975) fictional Miss Blue also belongs in this cast of teacher supporting characters. In the novel *Are You There, Miss Blue?,* the teacher dramatizes her science lessons in order to make them meaningful for students. She relates scientific principles to everyday life and she does so with spirit and imagination. The young hero, Flanders, reports: "I wasn't the only one under Miss Blue's spell in the classroom; most of us came away with the sort of full, silent feeling that you have after you've seen a really good movie and you have to walk back out into the real world again" (Kerr, 1975, p. 92). However, in keeping with the eccentric characterization, Miss Blue is a religious fanatic. She claims to have visited with Jesus in her room. Her fanaticism eventually becomes obtrusive and she is asked to leave.

These teachers provide the platform for young characters in books to test their own social power and go on in life to be somebody. The concern is not for accuracy or authenticity, but rather to enable youthful characters—and their reader counterparts—to be successful and survive. Youth itself becomes the real hero.

> All heroes and heroines help express something about this planet that the author needs to say. They also reflect the author's view of the world and the human's place within it. But even if these protagonists pop up overnight in the author's imagination ... they have not formed instantaneously, but have arisen after long gestation from a sort of elemental soup in the author's primal pot. This primal pot, this crucible of the psyche and its contents is what determines the kind of heroes the author will create, and the sort of stories that he or she will spin.   (Chetwin, 1995, p. 175)

It seems to me that teachers in young adult fiction are not resounding heroes. In fact, they are quite odd and at times downright unnerving.

In this chapter, I will examine three such teachers who, while they are not "the heroes" of the stories in which they find themselves, they do act in ways as to prompt heroism. They come from that "primal pot" described by Chetwin (1995) and bring the reader into unfamiliar teacher image territory. Madeleine L'Engle (1990) maintains that we might have a fear of fiction because it may be true. These teachers bring us to the edge of that fear and force us to face it.

Nonheroic Heroes: Teachers and the Battle Between Good and Evil

> I have tried to make the case that the function of literature as art is to open us to dilemmas, to the hypothetical, to the range of possible worlds that a text can refer to. Literature subjunctivizes, makes strange, renders the obvious less so, the unknowable less so as well .... (Bruner, 1986, p. 159)

The literary artists of our time are capable of unveiling compelling images of teachers because it is they who challenge readers to look beyond these physical images and to rethink what it means to be a teacher by creating characters who move into unfamiliar territory. Teachers in such school literature are not what we might expect, they are not what they appear to be on the surface. They pose questions that do not have clear answers and they appear in situations that are not easily recognized in a reader's own school experience.

There are three texts that have what I propose to call "nonheroic heroes"—that is, they do not behave as heroes should. Yet by their actions they point to issues in our modern society that we must address; they provoke our outrage and they instigate rebellion. Ray Bradbury's *Fahrenheit 451* (1951), Ernest J. Gaines' *A Lesson Before Dying* (1993), and Mel Glenn's *The Taking of Room 114: A Hostage Drama in Poems* (1997) are "episodes within a larger text" (Weber & Mitchell, 1995), depicting teachers as less than perfect, yet more than heroic. The tidy image labels do not fit these teachers.

Gaines' work of historical fiction is set in the 1940s; Glenn's drama in poem form takes place in the present, and Bradbury's science fiction novel is set in the future. The time frame sets each apart and serves as a further caution to one who would attempt to categorize. Yet each novel embodies ways of looking at teaching that might provoke those in the profession and will certainly intrigue those outside it. Each has a powerful message to deliver and calls for a response to the author's commentary on contemporary culture.

Teachers can remain teachers, presumably, only if they subscribe to the rules. We live in a society where teachers are expected to conform to patterns of conduct established by the administration and local community. Sometimes these rules are abhorrent; sometimes strong characters—or weak ones—must break them. Insubordination, alleged inappropriate demeanor, or even somewhat odd behavior is not typically tolerated by schools or communities. However, the teachers in these three texts resist, drop out, and defy. They run away, they clench fists, and they posture. The harsh realities of race, social class, and cultural confusion regarding the value of intellect push against these teacher images and stretch the definition of "teacher" in the minds of readers. Teaching becomes a social stance, a philosophical position, and a call to action.

How do we read these texts? Where do we begin for interrogating these images of schoolteachers (Weber & Mitchell, 1995)? It may well be that the point of entry is one's own sense of identity as a teacher and a learner in this society. We come to the text with society on our shoulders. Thus, an examination of these images might serve as a self-study, a theorizing of our own identity within this social context. The relationship between the reader and the text are primary to the experience of re-creating that text at each reading (Appleby, 1989). Weber and Mitchell write that image texts "can be agents of change and subversion, as well as invisible but powerful agents of reproduction and conservatism" (p. 128).

These texts for adolescents truly warrant a reading by us, too. Once we are brave enough to look at ourselves and begin to develop a deeper awareness of ourselves as teachers, then perhaps we can discover the truth, with a lowercase "t," in each work of fiction.

Revisiting an Old Friend

It is freshman year in high school. The year is 1966 and I am about to read Ray Bradbury's (1951) *Fahrenheit 451* for the first time. Most of us probably remember such an encounter; this is a text that is probably now safely labeled a classic in the American novel repertoire. When I asked a friend if she remembered the book, her reply seemed quite typical: "Oh yeah, wasn't that the one about the book burning?" Many readers recall the story of an anonymous government that remained in power by destroying civilization's link to knowledge, and therefore power, by burning all books. Some of us might even be able to recount how our high school English teachers led us through an analysis of this work as a political statement, connecting our reading to the Civil Rights era, the balance of power in the American government, and the *Declaration of Independence.* We might conjure up visions of essays written about the irony of a fire department employed to start fires rather than douse them or about the development of the main character, Montag, as he slowly begins to recognize who and what he has become.

How do our personal memories help us to revisit the teacher imagery in this text? Few of us probably remember Faber, the English professor who is the teacher figure in this story. Yet he is the cornerstone of the narrative. When we first meet Faber, he is in the city park, hiding furtively and very fearful of Montag. He tells the fireman Montag that he taught at the university 40 years ago, when they still had students in the liberal arts college. They talk for awhile "and when an hour had passed he said something to Montag and Montag sensed it was a rhymeless poem. Then the old man grew even more courageous and said something else and that was a poem too."

Finally, Farber confesses, "I don't talk things, sir .... I talk the meaning of things. I sit here and know I'm alive" (Bradbury, 1951, p. 103).

Each time Montag and Faber meet, the fireman learns something more about the essence of life and what his life has been missing. Faber teaches him the three necessary components of a meaningful intellectual life: the quality of information, the leisure to digest it, and the right to carry out actions based on what we learn (Bradbury, 1951, p. 113). These things can be learned from books, but they can also be learned from viable, real interaction among people, whatever the medium. It is awareness that is to be valued, not just the permission to read. "Remember, the firemen are rarely necessary. The public itself stopped reading of its own accord," notes Faber (p. 115).

The teacher is not the hero of this story, however, for Faber cannot muster up the courage to rebel all by himself. He has been in hiding, avoiding active resistance, until he meets Montag. This teacher needs a student to take the real action. It is through Montag that he uses his own creative energy, fully conscious of his own cowardice in the process. "See how safe I play it, how contemptible I am?" (Bradbury, 1951, p. 119). Because of Faber, the young fireman is able to find his way to other thinkers, to others who resist, to others who can walk the walk of resistance with him. Faber cannot be there, but he can get Montag to that place.

What can we make of this teacher image in Bradbury's novel? Adolescent and young adult readers need to begin to see the flaws in their teachers in order to grow and learn. Young readers deepen their understanding of the human experience by their encounter with adults in literature who experience conflict, indecision, and even paranoia. Faber teaches, not by being the hero, but by helping Montag see how he can be heroic. Faber fails in the responsibility of keeping his charge from harm, as much as he tries. He is not a savior; he is a cowardly human being, but he keeps the active critical awareness alive so that it can be passed on to Montag.

Fahrenheit 451 has recently been reissued in a 40th anniversary edition. Now, in the age of technology and information, Bradbury's tale is one worth reviving and retelling. This generation of adolescents and young adults can revisit Bradbury's teacher image and go beyond the mere story to a critical analysis of the nature of knowledge in today's technological society. These new readers of the now-classic novel can ask themselves, who are the Fabers in this generation who speak up for independent critical process and free access to real information? Who are the teachers?

Off the Deep End: Insights From Insanity

> Would I be a teacher?
> Not on your life.
> Who wants to teach these kids all day?
> They're animals.   (Glenn, 1997, p. 160)[1]

Images in contemporary texts are often reconstructions of images from the experiences and memories of other generations. But Mr. Wiedermeyer, in Mel Glenn's (1997) *The Taking of Room 114: A Hostage Drama in Poems,* may be as close to a unique teacher image as we are likely to get. Even though we have had teachers in literature who have had nervous breakdowns or psychotic moments (Kerr, 1975; Zindel, 1990), we have not encountered anyone quite like Wiedermeyer. Since the tragedy at Columbine High School, violence is a topic that has grabbed the headlines; nonetheless, it is not usually the teacher who erupts and threatens the safety of students.

Joseph Wiedermeyer never actually appears in Glenn's book. We only hear of him through the poems of his senior history class students, their parents, a few community members, and the occasional verse he writes himself. We learn that, on one of the final days of the school year, Wiedermeyer—finally frustrated beyond sanity by students' apathy, their personal challenges, and his own inadequacy—has taken his class hostage at gunpoint.

> I speak.
> Who listens?
> I teach.
> Who cares?
> There is little I can do to turn the tide.
> There is little I can do to make a difference.   (Glenn, 1997, p. 145)

The book consists of a series of poems that detail a single event in the life of an imaginary school. The hostage event is the catalyst for the narratives, but readers are introduced to much more than this single day as they wend their way through poems written during each high school year by each of the students held hostage. We learn of their issues and through their own poetry, we watch them grow up. We meet Esther Torres, whose mother "sleeps around," and Denise Slattery, who "don't need nobody" (Glenn, 1997, p. 111). We get to know Wing Li Wu, who writes about his family's escape from China, and Rhonda Ellis, who tapes all the "soaps." We read the story of Douglas Atherton, the perennial class officer, and Cory Deshayes, who writes, "There hasn't been a girl made/That I can't make" (p. 79).

And we meet Mr. Wiedermeyer as he discusses what he will pack in his book bag for school, naming essentials such as a box cutter, a switchblade, an ice pick, a can of Mace, a can of spray paint, a cherry bomb, and a razor blade—no pens, paper, notebooks, ruler, or apples.

> It's a tight fit,
> But I can throw out my texts.
> I don't need them for survival.   (Glenn, 1997, p. 134)

What seems particularly compelling about this teacher is how his persona unfolds. We learn whom Wiedermeyer has become, but not through events or through his own story. In fact, we do not hear about his son's suicide, which presumably pushes him over the edge of sanity until the very end of the book. Instead, the image of Joe Wiedermeyer, teacher and criminal, is unveiled through the poetic stories of his students. It is their 4-year journey through high school that provides the framework for this teacher's characterization. It is because the students are trapped in this hostage drama that they dare to look back on their high school years and wonder about who they are and why they are. This teacher, unlike his counterparts in films such as *Blackboard Jungle* and *To Sir with Love,* is not likely to end up being called a hero. And yet Wiedermeyer gives his students a context for taking stock of their own histories. In doing so, they reveal something about teaching, society, and the culture of 20th century schooling.

The Taking of Room 114 (Glenn, 1997) is a dramatic response to what schooling has become for many students and teachers. It seems to bring into sharp relief the challenges and dilemmas of teaching in the last decade of the 20th century and forces readers to listen—and watch—as the drama unfolds. Wiedermeyer's insanity provides a mirror for what schooling and teaching has become. In this worst-case scenario, only the students' own stories suggest hope for the future.

Tales Out of School: Teaching To Believe

> The project that grows out of a close reading is to imagine and realize other possibilities, ways to get beneath the stereotypes, sometimes, paradoxically, by embracing them. (Weber & Mitchell, 1995, p. 140)

In Ernest J. Gaines' *A Lesson Before Dying,* we meet a teacher who teaches in a one-room plantation schoolhouse in Louisiana during the 1940s. Grant Wiggins is a young African-American man who has left his rural community to attend the university and then returns to teach school in his hometown. The reader sees Mr. Wiggins in class with children where he is, at best, uninspired, at worst, punitive. He chafes at the treatment of Black people in the town, yet his anger is often silent and remains unexpressed. Then, Jefferson, a young, illiterate Black man, gets unwittingly involved in a liquor store holdup that leaves three men dead. Jefferson is falsely convicted of murder and sentenced to death by electrocution.

During the hearing, Jefferson listens as his defense attorney labels him a dumb animal, a hog. Jefferson's godmother and Wiggins' aunt begin a crusade to help Jefferson die like a man. They convince Wiggins, the schoolteacher, to visit the convicted man in jail over a period of months in order to help him find his humanity. As Grant Wiggins makes his weekly pilgrimages to the prison, he invites Jefferson to write in a notebook, which the teacher then reads.

Through the process of writing and the dignity afforded him by the young schoolteacher, Jefferson does die "like a man." Paul, the young deputy at the courthouse describes the death scene to Grant, who chooses not to attend the electrocution. "He (Jefferson) was the bravest man in that room today" (Gaines, 1993, p. 256).

> Paul tells Grant, "You're one great teacher, Grant Wiggins."
> Grant replies, "I'm not great. I'm not even a teacher."
> "Why do you say that?"
> "You have to believe to be a teacher."   (p. 254)

A Lesson Before Dying (Gaines, 1993) ends shortly after these words are spoken—Jefferson is dead; Grant is crying. As one reader of this text, I wanted to echo Paul's sentiment: Grant Wiggins was a great teacher. Though not a hero, he invited Jefferson to be one and he stood aside in order to let the convicted man articulate his thoughts, feelings, and ideas in his notebook. Wiggins resisted those trips to the jail; he resisted the old women's persistent belief in him as a savior for the imprisoned boy. He did not believe in this process, and yet he continued.

As with the Bradbury and Glenn novels, *A Lesson Before Dying* seems to convey an image of what it means to be a teacher through the lens of students—be they adult or children. Schooling takes place outside of the schoolhouse, just as it seems to in the before-mentioned texts. Schooling is about expression—in a series of dramatic poems, in the recitation of old books no longer accessible in print, and finally in a bedraggled prison notebook. Schooling is about lessons, but they are lessons not necessarily lived, or even believed in, by the teachers.

Sarah Smedman (1989), in her analysis of teachers in books for younger readers, notes the numbers of books in which teachers make a significant difference at critical times in students' lives (p. 149). The teacher images are then shaped by the impressions they have made and by the actions and reactions of their pupils. Grant Wiggins may not believe, but the imprisoned Jefferson does. Jefferson goes to his death believing that he is not a dumb animal, a hog, but rather a man who walks upright toward his fate. "By clarifying and displaying those images that we do not like, by articulating and sharing those that resonate deeply, we breathe new life into them and their power increases" (Weber & Mitchell, 1995, p. 140).

Bruce Appleby (1989) writes that there are three norms imposed on adolescents in this society: (a) conformity, (b) hostility to intellectualism, and (c) passivity. The three novels in this study portray teachers who challenge all three of these norms. The teachers in these stories face violence, discrimination, and apathy. The teachers themselves also demonstrate some of these same behaviors. They are not heroes, but neither are they victims. In some ways, young readers and the teacher characters—Faber, Wiedermeyer, and Wiggins—all are caught up in a critical interrogation of the social norms that they face. They do not win great wars against those norms; they fight—often unwillingly—only the smallest of battles. But, in doing so, they reveal their humanity and point the way toward our own.

When young people encounter these teachers, they have the opportunity to view themselves as political beings, actively choosing to select or resist social roles and responsibility. Umberto Eco (1979) observes that in any given literary message, there is both the sender and the addressee. This literature shows young readers that they can take part in the development of their own social power; although they may not be heroes or have more than supporting roles, the teachers in these texts—with all of their psychological afflictions and moral failures—show them the way.

NOTE

1. The point of view in this quote comes from the character of a parent in book. All quotations from Glenn (1997) are from *The Taking of Room 114*, by M. Glenn, 1997, New York: Dutton. Copyright © 1997 by M. Glenn. Used by permission of Lodestar Books, an affiliate of Dutton Children's Books, a division of Penguin Putnam, Inc.

REFERENCES

Applebee, A. N. (1989). *The teaching of literature in programs with reputations for excellence in English.* Albany: State University of New York, Center for the Learning and Teaching of Literature. (Report Series 1.1, 1–45, No. ED315753)

Appleby, B C. (1989). Is adolescent literature in its adolescence? *The ALAN Review, 17*(1), 40–45.

Beach, R. (1993). *A teacher's introduction to reader-response theories.* Urbana, IL: National Council of Teachers of English.

Bradbury, R. (1951). *Fahrenheit 451.* New York: Simon & Schuster.

Bruner, J. (1986). *Actual minds, possible worlds.* Cambridge, MA: Harvard University Press.

Carlsen, G. R. (1980). *Books and the teenage reader: A guide for teachers, librarians, and parents* (2nd ed.). New York: Harper & Row.

Chetwin, G. (1995). Creating ethical heroes who know how to win: Or muddling through. In S. Lehr (Ed.), *Battling dragons: Issues and controversy in children's literature* (pp. 175–193). Portsmouth, NH: Heinemann.

Dias, P. X. (1992). Literary reading and classroom constraints: Aligning practice with theory. In J. A. Langer (Ed.), *Literature instruction: A focus on student response* (pp. 131–162). Urbana, IL: National Council of Teachers of English.

Eco, U. (1979). *The role of the reader: Explorations in the semiotics of texts.* Bloomington: Indiana University Press.

Fish, S. (1980). *Is there a text in this class?* Cambridge, MA: Harvard University Press.

Gaines, E. J. (1993). *A lesson before dying.* New York: Vintage Books.

Gans, H. J. (1974). *Popular culture and high culture: An analysis and evaluation of taste.* New York: Basic Books.

Glenn, M. (1997). *The taking of room 114: A hostage drama in poems.* New York: Dutton.

Kerr, M. E. (1975). *Are you there, Miss Blue?* New York: Harper & Row.

Langer, J. A. (1992). *Literature instruction: A focus on student response.* Urbana, IL: National Council of Teachers of English.

L'Engle, M. (1990, March). Unnamed presentation, Wheaton College, Wheaton, IL.

Probst, R. E. (1988). *Response and analysis: Teaching literature in junior and senior high school.* Portsmouth, NH: Heinemann.

Rosenblatt, L. (1978). *The reader, the text, the poem: The transactional theory of the literary work.* Carbondale, IL: Southern Illinois University Press.

Smedman, S. (1989). Not always gladly does she teach, nor gladly learn: Teacher in Kunstlerinroman for young readers. *Children's literature in education, 20*(3), 131–149.

Taxel, J. (1995). Cultural politics and writing for young people. In S. Lehr (Ed.), *Battling dragons: Issues and controversy in children's literature* (pp. 155–169). Portsmouth, NH: Heinemann.

Weber, S., & Mitchell, C. (1995). *"That's funny, you don't look like a teacher": Interrogating images and identity in popular culture.* London: Falmer Press.

Zindel, P. (1990). Paul Zindel. In D. R. Gallo (Ed.), *Speaking for ourselves: Autobiographical sketches by notable authors of books for young adults* (pp. 228–230). Urbana, IL: National Council of Teachers of English.

10

"I Will Not Expose the Ignorance of the Faculty": *The Simpsons* as School Satire

Ken Kantor
Nancy Lerner Kantor
Josh Kantor
Mary Eaton
Benjamin Kantor

I n the opening credits for the hugely popular cartoon comedy, *The Simpsons,* Bart is seen in detention, writing a sentence on the chalkboard numerous times, apparently as punishment for one of his regular transgressions. "I will not expose the ignorance of the faculty" is one such sentence, in this case occurring at the end of an episode that takes on such educational issues as standardized testing, career education, gender bias, student rebellion, and teacher and administrator performance.

From its beginning, we were attracted to *The Simpsons* for several reasons. First, we liked its approach to comedy, in particular its balance between cynicism and sentiment, and its attention to both the stereotypical and multidimensional features of characters and events. Second, we were captivated by ways in which the show addressed educational and societal issues. The satirical treatment of such themes is often blunt and unflinching; viewers looking for a sanguine or sanitized perspective on American education may well be disappointed or offended. And third, we identified, in various ways, with the experiences of the Simpson family and teachers and students in school settings. The show manages to capture a sense of reality, even in far-fetched scenarios.

What is remarkable about *The Simpsons* is the wide range of issues—educational and beyond—that it addresses in penetrating and scathingly funny ways. Animation allows the show's writers to present characters and events in more fantastic and outrageous means than the typical situation comedy peopled by actors, which must generally adhere to a different level of reality and credibility. In this chapter we wish to provide an analysis and interpretation of the unique manner in which *The Simpsons* satirizes American schooling, as reflected especially in the episodes depicting Springfield Elementary School and its teachers.

Background and Sources

The Simpsons—which celebrated its 10th anniversary in December 1999—is the longest running comedy among current prime-time television shows and the longest running prime-time animation series in television history. It also has been named by *Time Magazine* as the television show of the century because of its revolutionary impact on this medium.

In this series, teachers are variously portrayed as lazy, uninspired, authoritarian, pessimistic, condescending, elitist, propagandistic, biased, lonely, insecure, depressed, dissatisfied, pathetic, defensive, fearful, reactionary, or, especially, incompetent. *The Simpsons* takes its place in the history of images of teachers in television situation comedies (see Kantor, 1994), as positive or sympathetic images make occasional appearances, but most often teachers are objects of ridicule.

The series centers on the lives and misfortunes of the hapless but resilient Simpson family: parents Homer and Marge, schoolchildren Bart and Lisa, and infant Maggie. Teachers, students, administrators, parents, and community members alike are skewered, their shortcomings and foibles exploited and displayed in the episodes depicting Springfield Elementary, the town's public school.

Our sources for this investigation have been primarily the television episodes themselves, especially those pertaining to Springfield Elementary School and its inhabitants, from December 1989 to July 1998. We have discussed these episodes intensively, searching for themes and nuances of meaning. As further reference guides, we've also looked to *The Simpsons: A Complete Guide to Our Favorite Family* (Groening, Richmond, & Coffman, 1997), the official web site (http://thesimpsons.com), and one of many unofficial web sites, "*The Simpsons Archive*" (http://www.snpp.com).

The satire of schooling derives from the work of *The Simpsons'* creator Matt Groening, notably in the compilation *School Is Hell* (Groening, 1987), a selection from his "Life Is Hell" cartoons. One cartoon in the *School Is Hell* collection, for example, describes nine types of grade school teachers: "The Good Mom," "Ms. Sunshine," "The Big Pal," "Jumpy," "The Bad Mom," "Grandma," "The Sarge," "The Martian," and "The Monster." The traits associated with these types can often be found in depictions of Springfield teachers. Between April 1987 and May 1989 there was also a series of 48 shorts on the initial Simpson family aired on *The Tracey*

Ullman Show. Though none of these took place in a school setting, they did reveal the evolution of the characters and relationships within the family. The success of *The Simpsons* further paved the way for other animated series, notably *Ren and Stimpy, The Critic, Beavis and Butthead, King of the Hill,* and *South Park.* The last three contain some portrayals of school situations, but we feel without the breadth or depth of *The Simpsons.*

Additionally, the contexts are not limited to home and school; they extend outward to community and society. As with any good television series, a single episode can stand on its own, but also increasingly becomes interwoven with other episodes, as characters, events, interactions, and themes are revisited and restructured. Roles in *The Simpsons* are often fluid and interchangeable, for example, when community members become substitute teachers during a teachers' strike. Indeed, the town of Springfield can be viewed as a character itself, as in the way the populace mythologizes its town's founder Jebediah Springfield. Events and dialogue can serve as platforms for penetrating statements on social, cultural, historical, economic, and political issues. Again, the animation medium permits this complexity and fluidity: The characters do not age (except in some flash-forward scenarios), they are absurdly resilient—continually bouncing back from what would otherwise be tragedies, and they can express exaggerated and even anti-social ideas, but still retain their believability.

Students: Bart, Lisa, and Classmates

An understanding of Springfield's school system and its teachers is best begun, we think, with an examination of its students, particularly Bart and Lisa. It is their character traits and interactions with teachers, family, and community members that provide the core of *The Simpsons* school satire.

Bart is the ingenious class clown, trickster, and avenger. He is both unpopular with other students and also admired by them because of his callow attitudes toward school. His pranks include defacing the walls of the school building, planting a cherry bomb in a toilet in the boys' bathroom (revealing his fondness for "the classics"), starting a riot by wearing a T-shirt that says "Down With Homework," changing a weather balloon into a semi-nude effigy of Principal Skinner, and shattering town windows with the use of megaphones he discovered on a field trip to the police station. He frequently cuts class and devises excuses to avoid homework and tests. His exploits usually backfire, and he is caught and punished. Sometimes he is embarrassed, as when bullies harass him for his mother being a substitute teacher or when he finds himself in over his head in a gifted class. He is indomitable, though, arising in the next episode to create more trouble. As he brags to his friend Milhouse, the two of them can accomplish anything "with your book smarts and my ability to exploit people with book smarts."

By comparison, Lisa is the ideal student—brilliant, talented, academically motivated, and socially conscious. She gets straight A's and high scores on standardized tests, plays jazz and blues on the saxophone, and speaks out passionately for the homeless and the environment and against corrupt government and corporate capitalism. But she is thwarted by her circumstances, unappreciated and unchallenged by her teachers, and often ridiculed by her classmates. She complains of "rotting away in second grade." When the music teacher, Mr. Largo, reprimands her for playing jazz riffs in the school band rehearsal, she claims to be "wailing out for the homeless," to which he callously responds that "none of those unpleasant people will be at the recital."

Lisa is also highly competitive. Threatened by transfer student Allison's superior ability, she sabotages her new rival's entry in the school diorama contest. She is obsessed with school; when the teachers go out on strike and school is closed, she suffers withdrawal symptoms. She pleads with her mother, "Evaluate and rank me!" and calms down only when Marge writes "A+" on a sheet of paper and hands it to her. Generally, though, Lisa is affectionate and compassionate, for example, in her kindness to Ralph, the class "dummy"—whether giving him a valentine or offering to share a presentation with him at a school assembly.

On the surface, then, Bart and Lisa contrast sharply in their traits and actions, especially their attitudes toward school. However, in some important ways they are not so different from one another. Bart's schemes reveal an intelligence equal to that of Lisa; it is simply directed toward nonacademic and disruptive ends. Lisa sometimes acts rebelliously, as when she challenges political conservatism or resists attempts by teachers and others to limit her opportunities. Moreover, Bart often feels and acts sympathetically toward his sister, as when he helps her with her fitness test during an episode in which the two attend a military school. Like many siblings, Bart and Lisa are friendly adversaries, linked in their search for identity and struggles against conformity. As such, both are hindered by the limitations of the school and the narrow-mindedness of their teachers and administrators.

Other students are more two-dimensional: dummy Ralph, the bullies Nelson and Jimbo, egghead Milhouse, teachers' pet and class snitch Martin, and rival Allison. Occasionally, however, we find instances in which one of these characters will reveal another side, as when Nelson develops a crush on Lisa or when Martin is enlisted to help Bart pass a big test. We also see adults in the roles of students, for example, when Homer goes to college for retraining and falls in with a group of "nerds." Even the family dog, Santa's Little Helper, must attend "Canine College" to learn obedience. Again, the show's genius resides not only in exploiting stereotypes, but also in moving beyond them and revealing more subtle and complex dimensions of character and role.

Teachers and Administrators

The two educators most elaborated on in the series are Bart's fourth-grade teacher, Edna Krabappel, and school principal, Seymour Skinner. Though the show continually mocks their shortcomings, we also see sides of them that enlist our sympathies. They are significantly more than two-dimensional stereotypes.

Mrs. Krabappel (emphasis placed cleverly on the second syllable) is a mostly authoritarian teacher, stating clearly that her classroom "is not a democracy" and in one instance calling on an unprepared Bart to answer every question she asks. She often plays favorites, as when she urges students to vote for brainy Martin over troublemaker Bart in a class election. She is condescending toward students and especially intolerant of Bart, who, through his misdeeds, ends up in frequent detentions. At times, she is casual toward her work; when Lisa's teacher Miss Hoover calls her for a happy hour in the teachers' lounge, she quickly marks B's on all the papers she is grading and rushes off.

In her personal life, Edna is embittered by her divorce, her husband having run off with their marriage counselor. She often reveals her desperation to find a man (she even tries at one point to seduce Homer); Bart exploits this weakness when he writes love letters to her in the name of a false suitor. Feeling remorse, Bart eventually writes a letter in which "Woodrow" lets her down easy. Her spirits lifted the next day, Edna suggests to Bart that they spend detention outside. We can see her, then, as a generally well-intentioned person whose life has been devalued by her own poor judgment and a career that discourages her aspirations and motivation. She is strict with students and contentious with colleagues, but is also romantic and softhearted at times. She reflects a stereotypical image of the historical spinster teacher, but with her own complexity.

Seymour Skinner is a Vietnam veteran who has brought his military style to his role as principal. He still lives with his mother, who dominates his life and calls him "Spanky." Bart is Skinner's chief nemesis, constantly challenging his authority and causing disruptions at school; Skinner's recommended punishments range from detention to deportation. He joins with Superintendent Chalmers and others in criticizing the students. At one point, with Chalmers' approval, he even mandates the wearing of uniforms; the students become docile and apathetic until a rainstorm washes away the drab surface, revealing psychedelic colors underneath and causing the students to run wild. Skinner is given to celebrating the mundane, as with his delight over "Diorama-Rama Day," "Hearing Test Thursday," the "schwa" sound, cafeteria "Tater-Tots," and a field trip to the box factory. He spouts platitudes like "There's learning afoot!" and shouts commands to the "soldiers" under his command: "You're in this man's army to learn!" The townspeople generally regard Skinner as a "weenie," but also acknowledge that he is "our weenie."

In a 1997 episode, Edna and Seymour come together in a romantic relationship. Having previously squared off against each other numerous times, including in a debate over school funding and a teachers' strike, the two find themselves attracted to each other. When their relationship is discovered by Bart, they bribe him to serve as their go-between by deleting infractions from his school records. Later they are caught kissing in the school closet, and the town is scandalized. Chalmers dismisses them, but Skinner confesses that he is a virgin, and they are forgiven and reinstated. The episode concludes with Skinner boasting, "That's what I love about elementary school, Edna. The children will believe anything you tell them." On the whole, however, Skinner is an ineffectual principal, unable to maintain order in the school and taking pleasure in random knowledge that no one else appreciates.

We must also mention Lisa's teacher, Miss Elizabeth Hoover, who usually reflects the worst of teacher traits; she is lazy, indifferent, cynical, reactionary, and given to panic under pressure. When the teachers' strike is announced, she flies out the door and off in her car, leaving the students bewildered. Though she is friendly with Edna Krabappel, she lacks her colleague's redeeming qualities.

Substitute teacher Mr. Bergstrom, who appears in only one episode, serves as a foil to other teachers. He takes over for Miss Hoover when she supposedly contracts Lyme disease (an illness that, in this instance, turns out to be psychosomatic). He enters the classroom dressed as a cowboy and shooting blanks from a gun. He plays guitar, tells stories (about Jewish cowboys), encourages students to make fun of his name, and praises their efforts, however immature or minimal. Lisa is smitten with him, and Homer suffers badly in her eyes by comparison. Bergstrom must eventually leave for another assignment and explain his departure to a distraught Lisa. He gives her a note that states simply, "You are Lisa Simpson." Returning to school and frustrated that Bergstrom didn't follow her lesson plans, Miss Hoover asks the class, "What did he teach you?" to which Lisa replies, "That life is worth living."

Mr. Bergstrom's appearance in this episode raises the issue of teachers (and parents) as role models. He is the committed, innovative, and caring teacher that Krabappel, Skinner, and Hoover are not, and the source of inspiration that Homer cannot measure up to. He is transient, though, and at the end of the episode, Homer wins Lisa's affection back through a pep talk and some monkeyshines. Though Homer's limited talent is no match for Bergstrom's, he ultimately provides a constancy that Bergstrom cannot, and his own kind of understanding and entertainment of his children.

Other individuals in Springfield also take on teaching roles at various times. Homer teaches an adult education course, ironically on the topic of successful marriage. Some community members, like the greedy owner of the nuclear power plant, Mr. Burns, come into classes as guest speakers. As head of the PTA, goody-goody neighbor Ned Flanders becomes principal at one point when Skinner is fired. Furthermore, during the teachers' strike, various citizens act as substitutes, the school emergency plan stipulating that teachers should be replaced "with super-intelligent cyborgs." Or "if cyborgs aren't invented yet, use people from the neighborhood." They are in various ways ineffective, like mad scientist Professor Frink who lectures far above the heads of the kindergartners, or Moe the Bartender who is easy prey for Bart's pranks, or senile old Jasper who lists behaviors that will result in punishment by paddling and later gets his beard stuck in the pencil sharpener. Eventually Marge takes over Bart's class, causing considerable damage to his reputation and well-being. Desperate to change the situation, Bart devises a way to lock Krabappel and Skinner together in the principal's office until they resolve the dispute that Bart himself instigated.

These teacher substitutions can be read as a critique of the profession: that virtually anyone (including a cyborg) can teach. However, most of them fail miserably, and Krabappel and Skinner find a way to settle the strike and restore the regular teachers. Flawed as they are, they are the enemies the students know. And the resolution is once again a hiatus, however temporary, against disruptions to the always precarious status quo.

Commonplaces

One of the major devices in *The Simpsons* is the use of what we would refer to as "commonplaces": characteristics, objects, and events of everyday life. Viewers are aware of them, perhaps only subconsciously, until they are brought to light as instances of what is known as "recognition humor." With respect to education, we do not know of any other television show that has so skillfully and thoroughly mined the commonplaces of school life. These include such matters as field trips, educational films, class elections, permission slips, the teachers' lounge, "Show and Tell," cafeteria lunches, extra credit, science fairs, book reports, tests and grades, permanent records, assemblies, the school bus, and even the teacher's marking pen (referred to affectionately by Mrs. Krabappel as "Old Red"). When the teachers go on strike, Lisa puts together a survival kit for herself containing a math book, a picture of the school, an audiotape of Miss Hoover speaking sternly, and fish sticks from the cafeteria. These commonplaces are part of the stock in trade for educators and recognizable by anyone who has ever been a student in American schools.

Especially fascinating are those commonplaces associated with subject matter areas—English, social studies, science, math, art, music, and physical education—in the school curriculum. These are fields of knowledge typically taken seriously by educators, but exaggerated or trivialized here to create the desired comic and satirical effects. Some examples follow. After attending a yo-yo performance at a school assembly, a student asks during a history lesson if the Pilgrims had yo-yos. When told he is failing English, Ralph cries, "Me fail English? That's unpossible!" Mrs. Krabappel tells her class that the primary reason for learning Roman numerals is to decipher the copyright date in movie credits. When Homer and Marge accompany Bart and Lisa on a visit to a military school, they witness students in an English class barking out lines from Keats' "Ode to a Grecian Urn": "Truth is beauty, beauty truth, Sir!" Marge reacts, "Well, they sure sucked the fun out of that poem."

Science gets a strong share of attention, in part because of Skinner's interest in astronomy and fondness for his telescope. At the science fair, he declares that "every good scientist is half B. F. Skinner and half P. T. Barnum." Students' projects include "Wasting Squirrels with B. B. Guns," "Making Milk Carton Ukuleles," and "Can Hamsters Fly Planes?" During Science Week, Skinner asserts that "there's nothing more exciting than science. You get the fun of sitting still, being quiet, writing down numbers, paying attention. Science has it all." And at the Springfield "Knowledgeum," attractions include the double-helix slide, earthquake simulator, and Velcro ceiling. This juxtaposition of the substantive with the mundane enables the writers to satirize the tendencies of teachers either to take traditional subject matter too seriously or to sugarcoat knowledge in the interest of motivating students to learn.

Among the commonplaces we also discover in *The Simpsons* are numerous references and allusions to popular culture, especially movies and television—the out-of-school curriculum that provides counterpoint to the in-school curriculum. In an early episode, for example, Skinner exclaims "Tomorrow is another school day," echoing the famous line from *Gone With the Wind.* In "Lisa's Substitute," Edna is seen posing in Mr. Bergstrom's classroom after school like Mrs. Robinson in *The Graduate,* leading him to say, "I believe you're trying to seduce me" (all the funnier since the voice for Bergstrom is that of an uncredited Dustin Hoffman). In college, Homer watches a TV movie entitled *School of Hard Knockers,* based clearly on the film *Animal House* and its various B-movie imitators. In the same episode, the "nerds" work out of Room 222, the name of the popular 1970s TV show about a high school. In what may be seen as the ultimate "tongue-in-cheek" comments on the effects of popular culture, Bart at one point concludes that television watching has shortened his attention span to 8 seconds and at another point that "TV has ruined my imagination."

Self-Fulfilling Prophecies

At the yo-yo performance, Mrs. Krabappel and Miss Hoover sit at the back of the auditorium, casually smoking cigarettes. Miss Hoover questions the educational value of the assembly, to which Edna replies that it will probably provide good memories for the students later in life when they are pumping gas for a living. This is one of many reflections in the show of a deterministic, self-fulfilling prophecy—the idea that few if any students (or for that matter Springfield residents) can rise above their present limited abilities or stations in life. A priority of these educators, then, is to prepare students for the bleak futures they face while pretending that those destinies are promising. The sign on the Springfield Youth center sums up this attitude in ironic fashion: "Building Unrealistic Hopes Since 1966."

Skinner and Chalmers are especially busy purveyors of this fatalistic message. When Krabappel confronts Skinner in the cafeteria about his cutbacks selling out the children's future, he responds loudly, "We both know these children have no future!" The room becomes abruptly silent, all eyes turning toward him, and in a nervous attempt to cover up his faux pas he states, "Prove me wrong, kids. Prove me wrong." Similarly, when wearing uniforms causes students to become docile, Chalmers happily proclaims that the experience will help prepare them for "positions in tomorrow's mills and processing facilities." Skinner even shows a sense of his own predestination, when he acknowledges that it's too late to do anything about his winding up in elementary school.

Not surprisingly, Bart in particular receives the brunt of these deterministic judgments. In a flashback to Bart's first days of school, he adds an extra clap while singing "Bingo," and the teacher designates him as "not college material." When he misses the letter "F" while reciting the alphabet, the teacher says sarcastically, "Believe me, you'll be seeing plenty of 'em." Skinner and Krabappel try to convince Bart that his school record will qualify him only for the "hottest and noisiest jobs" in a "gloomy and windblown future." Failing in school and resigned to his fate, Bart announces, "I am dumb, okay?"

Of *The Simpsons'* characters, then, Lisa clearly stands the best chance of transcending her circumstances and succeeding. In a future college scenario, she emerges as the only Springfield Elementary School graduate to read at an adult level. However, Lisa's intelligence and imagination are constantly suppressed by the narrowness of her teachers. When she improvises on the saxophone, Mr. Largo warns her about "another outburst of unbridled creativity." When she objects to Skinner about the outdated films and lengthy "magazine time" in Miss Hoover's classroom, he contends that if the class were more challenging, the less-able students would complain. Of her teachers, only Mr. Bergstrom seems to appreciate Lisa's potential, as he tells her that intelligence is an asset.

Bart and Lisa's horizons appear limited by their heredity as well as their environment. A psychologist, upon meeting Homer, describes Bart's perceived giftedness as a "total mystery." Similarly, a judge of a student essay contest, after testing Homer, gives Lisa five extra points for overcoming the adversity of her father's influence. Confronted with the deteriorating mental state of family members and her grandfather's explanation of the "Simpson gene," Lisa wonders whether she will go through a process of "dumbening." Fortunately, with the unwitting help of Homer in gathering his relatives together, she discovers that women in the family have achieved success and prominence in a number of fields. Most often, though, the messages from adults are like the advice given to Bart in kindergarten: "Learn to be less of an individual, and more a faceless slug."

A major device for carrying out the self-fulfilling prophecy is the system of record-keeping, grades, testing, and tracking in Springfield Elementary School. Administering a standardized test, Mrs. Krabappel "consoles" her students by telling them that the test will "merely determine your future social status." Identifying a busboy in a restaurant as a former student, Skinner comments that "standardized testing never lies." At another point, he establishes an "Academic Alert" program, so that parents will not have to wait until report-card time to punish their children. When Bart brings home a stack of these warnings, Homer praises him for not forging his signature. The continuous accumulation of grades, test scores, and reports in school records is what helps to point students like Bart to their bleak destinies.

These academic records in turn become the basis for ability grouping and tracking. In an early episode, Bart is placed in the gifted program because he has switched his IQ test with that of Martin. Unable to meet the demands, he must confess his crime. At another point he is placed in the remedial "Leg Up" program at another school. Puzzled by the dumbing down of the class, he asks, "You mean we catch up by going slower?" We can hardly imagine a more incisive critique of ability grouping in American schools.

The ultimate effects of tracking can be seen clearly in how things turn out for Springfield students in later life. A dramatic example can be found in the resolution to the teachers' strike and funding crisis. Locked in the principal's office, Krabappel and Skinner find they are "prisoners in our own school." This realization gives them the idea to generate revenue by adding a prison to the school building, with fences and guard towers. The prisoners occupy cells at the back of the classroom. One prisoner named Snake points to a desk and says, "Yo, I used to sit right over there." The metaphor of the school as prison is a venerable one, but also serves here to confirm the self-fulfilling prophecy, as students are from early on locked into tracks that will lead them nowhere.

On the surface, then, we see a reproduction model: The school creates the structures and categories that predetermine future occupations and roles in society. This view clearly challenges liberal myths about education as the key to mainstream success and social mobility. At the same time, though, not all is predestined. The characters, in their odd and flawed ways, show resilience and resistance. They are not discouraged long by setbacks; they come back to try again another day. It is this sentiment for the buoyant side of human nature that tempers the cynicism of the show, and keeps the comedy fresh and upbeat (and the viewers returning to watch). As Edna Krabappel reassures parents at the school open house, "even the poorest student can end up becoming, oh, say, Chief Justice of the Supreme Court." And Bart, in one flash forward, does indeed become Chief Justice, once again demonstrating the multiple levels of satire on which The Simpsons operates.

School, Community, and Society

At the same Parents' Night mentioned earlier, a sign proclaims, "Let's Share the Blame." The school is both a microcosm of the larger community and an extension of it. Springfield ranks "dead last" in science and culture, not surprisingly, given the lack of value attached to them. The events of Springfield school life often take on larger meanings—social, cultural, historical, religious, economic, and political.

The politics of educational trends receive particular attention. The traditional methods espoused by Krabappel, Skinner, and Hoover, for example, contrast with so-called progressive approaches. The teacher in the gifted program Bart is mistakenly assigned to is the "learning coordinator," who encourages students to make their own rules and "discover" their desks. Ironically, she expresses shock when she finds a comic book hidden among the classics on the bookshelves. Relatedly, when Ned Flanders becomes principal, students take advantage of his permissiveness, and Skinner is welcomed back. Though the political tone of the show is generally liberal, progressive approaches to education are treated as no less shallow and misguided than traditional ones.

Religious education also receives its share of barbs. A local Christian school advertises itself as putting the "fun back in fundamentalism." When confronted with the issue of school prayer, Superintendent Chalmers declares that "God has no place within these walls, just as facts have no place within organized religion." Two students whose religion prohibits them from participating in sex education classes are permitted to go outside to pray for the souls of their classmates. Moreover, a Sunday school teacher whose students are driving her crazy with questions desperately cries, "Is a little blind faith too much to ask?" Many of these references parody the religious Right, but also raise issues about both freedom of religion and students' needs to think critically. At the end of a film on sex education, the narrator warns, "Now that you know how it's done, don't do it." When students, especially Lisa, express their own ideas, Miss Hoover sounds an "independent thought alarm," a device no less restrictive than the imposition of religious dogma.

School matters often are tied to economic issues, especially as related to cutbacks in funding, the interests of big business, and discrepancies between the "haves" and "have-nots." When money goes toward the establishment of a town monorail, Skinner decides to cut science, music, and art from the curriculum. The school bus is in a shambles; cafeteria food includes grade F meat, ground-up gym mats, cow hearts, shredded newspaper, horse testicles, and a milk substitute named "malk" with vitamin R; and the only books available are those banned by other schools. Miss Krabappel informs her students that the worse they do on a standardized test, the more likely the school will be to receive additional funding.

In actuality, though, the rich get richer. When Springfield students go on a field trip to see a Civil War reenactment, Skinner is surprised to discover that there is an admission fee. The ticket lady points to the sign that reads, "Diz-Nee Historical Park. Sorry, But There's Profit to Be Had." At that moment a fancy double-decker bus from a private school arrives, and its administrator, Principal Valiant, pays the admission plus an additional amount to the ticket lady to "see that they get a little extra education." Since Skinner refuses to pay the admission charge, Springfield students must peer over a wall to view the battle enactment. Seeing this, a soldier shouts, "Hey, they're trying to learn for free!" The economic inequities here can hardly be more dramatic.

Distinctions pertaining to race, gender, and class also surface in school situations, as individuals reveal their biases and stereotypes. "For a school with no Asian kids, I think we put on a pretty good science fair," Skinner proudly boasts in one of Bart's dreams. Introducing Adil, an Albanian exchange student, Skinner urges the students to give him the benefit of the doubt, even though they may find his language and culture strange and offensive. Tolerance is necessary, he asserts, "to better understand our backward neighbors throughout the world." His xenophobia thinly disguised, he exposes his true feelings toward multiculturalism, reflecting the problems of personal resistance to that movement.

As historical background for gender issues, we learn that as a high school student, Marge first met Homer in detention after giving a speech on women's liberation and burning her bra. On the day designated for parents taking children to the workplace, school policy disallows Bart from staying home with Marge, on the premise that homemaking is not real work. When Bart is forced to take ballet, he is mercilessly teased by other boys. Lisa suffers discrimination in military school at the hands of a sergeant who gives her a whistle in lieu of a gun and patronizingly tells her to blow on it if there's a war. Throughout the series, Lisa and Marge's ambitions are repeatedly constrained by the narrow attitudes of others toward females.

Lisa bravely continues, however, to protest undemocratic processes. She is the iconoclast, the social activist, and the crusader against injustice. As in many media portrayals of schooling, students often are more insightful and heroic than the teachers or other adults. When oil is discovered on school property and administrators establish Oil Appreciation Day, Lisa speaks out against corporate propaganda. She confronts the ruthless Mr. Burns on his dumping of toxic waste and disdain for recycling. She writes a school essay decrying corruption in government. A vegetarian, she protests the showing of a school film titled "Meat and You: Partners in Freedom," in which a gullible boy named Jimmy is persuaded that eating meat is healthy, patriotic, and necessary for survival.

Reactions to Lisa's militancy are generally hostile, in part because of the threat that it poses to complacency. When, in another essay, she exposes the town founder Jebediah Springfield as a murderous pirate and fraud, Miss Hoover gives her an F and condemns the paper as "dead White male bashing from a PC thug," preventing women like herself "from landing a husband." Banned from the historical society and ostracized by the townspeople, Lisa bravely pursues her investigation, but ultimately sees that the myth of Jebediah is just as important and "truthful" to the townspeople, so she publicly pronounces him "great" and ends up leading the parade in his honor. Lisa's truth-seeking and social activism are no match for the entrenched beliefs of Springfield society. Teachers, and townspeople in general, do not want change; they like things the way they are and always have been. Lisa, despite her brilliance and courage, is still a child, vulnerable to adult authority, peer pressure, and at times her own immature or knee-jerk impulses. She is a countercultural presence, but is culturally bound.

Social, political, and economic class inequities, then, are prevalent and abiding. Leaving to teach in the projects of Capitol City, Mr. Bergstrom explains to Lisa, "That's the problem of being middle class. Anybody who really cares will abandon you for those who need it more." In general, though, discrepancies between the advantaged and disadvantaged are highlighted, as with students in gifted programs or private schools versus those in remedial programs or the underfunded Springfield Elementary. Class distinctions within the school parallel those outside the school. As Bart incisively points out to Marge in his objection to playing with the dimwitted Ralph, "The social order of elementary school is densely layered."

Case in Point: "Separate Vocations"

One episode in particular, "Separate Vocations," brings together many of the themes we have discussed so far. We would like to focus on it here as a case in point. A brief synopsis follows.

Students take the Career Aptitude Normalizing Test (CANT), and the results indicate that Lisa is best suited to becoming a homemaker. She is distraught; Marge tries to convince her that homemaking can be creative, but she remains unconvinced. She becomes rebellious at school, defying her teacher and falling in with the group of "bad girls." Bart's test results, meanwhile, indicate that he should be a policeman, and he gets to ride along with officers Lou and Eddie to see what the job is like. Later Principal Skinner enlists Bart as a hall monitor, and he both enjoys and abuses his authority, leading Milhouse to lament, "Sure, we have order, but at what price?"

Meanwhile, Lisa becomes even more disaffected and decides to show how little the teachers know by stealing the teachers' editions of the textbooks. The teachers, particularly Miss Hoover, are upset—at a loss for what to do in their classrooms. In desperation, one teacher nervously tries to interact with students, asking them if they want to hear about the 1960s. Skinner has Bart conduct a locker search for the stolen books; when Bart discovers them in Lisa's locker, he talks to her and then takes the blame himself. He is defrocked as hall monitor, given 600 days detention, and required to write repeatedly on the blackboard, "I will not expose the ignorance of the faculty."

Bart and Lisa's reversal of typical roles in this episode provides a catalyst for the satirical humor. As police assistant and hall monitor, Bart becomes the responsible figure, though police officers Lou and Eddie's interests in beer drinking, intimidating suspects, and "hot and cold running chicks," make them less than ideal role models. When Bart asks them if he needs A's in school to become a cop, they laugh uproariously. Lisa's behavior, meanwhile, is even more defiant and disruptive than what we usually see from Bart. When Miss Hoover tells Lisa to put sprinkles on her paste, Lisa retorts, "Shove it!" Later, in a history lesson, when Miss Hoover relies on the answer key in the teacher's edition of the textbook, Lisa remarks sardonically, "Well, you're earning your 18 grand a year." In the end, however, the players reassume their accustomed roles—Lisa as the good and innocent student, Bart as the deviant, and the teachers as indifferent and ignorant. What is appealing here is the understanding and loyalty the siblings show for each other. When Lisa asks Bart why he took the blame, he tells her (much like Mr. Bergstrom did) that she has the ability to do whatever she wants, and he didn't want her to ruin her life. To show her gratitude, Lisa plays the saxophone for Bart outside of his detention room.

We also see further revelations here of Edna Krabappel's and Seymour Skinner's characters. Introducing the aptitude test, Edna informs her students that some of them may discover wonderful occupations, while others may find that life isn't fair: "In spite of your master's from Bryn Mawr, you might end up a glorified babysitter to a bunch of dead-eyed fourth graders while your husband runs naked on a beach with your marriage counselor." Her bitterness is too much to contain. When the bad girls, at Lisa's suggestion, toilet paper and egg the statue of the school mascot, Skinner reacts, "I saw some awful things in 'Nam, but you really have to wonder at the mentality that would desecrate a helpless puma." He concludes that the "no-goodniks" are controlling the school. Of interest here are the ways in which the past experiences of Skinner and Krabappel have caused them to react viscerally to present events; this insight enlists sympathy for them, at the same time poking fun at their obsessions.

The commonplaces of school life are apparent everywhere in this episode; they include testing (note that the agency headquarters is in Proctorville, Iowa), hall monitors, the girls' bathroom, history lessons, the teachers' lounge, disciplinary reports, and the *Daily Fourth Grader,* boasting in its headlines Bart's accomplishment: "Foodfight Foiled/Fishsticks Seized." Especially impressive is the detailing of multiple choice questions on the aptitude test: "If I could be any animal I would be: (a) a carpenter ant, (b) a nurse shark, (c) a lawyer bird." The writers here have ingeniously taken a commonplace of testing format and given it a ludicrous twist, thus revealing the inherent flaws of tests like these in general.

The self-fulfilling prophecy is at work in this episode as well, especially in the occupational roles determined by the aptitude test. The sign at the entrance to the testing agency reads, "Controlling Your Destiny Since 1925." Lou and Eddie are prime examples of this determinism; they are products of the educational system, little different from the prisoners who once sat in the same school desks. In this episode, Lisa expresses her vision of becoming a famous jazz musician, revered in France, and having "several torrid love affairs." When Marge takes her to a music school, however, the teacher there tells her that she cannot become a great musician because she has inherited stubby fingers, probably from her father's side. Again, assumptions about heredity as well as environment have conspired against Lisa's aspirations. Her resistance in this case proves futile; her consolation is the faith that Bart expresses in her intelligence and talent.

Implications

Renee Hobbs (1998) describes her use of *The Simpsons* in conjunction with the works of Mark Twain in her English classes. She sees the two as closely related in their treatment of hypocrisy, greed, stupidity, and self-indulgence. We would agree that the show deserves a place alongside the works of Twain, who, as quoted by biographer Justin Kaplan, described the function of satire as "the deriding of shams, the exposure of pretentious falsities, and the laughing of stupid superstitions out of existence" (Kaplan cited in Hobbs, 1998, p. 50).

When Bart writes "I will not expose the ignorance of the faculty" on the blackboard, he refers explicitly to what *The Simpsons* does. When we witness Edna Krabappel's favoritism, Seymour Skinner's pedestrianism, or Miss Hoover's incompetence, we feel our own superiority and snicker at their limitations while forgetting about our own. At one point, while carrying out yet another devious scheme, Bart momentarily feels sorry for teachers, but then reminds himself that "they're trying to teach." One interpretation, then, is that the depiction of schools and teachers and administrators in the show constitutes an indictment of the profession; there is little to suggest that any meaningful learning is taking place at Springfield Elementary. (We might speculate, then, as to what the writers attribute their own success, if not to the dismal schooling they recall so clearly).

If that negative view were the only representation, we think the show would lose much of what makes it work. There are saving graces: We can sympathize with Edna and Seymour's loneliness; we can hope that Lisa will realize her dreams despite the odds. If we are teachers, we might wince when we see Miss Hoover do something that we have done in some form, or at the unhappy revelation of teachers earning $18,000 per year. Or we might laugh at our memories of ourselves as students like Bart or Lisa or their classmates. But these are, after all, fictional cartoon characters, so we really don't have to identify much with them one way or another. It is the satirical humor that is important, the ways in which the jokes interweave with one another, and the larger meanings suggested by this interweaving. Thus the characters become abstractions; we can laugh at their pretensions and shortcomings while still retaining our faith in teachers and schools.

At the same time, there are implications here for what is wrong with American schooling and what might be corrected. *The Simpsons* takes a sharp look not only at commonplaces of school life, but also at current educational themes and controversies. It offers penetrating commentary, quite different from that which we typically find in academic journals, on such matters as critical thinking, multicultural education, gender bias, business–school relationships, cultural literacy, ability grouping and tracking, school funding and access to resources, private versus public schools, the separation of church and state, and traditional versus progressive approaches to teaching and learning.

In a sense, Springfield gets the worst of it; a truly good education does not exist there—that is the null curriculum. Resources are limited, in part, because the community attaches little value to them. Individuals at times perceptively articulate the problems of the school and community, but are powerless to do much about them; they wander about in a maze with no apparent escape path. They are confined by cultural boundaries and power that resides elsewhere. As Bart says, "the social order ... is densely layered," but rarely to the advantage of Springfield residents.

Nonetheless, there are intimations of hope, much like the bright colors just underneath the drab surface of the school uniforms. This hope lies especially in Bart and Lisa's resistance to conformity and the hint that there are more teachers like Mr. Bergstrom out there who appreciate and encourage students' individuality and creativity and social commitment.

The Simpsons reminds us, though, that educators like Bergstrom are impermanent and that those like Krabappel, Skinner, and Hoover survive. Like Wile E. Coyote in the Roadrunner cartoons, they quickly regain their shape and form and intentions after falling off various cliffs and being crushed by oncoming trains. Matt Groening and the show's writers have brilliantly captured the commonplaces and clichés of school life, as well as the pretensions and shortcomings of teachers, and attack them all with precision and gusto. Despite constant disruptions, the culture of Springfield and its educational system remains intact; the show offers few solutions to educational problems or proposals for change. Its genius lies instead in exaggerating the situations and dilemmas that we all face as teachers and as citizens. The rewards are in the critical insights we gain and the laughter at our all-too-human foibles.

REFERENCES

Groening, M. (1987). *School is hell.* New York: Pantheon.

Groening, M., Richmond, R., & Coffman, A. (1997) *The Simpsons: A complete guide to our favorite family.* New York: HarperCollins.

Hobbs, R. (1998). The Simpsons meet Mark Twain: Analyzing popular media texts in the classroom. *English Journal, 87*(1), 49–51.

Kantor, K. (1994). From Our Miss Brooks to Mr. Moore: Playing their roles in television situations comedies. In P. B. Joseph & G. E. Burnaford (Eds.), *Images of schoolteachers in twentieth-century America: Paragons, polarities, complexities* (pp. 175–189). Hillsdale, NJ: Lawrence Erlbaum Associates.

The Simpsons official web site: http://thesimpsons.com

The Simpsons archive/unofficial web site: http://www.snpp.com

11

A Teacher Ain't Nothin'
but a Hero: Teachers
and Teaching in Film

William Ayers

C urled up in a well-worn seat in a large dark theater, wrapped around a box of stale popcorn, and illuminated by the eerie flicker of moving pictures across a silver screen, I search in shadows for images of teachers and teaching. This is a private screening, a lonely marathon of movie madness, and my mind and body begin to ache. But I am an explorer, I remind myself, and even bruised or battered I must go on. *Blackboard Jungle* blinks off and *Stand and Deliver* starts to roll.

I feel punchy, and I begin to wonder what a visitor from outer space would conclude if the dozen or so films I subject myself to were her only point of reference. Without experience or memory, prior knowledge or teacher autobiography, this visitor would be in an interesting position to help me get beyond my own distorting spaces, to read what the movie makers—these "writers with light"—make of teaching, to see what is actually there.

What is actually there? The movies tell us, to begin with, that schools and teachers are in the business of saving children—saving them from their families, saving them from the purveyors of drugs and violence who are taking over our cities, saving them from themselves, their own pursuits and purposes. The problem is that most teachers are simply not up to the challenge. They are slugs: cynical, inept, backward, naive, hopeless. The occasional good teacher is a saint—he is anointed. His job—and it's always *his* job because the saint-teacher, and most every other teacher in the movies, is a man—is straightforward: He must separate the salvageable students from those who are beyond redemption and he must win them over to a better life, all the while doing battle with his idiot colleagues, the dull-witted administration, and the dangerously backward parents. He is a solitary hero. The saint-teacher's task is urgent because he must figure out who can be saved before it's too late, before the chosen few are sucked irredeemably back into the sewers of their own circumstances. Giving up on some kids is OK, according to the movies, but the bad teachers have already given up on all kids. That's their sin.

Blackboard Jungle

These themes are articulated in a very loud voice in Richard Brooks' 1955 classic, *Blackboard Jungle,* a film that manages to exploit perfectly the tinny patriotism and surface smugness of its era while reflecting and, in a sense, prefiguring the underground conflicts and tensions about to burst to the surface. *Blackboard Jungle* says it all—beginning with its title, it taps into deep racial stereotypes and captures the sense of civilization doing battle with savagery, of white chalk scraping along a black surface. It plays excitedly to all the received wisdom of teaching and schooling, as well as to the wider fears—racial and sexual—of a precarious middle-class. Its portrait of the idealistic teacher struggling to save the delinquent boy with the good heart is imprinted on our collective consciousness—it is a major myth. Much of our cultural common sense, as well as every popular film since, is in a sense derivative. The fact that the police were called in to control violence in theaters across the country when it opened (a first) set a pattern that has also become a cliche.

Blackboard Jungle opens with a straight-laced if disingenuous apology read against a military drumbeat:

> We in the United States are fortunate to have a school system that is a tribute to our communities and to our faith in American youth …. Today we are concerned with juvenile delinquency—its causes—and its effects. We are especially concerned when this delinquency boils over into our schools.
>
> The scenes and incidents depicted here are fictional. However, we believe that public awareness is a first step toward a remedy for any problem. It is in this spirit and with this faith that *Blackboard Jungle* was produced.

But the filmmakers don't mean it. The moment passes and we are thrust into an urban schoolyard where tough-looking youngsters jitterbug and jostle one another to the pounding rhythm of Bill Halley and the Comets' "Rock Around the Clock." It is sexual and chaotic, and the audience is whiplashed, threatened.

Enter Richard Dadier (Glenn Ford), wide-eyed, shy, a young Korean War vet looking for a teaching job. Dadier, to his delight and surprise, is hired quickly, but he turns to the harsh and aloof principle with "just one question: the discipline problem." His voice trails off uncertainly, but the response is loud and clear. "There is no discipline problem—not as long as I'm principal." We are not reassured.

The principal's bravado is mimicked and mocked by the teachers: "There's no discipline problem at Alcatraz either"; "You can't teach a disorderly mob"; "They hire fools like us with college degrees to sit on that garbage can and keep them in school so women for a few hours a day can walk around the city without being attacked." Dadier is awed, but he can't resist the rookie's question, "These kids … they can't *all* be that bad … ?"

Oh no? Opening day is anarchy. The new teachers sit blinking at the barbarians, while the tough assistant principal snarls and cracks the whip. The auditorium pulsates—kids fighting and pushing one another, smoking and shouting. It is a mob scene. When the innocent Miss Hammond is introduced the crowd goes wild, and, with the camera playing on her ass, everyone leers. The film is ambivalent about the attack that follows later: She really shouldn't dress that way, it says, look that way; … but at the same time, these boys are clearly animals—can't they draw the line between wolf whistles and rape? All of Mr. Dadier's students shun him for his heroism in saving Miss Hammond and capturing her attacker.

Mr. Dadier struggles on. He means well, of course, and he cares. Within a certain framework, he even tries. He shows his students a cartoon to accompany his homily on thinking for themselves; he encourages them to see the importance of English if they want to become a carpenter or a mechanic. He encourages Gregory Miller (Sidney Portier), the good delinquent ("a little smarter, a little brighter"), to play piano and to sing in the Christmas show. This is, of course, all part of the Hollywood dream: Blacks sing and dance, aspirations for working class youth are appropriately low, and White liberals are loved for their good intentions. There is no hint that the problems facing these young people include structures of privilege and disadvantage, social class, racism, or the existence of two societies, separate and unequal. In fact, Mr. Dadier tells Miller to get the chip off his shoulder, that racism is "not a good excuse" for failure … "Dr. Ralph Bunche proved that."

Here is a short list of what Mr. Dadier endures: He is mugged and badly cut in an alley by a group of delinquents, his best friend on the faculty has his priceless collection of jazz records smashed up by the kids, he and his pregnant wife are almost killed by youngsters who are drag-racing, he is accused of racial prejudice after attempting to teach the ignorance of "name-calling," and his wife goes into labor prematurely as a result of anonymous notes and phone calls indicating that Miss Hammond and Dadier are having an affair. Dadier bends, but he never breaks; he perseveres. At his lowest point (with a new job offer in hand), his wife reminds him that "kids are people … most people are worthwhile. We all need the same things: patience, love, and understanding." Her list is missing, of course, other possibilities: justice, power, and collective solutions.

Mr. Dadier is wide-eyed much of the time, unable to believe the depths to which humanity can sink. About to give up, he revisits his old professor and seeks advice. It is pure corn. With the "Star Spangled Banner" playing in the background, Dadier watches well-mannered students attending well-run classrooms; he questions how he can teach "kids who don't want to learn," have "IQs of 66," and act like "wild animals." The sage old man reminds him that most people want to be creative, and that

Dadier is called to "sculpt minds" in a school where he is badly needed. "For every school like yours, there are hundred like this. This school could use you; your school needs you." Dadier and the professor join in the last lines of the national anthem, and, as he prepares to leave, Dadier thanks his mentor: "I think I'll take another crack at my jungle."

Back in the jungle, Dadier's efforts are paying off. He works on Miller, urging him to use his influence ("I've been looking at your file, and you're a natural leader") to break the grip of the gangs and especially the power of the disturbed Artie West (Vic Morrow). When West pulls a knife on Dadier, Miller backs his teacher. The tide turns. One student breaks West's knife while another pulls the American flag from its wall brace and knocks West to the ground. West and his gang are finished. Dadier exhorts the whole class to take them to the principal: "There's no place for these two in our classroom." With the bad delinquents gone, the good delinquents can get on the serious business of learning: copying sentences from the board and so on. Miller gets the last word: "Everyone learns something in school ... even the teacher."

Conrack

Fast forward to 1974. In Pat Conroy, the teacher as savior—the "Christ complex"—is fully realized. Based on *The Water is Wide,* the movie *Conrack* (directed by Martin Ritt) is billed as a "true story"—an account of Conroy's 1-year sojourn as a teacher on the Sea Islands off South Carolina in 1969. It is, of course, true in the sense that the later *Lean on Me* or *Stand and Deliver* are true—a few ready-made verities, a handful of simple formulas, a couple of slogans thrown out and passed along. It is a comfortable kind of truth, a painless and uncomplicated romance, and an easy belief.

The film opens with the humane and gentle Pat Conroy (John Voight) waking up in his comfortable and vital home, feeding his fish, birds, and plants, and gathering his belongs to venture across the wide water to awaken his Black brethren on an isolated island off the coast. As the titles roll, they too awaken, but in poverty, simplicity, suspicion, and backwardness. But Conroy is coming: he is the missionary, full of light and love.

False prophets are everywhere. The White superintendent, Mr. Skeffington (Hume Cronyn), who "never accepted Appomattox," preaches that the important things are "order, control, obedience," and urges Conroy to beat the children: "Just milkin' the rat." "Mad Billy" (Paul Winfield) raves about the dangers of White folks. And the dreadful principal, Mrs. Scott, tells Conroy, "You're in a snake-pit, son. Treat your babies tough. Step on them. I know colored people better than you." But, of course, she doesn't. Later she tells him she's "making 'em tough, because it is tough. What do you know about it? You got that thin white skin. I don't have your advantages."

Conroy believes he has a direct line to the light, and he's not listening to blasphemy. He knows better. "We're off the old plantation, Mrs. Scott," he tells her, all shiny and smiling (a model for Bill Clinton, Al Gore, and the "new South" to come). True enough, the plantation days are gone, and, instead of overseers, the field is crowded with self-righteous, self-important, self-anointed professional saints. Pat Conroy, sugary and sweet, is the model.

Conrack reflects the deficiencies created in education with dangerous generalizations; we then compete for resources based on our deprived and degraded condition. The object of everyone's ministrations has no name, simply a condition. Professionals—saints and otherwise—need clients. In fact, professionals turn us into clients—we become defined by our weaknesses, our deficits, and our shortcomings. In *Conrack,* only Conroy has a name. (Although no one is smart enough to even get it right. Mrs. Scott calls him "Mr. Patroy" throughout, and the kids slaughter his name consistently, calling him "Conrack.")

If the indistinguishable mass of youngsters have any name at all, it is "Ignorance." Conroy initially asks the kids what country they live in. Blank stares. "Come on, gang, what's the name of this little red, white, and blue country of ours? Land of the free and home of the brave?" Nothing. "Honey," he turns to one of the girls. "How much is two and two?" There is nothing there. Conroy's heart is breaking as the scene fades.

Here are some of what the kids living on this island don't know: They don't know how to cook or make biscuits, they don't know how to play games of any kind, they don't know how to differentiate foxfire from baby's breath from Queen Anne's lace, they don't know the name of their island, and they don't know how to build a fire or camp out or sing. They've never been in a boat or in the water. It's amazing they can even get up in the morning … they are that backward.

It never occurs to Conroy, of course, to find out if they have their own names for Queen Anne's lace or for their own land. He knows best. So, instead of assuming an intelligence in youngsters, instead of investigating and questioning as a step toward authentic teaching, he launches a campaign of cultural literacy that would make Allan Bloom proud. "Who's the home run king? … Babe Ruth." "Who led the barbarian hordes? … Atilla the Hun." And so on.

Teachers

Next, we jump to 1984 and the film, *Teachers.* Here is the inheritor of *Blackboard Jungle*; the corny sincerity and idealized chivalry of 1955 yield to a kind of hip idealism, but the messages are intact. Take the question of women. In glaring contraction with reality, teachers in the movie are men. The occasional woman teacher is a prop—something to look at or rescue: "Bright kid; great ass," thus the sensitive Alex Jerrel (Nick Nolte) describes one of his favorite former students (Jobeth Williams) in Arthur Hiller's star-studded film. The student is grown-up now, and, being a modern woman, she's got it all—a law degree and a great body. The line back to *Blackboard Jungle* is direct: only this time the hero-teacher can go ahead and fall for her; they can hop in bed and together they can fight for school reform. The hero again rescues a woman in distress; only this time, it is a student (Laura Dern) suffering abuse from a teacher, and the rescue involves a trip to the abortion clinic. The more things change, the more they stay the same.

Or take the question of barbarians at the gate. *Teachers* opens with cops literally unlocking gates and unruly kids swarming into school. Once again, chaos. The principal hides in his office, teachers (one of whom is the school psychologist) go nuts fighting each other over the mimeograph machine, one child sits bleeding in the office waiting for someone to call an ambulance, the union rep is making some inane point to report at 7:35 a.m. and the necessity of holding out until 7:38 a.m., and the assistant principal (Judd Hirsch), desperate for substitutes, tells his secretary to "scrape the bottom of the barrel."

Alex's phone rings. He stirs slowly, hung-over and partied out, picks up the receiver, and is summoned to school. The woman with whom he is sleeping is incensed to discover that he's only a schoolteacher, and dresses hurriedly. This is apparently Alex's life: drinking, carousing, losing women (in one drunken scene he tells a friend that his wife left him because she wanted more than a teacher can provide—"food, clothing, shelter"), and dragging himself to school.

Alex battles a rogue's gallery in the school: a frightened principal, a union hack, incompetent colleagues, mindless bureaucrats, one teacher called "Ditto" who passes out work sheets and sleeps behind his newspaper (dying one day and no one notices), another who appears as a popular and creative history teacher but in fact has recently escaped from a mental hospital, and an old friend (Judd Hirsch) who once shared Alex's zeal but burned out long ago ... ("We are not the bad guys; we do good with what we got").

As in *Blackboard Jungle* where there is "no home life, no church life [and] gangs are taking the place of parents," Alex must do hand-to-hand combat with the putatively pathological parents. At one point, he explodes, "the parents and the system so fucked up this kid that I don't think I can ever reach him!" Moreover, he asks a mother, "Don't you care about your son's education?" She replies, "Isn't that your job, Mr. Jerrel?" Alex's project is Eddie (Ralph Maccio), the bad kid who will come around in spite of the lure of the streets and his parents' indifference ... in spite of the official judgment that he's a lost cause. Only Alex cares and, when he's called crazy, he responds, "I can't help it ... I'm a teacher."

Lean on Me

Connection, connections. *Lean on Me,* the 1987 film—that made Joe Clark, the baseball bat-toting, bullhorn-exhorting, real-life principal of Eastside High in Paterson, New Jersey, the most famous principal in the world—opens to the pounding hard-rock rhythms of Guns 'n Roses' "Welcome to the Jungle." Again, the montage of open drug deals, teachers being assaulted, a woman's clothes being ripped from her body. Again, the barbarians at the gate. Again our hero saving kids from their parents ("Why don't you get off welfare? Why don't you help your kids with their homework?"). And again, we see Morgan Freedman—in *Teachers* he was a toady lawyer for the superintendent; here he is the strutting "Saint Joe."

Joe Clark harangues, batters, and bullies everyone around him ... but for a purpose. Clark cares in his megalomaniacal way. He tells the kids that the larger society believes they are failures—"a bunch of niggers and spicks and poor White trash"—but that society is wrong. "You are not inferior," he insists. And this is his appeal. When Joe Clark says, "If you do not succeed in life—I don't want you to blame yours parents, I don't want you to blame the White man ... I want you to blame yourselves," it resonates quite the opposite from Richard Dadier's invocation of Ralph Bunche. One hopes at this point that Clark is going to organize the youngsters to overthrow the system that perpetuates their oppression or that he will at least find some way to unleash their energy and intelligence; alas, he urges them to do a better job on the standardized tests.

Clark begins his tenure with the famous event that frames his career. He assembles "every hoodlum, drug dealer, and miscreant" on the stage of the auditorium and, in front of the whole school, expels the bunch. "These people are incorrigible," he shouts above the din. "You are all expurgated, you are dismissed, you are out of here forever." He turns then to the remaining students: "Next time it may be you. If you do no better than them it will be you." It's dramatic—an attention-getter. However, the drama is repeated one way or another in every popular film on teaching.

Joe Clark is at war—"a way to save 2700 other students." He's in the trenches, on the front lines, fighting man to man to save the good ones. He doesn't want to hear about the miscreants; let them go to hell, let the liberals bleed for them. The film ends with his vindication: The school retains its accreditation because the kids pass a basic skills test. In the final analysis, we never really learn how many kids drop out before graduation, and how many more are pushed out by the principal. The message seems to be we can believe in some kids, but the rest are indeed trash. Say it isn't so, Joe.

Stand and Deliver

Stand and Deliver (1988) is "based on a true story," too, this time the story of Jaime Escalante (Edward James Olmos), the renowned math teacher from Garfield High School in Los Angeles. Escalante battles the ghetto, the gangs, and the low expectations. He teaches pride—we get glimpses of the Che Guevara mural and of graffiti proclaiming "Not a Minority," and we hear him tell his students that "your ancestors, the Mayans, contemplated zero ... math is in your blood." He also teaches *ganas*—desire. "You already have two strikes," he says, "Your name and your complexion .... Math is the great equalizer .... I don't want to hear your problems. If you have *ganas,* you can succeed."

Escalante chases the bad delinquents away, humiliates them, and drives them from his class. Angel (Lou Diamond Phillips) is the good delinquent to be saved. Escalante gives him a set of books to keep at home so his gang-banger pals won't know he's studying. Angel cares for his sick grandmother who has no idea of the importance of school to him. Other parents are worse: One student has to stop studying when her mother comes home from work, another is pulled from school to become a waitress in the family-owned restaurant, and a third is told by her mom that "guys don't like it if you're too smart."

Escalante fights the parents' ignorance and he aims to turn the school around. His strategy is "to start at the top." (Perhaps the trickle-down theme of social progress is one reason the Reagan–Bush administrations, 1981–1993, embraced this film so whole-heatedly.) He wants to teach advanced placement calculus. The principal laughs and the chair of the math department scoffs, "Our kids can't handle calculus." But they can and they do, and Escalante practically kills himself making it true.

Unlike Joe Clark whose wife divorced him, Escalante's obsession is dutifully tolerated at home. Escalante works 60 hours a week, teaches ESL at night, and never takes a vacation. Like all the saint-teachers, he has no life … he is never learning something new, coaching little league, making art, and pursuing political projects. He doesn't need to reflect or consider or weight or wonder—he is living an irrational life with a powerful pull. He is sacrificing himself for his students alone. Whereas Clark casts himself as crucified for his commitment, Escalante is downed by a heart attack only to rise again on behalf of inspiring his students to win their confrontation with the test.

Discussion

From *Blackboard Jungle* to *Stand and Deliver,* these popular teacher films are entirely comfortable with a specific common stance on teaching. This stance includes the wisdom that teaching can occur only after discipline is established, that teaching proceeds in stages: first, get order; then, deliver the curriculum. The curriculum is assumed to be stable and good—it is immutable and unproblematic; it is disconnected (but important) bits and pieces of information. The movies assume that anyone with any sense would agree, and so they toss off the familiar phrases, and we can add ones of our own: Don't turn your back on the class; don't smile until Christmas; if you can't control them—you can't teach them; establish authority early; and survival in the trenches requires good classroom control. And so on. Everyone believes it—experienced teachers mimic it—and so beginning teachers grasp for anything that will help them with "classroom management," the assumed first principle of teaching.

The only problem with this prime piece of received wisdom is that it is not true. In fact, real learning requires assertion not obedience, action not passivity. It is an intimate act, an ambiguous and unpredictable act. It is deeply human. Teaching demands some connection between the knowledge, experiences, and aspirations of students, and deeper and wider ways of knowing. Teaching is intellectual work—puzzling and difficult—and at its heart it is ethical work. It is idiosyncratic, improvisational, and most of all relational. All attempts to reduce teaching and learning to a formula, to something easily predictable, degrade it immeasurably.

Concerns about classroom management must be reconsidered in light of concerns about curriculum—about what knowledge and experiences are of most value—as well as concerns about students as whole people with their own minds, bodies, feelings, spirits, hopes, and dreams. This is a complex process and it involves our learning how to see beyond the blizzard of labels and stereotypes—how to embrace students as dynamic beings and fellow creatures. It requires building bridges from the known to the not-yet-known. In addition, it demands liberating schooling from its single-minded obsession with control, obedience, hierarchy—and everyone's place in it. Alas, the movies are of no help in this regard. On the contrary, the ready-made clichés and empty repetitions feed our collective powerlessness and manage our mindless acquiescence.

Common sense can be more dogmatic than any political party, more totalizing than any religious sect—it is insistent in its resistance to contradiction or even complexity. It wants to be taken on faith—there isn't room for either reflection or objection. Take it or leave it. Films on teaching fall into step ... they are all about common sense and they immunize against a language of possibility—for students, teachers, parents, and the public.

Becoming an outstanding teacher is exceedingly difficult work. The first step is a commitment to teach all children, regardless of condition or circumstance. Movie-star teachers make no such commitment. They are invested in some youngsters and willing to drive away many more. A second step is to find common cause with youngsters, their families, and their communities. Again, movie teachers despise families and can barely tolerate communities. The common wisdom is that children of the poor are lost in islands of nothingness and that school will lead them into the human family. In many real life schools, nothing about the presence of poor youngsters—and especially African American youngsters—is considered valuable or important; their presence is conceived as a problem, an encumbrance, a deficit, an obstacle. Contempt, fear, and condescension are not a strong foundation for real teaching.

Outstanding teachers need to question the common sense—to break the rules, to become political and activist in concert with the kids. This is true heroism, an authentic act of courage. We need to take seriously the experiences of youngsters, their sense making, their knowledge, and their dreams; and particularly we must interrogate the structures that kids are rejecting. In other words, we must assume an intelligence in youngsters, assume that they are acting sensibly and making meaning in situations that are difficult and often dreadful—and certainly, not of their own making. In finding common cause with youngsters, we may also find there our own salvation as teachers.

NOTE

Thanks to Zayd Dohrn, Lamya Khalidi, Craig Segal, and Yolanda Wilson for sneaking into the movies with me.

12

Teachers as Saviors,
Teachers Who Care

Robert Lowe

angerous Minds was a major box office attraction that failed to win over film critics. They viewed it as a predictable, trite, saccharine, credulity defying retread of movies that showcase a teacher confronting the educational problems of urban children (see Maslin, 1995; Wilmington, 1995). In contrast, *High School II,* Frederick Wiseman's film of East Harlem's Central Park East Secondary School (CPESS), won plaudits for the director, the school itself, and for Deborah Meier, the school's founder and perhaps the most renowned educational reformer in the United States today (see Bromwich, 1994; James, 1994; Matthews, 1994). These contrasting reviews are hardly remarkable, given the different genres the films represent. One is a Hollywood confection successfully designed to reach a large audience. The other, a PBS-aired documentary by a distinguished filmmaker, is stripped of viewer-friendly conventions. Without narrator, music, or a focus on the dramatic, it sets down nearly 4 hours of footage that captures the interactions between teachers and students.

Yet there are similarities between the two films that go beyond matters of educating urban children. Each, for instance, is closely tied to a book. *Dangerous Minds* is based on *My Posse Don't Do Homework* (1993), LouAnne Johnson's narrative of her teaching experience, and Deborah Meier's (1995) *The Power of Their Ideas* explicates the work of CPESS. More important, both films depict White educators who are dedicated to working with children of color. If this were standard practice for White people, there would be little interest in films that portray such a dynamic. Instead, White educators too often question the intellectual capacities of such children and write them off.

On the face of it, then, these films appear to offer White teachers models to emulate that might advance the project of racial justice. Yet how the work of these educators is framed can either support a vision of racial equality or justify White supremacy. This essay views the latter as the dominant message. It will contend that *Dangerous Minds* is a blatantly racist film that counterpoises LouAnne Johnson's commitment to educating her students to African-American adults' indifference or even hostility to this effort, and, more controversially, it will argue that the text of *High School II* captures a subtle racism within CPESS that appears to stem from a failure to question the power relationship between the school's White leaders on one hand and students and parents of color on the other. In both films, the construction of White teacher-heroes depends on distorting or silencing the voices of African Americans and Latinos. Ironically, the essay will maintain, the sometimes repugnant *Dangerous Minds* partly subverts the dominant framework by evoking a strong ethos of caring that appears to be largely absent from the sophisticated but sterile practice revealed in *High School II*.

Trials of a White Hero

The opening footage of *Dangerous Minds* captures in black and white a scene of early-morning urban desolation and desperation. Students board buses in this hopeless-looking environment and when they arrive at LouAnne Johnson's school in the sunny suburbs, the film turns to color. The point of debarkation bears no resemblance to the real East Palo Alto, California, where many of Johnson's African-American and Latino students lived. Though economically stressed, it is physically beautiful and maintains the semi-rural feel of the utopian farming community it once was. Dramatically speaking, however, the racially suggestive play of dark and light over urban wasteland and lush suburb prepares the viewer to identify with LouAnne Johnson and the teaching challenge she will face.

In perfect keeping with such imagery, this refined White woman, a novice teacher played by Michelle Pfeiffer, meets an out-of-control class of color that has driven away her predecessors. A candidate for the same fate, Johnson succumbs to taunts on her first day, fleeing the room minutes after the class begins. That night she strategizes, considering and then rejecting as absurd the assertive discipline technique of writing down students' names who misbehave. Instead, she chooses to pose tough, telling the students she was a marine and offering to teach them karate moves. This captures the students' attention, and, with the exception of the Black males in the class who consistently are portrayed as clowns or borderline thugs, the students quickly become attractive individuals whom Johnson encourages to perform by offering them extrinsic rewards like candy, a trip to an amusement park, and dinner at an elegant restaurant. Many fine teachers offer similar bribes, but Johnson does not have a very sophisticated sense of pedagogy to counterbalance the crudeness of this sort of incentive to achieve. What she does academically is sketchy, however. There is some conjugation of verbs, some Bob Dylan poetry, and later some Dylan Thomas, but there is little evidence of probing discussion, serious writing, or literature that ties into the cultures of her students.

Yet what Johnson does is a far cry from the transmission of inert information. She teaches her own passions, which happen to include Dylan's lyrics, and, though these are distant from cultural expressions of her students, it is perfectly plausible that her emotional connection with the words and cadences of Dylan's songs will be infectious and a legitimate way of evoking an understanding of metaphorical language. She also at times connects her preferred literature to themes that resonate to the experience of her students. Furthermore, as the movie progresses, Johnson relies less on extrinsic rewards, more on the intrinsic value of learning. At one point when a student asks what the prize will be for making sense of a poem, she responds, "Knowing how to read something and understand is the prize. Knowing how to think is the prize." She continues in this vein, identifying ideas with power in much the same way the Deborah Meier talks about the power of ideas at the end of *High School II.*

Whatever its limitations, it is not the curriculum that makes the film offensive educationally, but adult interactions that conspire to portray LouAnne Johnson as the only caring educator in the school. The ones who do not care include the pinched looking assistant principal who tosses an underprepared Johnson to the students who have devoured their previous teachers, and they include Hal, her closest (and apparently only) colleague, whose cynicism suggests an idealistic teacher gone sour.

Although both these characters are White, an absence of caring is not identified as a characteristic of White people in general, but it is identified with African Americans. The two Black adults in the film are portrayed as the greatest obstacles to Johnson's efforts to teach her students effectively. One is a parent. When Johnson visits her house, concerned about the weeklong absences of her two sons, this woman refuses to shake Johnson's hand and says, "You're that white-bread bitch messing with my babies' minds. My boys don't go to your school no more and that's going to be it ... I saw what they were bringing home, poetry and shit, a waste of time." To Johnson's suggestion that graduating from high school would be an advantage for the young men, she replies, "That's not in their future. I ain't raising no doctors and lawyers here." This bizarre inversion of African Americans' perennial struggles for educational access and equity casts the sole "militant" Black person in the movie as someone who appears to be more militantly against education itself than hostile to the educational orientation of a White teacher (see Anderson, 1988; Lowe & Kantor, 1995).

An equally unfortunate portrayal is that of the African-American principal, Mr. Grandey. He fits the too-familiar stereotype of Black male as cardboard martinet. When Johnson wants to jettison *My Darling My Hamburger* as too infantile a novel for the students, Grandey objects, telling her she must teach the approved curriculum. Grandey's commitment to rules rather than students comes through most forcefully in the way he treats Emilio, the class rebel whose intellectual gifts Johnson has helped tease out. In mortal danger, Emilio musters the courage to enter

Grandey's office to ask for help, but the principal summarily dismisses him for failing to knock before entering. Emilio's murder ineluctably follows, and Grandey's callousness is responsible.

These blatantly racist representations are not present in *My Posse Don't Do Homework*. The African-American mother simply does not exist, and Mr. Grandey (Mr. Grady in the book) is more humane. He appears to be somewhat stiff and rule bound, but allows Johnson to bend the rules when doing so could help a student. Thus, he permits her to keep a student who officially faces mandatory expulsion. In addition, the conflict between Johnson and him over requiring *My Darling My Hamburger* does not occur. In fact, it was Johnson who introduced the book to a class that considered it too juvenile, and consequently her students chose a work by Shakespeare instead. Furthermore, the episode in the movie when Grandey refuses entry to Emilio does not take place in the book, and Emilio does not die.

Unlike the book, the film version of Johnson's experience panders to the stereotype of Black men in authority by portraying Mr. Grandey as an unfeeling disciplinarian. For good measure, it plays to the stereotype of uncaring Black parents by inventing an African-American mother who has no regard for the education of her children. The viewer is invited to feel contempt for characters that represent Black leaders and Black parents. These obdurate figures serve as foils for Johnson who quite alone and through heroic effort must save her class that mostly comprises African-American and Latino students.[1] *Dangerous Minds,* then, conveys the message that only heroes are capable of educating children of color, that these heroes are properly White, and that they must battle against reactionary African-American parents and educators to rescue their students. In the world the film creates, educational change cannot take place beyond the good things that can happen in the isolated classroom of a White teacher.

An Innovative School

In a number of respects, *High School II* presents a more optimistic vision of educational possibilities for those who have been poorly served by schooling in the United States. While the opening frames of *Dangerous Minds* stress the neediness of students' home environment in order to help set up LouAnne Johnson as their hero, *High School II* begins by presenting a vista of East Harlem on a sunlit morning that banishes thoughts of dire living conditions. CPESS appears to be housed in a structure as plain as the buildings that surround it, save for the brightly painted student work on the entrance that hints at transforming educational practices within. The film proceeds to capture scenes from CPESS, a highly praised model of educational reform, which show a staff that is unified behind a commitment to the intellectual development of students. Before graduating, students are expected to be accomplished in exercising five habits of mind, which co-director Paul Schwarz lists early in the film. They include understanding the perspective through which a subject is being presented, examining the evidence that undergirds a position, recognizing the interconnectedness of knowledge, speculating on how things might have been different, and contemplating why an inquiry matters.[2] These generic elements of intellectual engagement are far too infrequently called upon in college-level work, let alone in most high schools.

What takes place in scenes from classrooms predictably often falls short of these goals. In a seminar on *King Lear* that turns to a discussion of different types of love, it is obvious that most of the students have read the play, but the teacher cannot elicit much thinking of any sort on the part of students. Often the nature of teachers' questions appears to shape the extent to which students' thinking is released. Thus, on the one hand, perhaps the best work is being done by a science teacher whose questioning guides a student in accurately projecting what percentage of fruit flies will have vestigial wings under different circumstances. It is clear that he is really learning something about genetics. On the other hand, a student is completely stumped by the requirement that she produce a thesis statement for an essay. The teacher patiently explains what a thesis statement is, but the real problem, I think, is that the student, understandably, has no convictions about and no access to ways of thinking about the question that was to prompt her thesis: "How and why do law and morality affect changes in each other?" Elsewhere opinions are offered and teachers probe for evidence, but the disciplined inquiry proposed by the habits of mind is rarely evident.

Whatever the gap between intellectual vision and practice, however, the lecturing and rote learning that typify instruction in most high schools are absent, and the school is organized to promote engagement. In fact, the configurations of staff members and students look downright unfamiliar, unschool-like. By using space in ways that suggest elements of both kindergarten and graduate school, CPESS defies our sense of a "real" high school, an institution that has been notably resistant to waves of progressive educational reform that have sought to make schooling more student-centered.[3]

Rather than the large body of students LouAnne Johnson and most other high school teachers face and must often treat as an undifferentiated mass, students stand out individually at CPESS. In much of the film, for instance, there is no evidence of traditional classes taking place. Students either work independently or interact with teachers individually or in small groups. In counseling sessions, students typically are outnumbered by the staff members present. The work of the school also reflects this focus on the individual. Instead of completing paper-and-pencil tests for passing grades required to graduate, each student is expected to complete a number of exhibitions that demonstrate in-depth knowledge and presumably showcase their acquisition of the habits of mind. At the beginning of the film, a student engages in one such exhibition, acquitting himself fairly well in an attempt to argue from a socialist perspective that class is a far more meaningful social category than race. In this exercise, three adults are present to probe the understanding of a single student.

Meier (1995) explains in *The Power of Their Ideas* how the school is able to maximize contact with students. Part of this explanation is purely logistical. The school is small, and most teachers are expected to teach two subjects to the same group of students, allowing interdisciplinary classes that effectively halve the number of students they otherwise would teach. In harmony with the perspective of the Coalition of Effective Schools, of which CPESS is a vital part, course offerings are limited, as depth rather than breadth is emphasized, and blocks of time for the courses exceed those of conventional schools. In addition, all staff members work with students in counseling/tutorial sessions, bringing the teacher–student ratio down to 1 to 15 for such activities. Organizing the work of the school differently from conventional public schools is not the whole story, however. Teachers are committed to the mission of the schools, choose their own colleagues (a privilege typically denied by union contracts), and clearly are willing to work unusually hard.[4]

Setting up the school to maximize contact between faculty and students can facilitate positive relations between the two. Meier (1995), for instance, writes eloquently of caring and compassion (p. 63), and, by refusing to let students slip through the cracks and demanding that they perform, the teachers at CPESS demonstrate that they care more than teachers who forgive poor performance because of children's unfortunate life circumstances. The opportunity to know students well also pays off in a remarkable scene from the film where an English instructor is helping students with essays. She is addressing one student whose face is almost completely hidden in the crook of his arm. Somehow the teacher resists the impulse to scold him—hardly easy under normal circumstances, but particularly tough given the presence of a camera that records this apparent lack of respect for her and her lack of control over his behavior. It ultimately becomes obvious, however, that the student is paying close, if unconventional, attention, and that a reprimand from the teacher would likely have broken their connection. Here an understanding of a student's idiosyncratic behavior and an ethos of caring enable the teacher to avoid a disruption of teaching and learning that would result from mistaking form for substance. Unfortunately, this moment in the film is exceptional. Though the vessels for positive interactions are in place, the exchanges that fill them at times suggest that the anonymity of conventional high schools has its solaces. This is particularly the case in counseling sessions led by either of the co-directors.

Meier (1995) writes that "new students often find so many caring adults a nuisance—'in my face,' as they say" (p. 32). But the "in your faceness" of the staff often seems less about caring and more about control or surveillance of students who implicitly are viewed as a danger to the smooth running of the institution. Meier, who like co-director Paul Schwarz can properly be seen as a lead teacher in the original sense of "principal," first appears some 30 minutes into the film. Indistinguishable from the other teachers in attire, occupying no authority-conferring space, and referred to on the same first-name basis as the other adults, she is part of a group of four White staff members meeting with a Latina student who recently had a baby.

The student is accompanied by her brother, who also goes to CPESS, and her mother. Meier seems remarkably different from the author who writes so persuasively of caring and of knowing the students well. Her voice lacks warmth; her introductory chitchat appears forced; and she seems to know little about the new mother and her brother. She wrongly guesses the gender of the baby, for example, and, after being corrected, she repeats the error. Her questioning suggests that she is not so much interested in how to support the sister and brother, but how to avoid disruption. She is quite concerned that the brother might get into a physical confrontation, most likely with Frankie, the child's father, who is a student at CPESS as well. The brother quite convincingly maintains that Frankie is not completely to blame, and, if trouble did begin, he would try to avoid it. Nonetheless, Meier continues to press the brother for assurances.

It does not occur to Meier and the other staff members to ask him how they might help him cope with the situation. An absence of support, however, is more glaring in the case of the teenage mother (whose name nobody mentions). Although she makes it clear that she wants to continue at CPESS, Meier not only offers her no real encouragement to do so, but also suggests she might be better off transferring to a school where students can bring their children. The student's mother responds by saying that she will take care of the baby during the day, but Meier again raises the possibility of a transfer.

Whose Power? Whose Ideas?

There was no overt racism in the way Meier treated the Latino family, but there was a distinct absence of caring and compassion, and there was a concern with security that may have been heightened by racial assumption about the students' volatility. In this and other situations, the existence of a pervasive, if subtle, racism may account for the somewhat claustrophobic, faintly punitive, and totally humorless feel of the school. The case for racism starts from the assumption that this is a tendency among White people in a society where persistent racial inequality is a defining feature. Confronting racism, then, becomes a necessary counterweight to such a tendency. This especially is the case in a staff-controlled school like CPESS whose co-directors and majority of faculty are White, and whose governance structure yields no authority to parents who mostly are not White. Yet like the student exhibition mentioned in the last section that trivializes race in understanding how society is organized, matters of race simply are not taken seriously in the practices of the school the film recorded.

Accordingly, much of the curriculum, like that of LouAnne Johnson's, appears to be at significant remove from the voices, experiences, and struggles of the majority of students. Only one work by a person of color is discussed—Lorraine Hansberry's *A Raisin in the Sun*. Moreover, the part of that discussion the film captures considers the American dream without any reference to race. Another sign that race is inadequately addressed is Meier's reluctance to support a student demonstration in the aftermath of the Rodney King verdict because she questions its educational value. Here her habits of mind—assuming that is what she means by educational—have no more vitality than worksheets, and they discredit a passionate response to racial injustice by shrinking the King case into an academic exercise. Ironically, in the entire film the most eloquent, thoughtful discourse by students takes place when two of them debate how best to protest the acquittals of the cops who had beaten King.

What appears to be a conviction that race does not matter is communicated on a more personal level when co-director Paul Schwarz, accompanied by another colleague, conducts what is more an interrogation session than a counseling meeting with an African-American student and his mother. Schwarz begins the session by stating that "It's a high school that works best for those people who really want to be here." Then he quickly becomes accusatory when he asks the student, "Do you see this as a White school, as a school run by White people? Would it be different for you if more teachers were Black or Latino?" Cowed a bit by the proceedings the student rather meekly agrees and says he thinks he would be more likely to respect Black teachers. This could be an opportunity for the two White staff members to uncover through careful questioning why the student feels the way he does, and this line of inquiry might enable them to help the student cope better, or it might even lead to changes in the school. But Schwarz clearly is not interested in what the student has to say or why he says it. Rather than giving him the opportunity to express himself fully, Schwarz retorts, "I disagree." Since Schwarz cannot be disagreeing that the school is run by White people, he must be saying that this fact makes no difference. The student has been effectively silenced. His mother, like all the parents who are present in the film, supports the position of the staff.

Perhaps she is speaking from the heart, but the power relations evident here would have made dissent difficult. Meier (1995) asserts in her book that "kids and parents show up at family conferences to complain about things to our faces and risk the necessary confrontations" (p. 58). This does not take place, however, in any of the conferences captured by the film. Rather, the dynamics of these conferences suggest that it would take exceptional courage to risk those confrontations since staff members are unwilling to listen to the students.[5] Furthermore, the White staff dominate all these sessions but one. The insistent message that the school belongs to the White educators who unequivocally know what is best for students is hardly likely to encourage overt disagreement from students and their parents.

Meier most likely would reject this characterization of the social relations of the school. She takes pride in the democratic deliberation among faculty members that students have the opportunity to witness and model. She writes, "The deep immersion in a value system that places mutual respect first and encourages a climate of diversity and disagreement becomes enormously powerful over time, and not just for the staff. The kids know we're serious" (Meier, 1995, pp. 58–59). Even if rich democratic discourse does take place among the faculty, however, the film nonetheless conveys a sense that "the power of their ideas" should properly refer to ideas of a predominantly White staff who unself-consciously exercise power over the, mostly, students and parents of color.[6]

Certainly the selection of scenes Wiseman included in the film might distort the way CPESS deals with matters of race, and these scenes are open to interpretations quite different from my own. Yet Meier's (1995) comments on race in *The Power of Their Ideas* tend to confirm a failure to come to terms with the matter. For instance, she states:

> We know that the school's pedagogy doesn't always rest easily with parents, some of whom wonder if we're not creating difficulties for children already handicapped by racism or poverty. We're not always going to be convincing but we need to provide evidence that where we disagree we do so respectfully, that we're not out to frustrate the aspirations parents have for their kids, or to blame them for what goes wrong .... At their best, family and school are allies, however cautiously, but the kid is the performer. (p. 52)

Meier, it appears, is referring to the concern of many parents that a progressive approach to education might not require students to master necessary content and skills (see Delpit, 1986). She is suggesting, however, that there is no problem with the school's pedagogy, but merely with parents' understanding of it. Teachers should try to convince the parents that they are right, but whether or not they succeed, parents have no standing to challenge the teachers' approach to education. Here is a notion of a good school based on the faculty's pedagogy. It is a notion quite different from the good school that derives its reputation from community support. Vanessa Siddle Walker (1993), for instance, writes about the good segregated school in the pre-Brown era. She emphasizes the seamless relationship between the Caswell County Training School and the surrounding community, maintaining that the school incarnated the aspirations of Black parents. Meier, in contrast, assumes an opposition between school and community where families at best are allies and where the school merely tries not to frustrate the aspirations of parents. This perspective has colonial implications since the school derives its legitimacy not from the values of parents of color, but from the pedagogy of White educators.[7] Meier, however, does not appear to see the disenfranchisement of parents as evidence that racial inequality is woven inextricably into the skein of the school.

Meier (1995) does allow that "The gap between the racial, ethnic, and class histories of the school' staff is often substantial .... It's a gap we cannot bridge by good intentions alone" (pp. 51–52). But shortly after, she states: "We can't do away with the likelihood that some of our students' families see White teachers as inherently suspect, but White teachers can reconsider our own reactions, offer alternative possibilities, and challenge some implicit assumptions" (p. 52). Again, the staff bears no responsibility for the race and class gap, but rather the gap appears to be created by the inappropriately suspicious attitudes of families. The burden on the staff, then, is not to address its own classism and racism in order to better serve students and their families, but to try to convince the families that their suspicions are ill informed.

Several pages later Meier (1995) appears to be moving toward real self-examination around race matters. She states:

> Unresolved also is our effort to deal with racism .... We must deal with the issue over and over if we are to help kids who desperately need to be able to talk with adults about such difficult matters, and must do so before we have "solved" them. We need to take chances even though making mis-

takes can be dangerous. We've called in outside experts on racism as well as experts on group relations to work with us on both a regular basis and in times of crisis, when these issues seemed likely to split us apart. (pp. 57–58)

But then she pulls back: "A bitter charge by some parents that a White teacher was not only a racist but out to injure children of color, and the overtones of anti-Semitism that went with it, didn't produce the same instinctive response in all of us. We didn't reach a consensus, except on how to get through it safely" (p. 58). Although Meier tries to take racism seriously, she never really acknowledges that it exists within the school, and she essentially dismisses the parents' conviction that a teacher is racist by merely calling their charge "bitter" and by saying it carried "overtones of anti-Semitism." Whatever the merits of the parents' charge, it is the predominantly White staff who get to define racism, and it is they who get through the matter safely. How safe the parents felt is left unrecorded.

Meier's thinking about race seems to have evolved little since she taught in Harlem in the late 1960s. She then wrote about attending a meeting with 100 African-American and Latino parents who were angry about the teachers and the schools: "Vengefulness and suspicious fury had dulled their ability to distinguish targets. Anything said against schools was guaranteed to produce enthusiastic anger. Speaker after speaker expanded on how the teachers destroyed children, and the audience cheered, stomped and shouted 'You tell 'em!'" (Meier, 1968, p. 131). Though she never specified who or what she thought was the appropriate target, she apparently believed that these parents—and the whole community control effort—were irrational if not hysterical in their criticism of innocent teachers. Furthermore, in talking about her support for the strike of the United Federation of Teachers (UFT) the previous spring, she made it clear that parents of color had no idea what was best for their children: "While I wholeheartedly supported the UFT and felt proud of the teachers for going out on non-wage demands, their position seemed impossible to communicate to the people who most needed just what the UFT was demanding" (Meier, 1968, p. 134).

As troubling as Meier's writing about race is, she certainly does not subscribe to either the notion that African-American and Latino children cannot benefit from an academic curriculum or that it would be unfair to place strenuous demands on children because their lives already are difficult. At CPESS, students are expected to learn, and teachers rightly do not countenance excuses from children for not applying themselves. Yet a school where the predominantly White staff rules and somehow views itself as unmarked by societal racism denies itself the opportunity to be educated by children and their families in ways that could close the class, race, and ethnic gaps that Meier acknowledges, and this denial is likely to inhibit the forging of the genuine community that Meier values. Certainly, data that document the impressive graduation rates and low dropout rates of CPESS students have been disseminated widely. Although I do not question these numbers, my analysis invites questions about how self-selection may influence the successes of the school, what part of themselves students may have to give up in order to participate in the community at CPESS, and how many students survive but do not thrive because they are unwilling to assimilate to the institution.

Who Cares?

The imaginative ways CPESS augments contact between staff and students at times appear in *High School II* to maximize control rather than closeness, to suggest more Jeremy Bentham's panopticon than a caring community. In contrast, *Dangerous Minds* depicts the development of a very warm connection between LouAnne Johnson and her students. Pedagogically unsophisticated and ignorant of her students' cultures—though her Spanish is deployed to good effect—she nonetheless cares about her students in a way that superior teachers do in real schools. Johnson appears to operate from the heart, and this may serve her better than pedagogical knowledge. The infectious warmth Johnson exudes in part manifests itself in physical contact with students, something that occurs only once in all of *High School II.* In *My Posse Don't Do Homework,* Johnson (1993) notes that such behavior violates proper decorum for high school teachers:

> "Never touch a student" was one of the first rules I'd learned as a high school teacher. It's a good rule and a sensible one, too, because it presents legal complications, personal confrontations, and inappropriate familiarity between students and staff. But it was a rule I couldn't follow, and breaking it was one of the best things I ever did as a teacher. (p. 141)

Johnson's warmth contrasts with the mere pleasantness of most teachers at CPESS and the coolness of their leaders.

Johnson also expresses regard for students by addressing problems in strikingly different ways from the staff of CPESS. As noted previously, Paul Schwarz dismissed a student's concerns with the racial makeup of the staff and made it clear that it was up to the student to adjust to the school. In contrast to this oppositional approach to students, LouAnne Johnson, in both the film and her book, found ways of expressing her solidarity with students and their parents, even when students' behavior had been disruptive. When Raul had been suspended for fighting, for instance, Johnson visited his home, but she did not offer the litany of wrongdoings expected by both Raul and his parents. Instead she said to his parents, "I just wanted to tell you personally what a pleasure it's been having Raul in my class this semester. You must be very proud. He's very bright, funny, articulate. The truth is he's one of my favorites." This simple but surprising act solidified bonds between student and teacher, parents and child, and family and school in a way that was far more likely to spur Raul's academic achievement than admonishments.[8]

Another example of Johnson's support for students involved a situation more directly analogous to what took place at CPESS. With less subtlety than Meier's suggestion that the teenage parent transfer out of CPESS, the administration at Johnson's Parkmont High School pressured Callie, perhaps Johnson's brightest student, to transfer out when she became pregnant.[9] Recognizing that a transfer could limit Callie's chances for academic success, Johnson intervened in her behalf. In contrast to the leader of CPESS and the administration at Parkmont, Johnson put the interests of the student before the convenience of the school.

Unlike Meier, who had a formidable influence on the curriculum of CPESS, LouAnne Johnson acknowledged in her book that she followed an unimaginative, mandated curriculum:

> When the students truly believed that I liked them just as they were, it was no longer Teacher versus Students. It became Teacher and Students versus Curriculum. Together, we hated vocabulary exercises, grammar exams, reading proficiency tests, and spelling quizzes, but we had to do them. Teaching was the best thing I had ever done in my life. Before I knew it June raced around the corner and crashed into the classroom, spinning all my students out into the summer sun. (1993, p. 68)

Viewing the curriculum as an enemy that must be fought rather than transformed is not likely to inspire the highest level of intellectual engagement. Yet what perhaps mattered much more than the content of the curriculum was the solidarity between teacher and student, the conviction that kids could succeed academically, and the understanding, articulated by Meier as well, that caring meant not letting students off lightly.

In *My Posse Don't Do Homework,* Johnson (1993) considers shortening an assignment and decides against it: "I loved them too much to make it easy on them" (p. 258). Even Meier (1995) considered the proposition that the success of students at CPESS was not so much grounded in pedagogy as in the creation of a caring environment for kids: "Maybe our success is not related to our highly praised curriculum or pedagogy but to creating an intensely personal and stable place that's always there for kids" (p. 177). Yet that personal dimension often comes across as carping rather than caring in *High School II,* a film that tells us much more about pedagogy and school organization than matters of the heart.

As important as caring is to good teaching, unilateral caring is unsustainable. *Dangerous Minds* conveys a sense that Johnson has genuine feelings for her students by showing that they reciprocate. She is not merely sacrificing the possibility of a personal life for the sake of the kids. The kids care back and keep her from resigning at the end of the year. When her friend Hal asks why she decided to return, Johnson, who had previously given her students sweets and helped them discover the Dylan Thomas passage, "You've got to rage against the dying of the light," replied, "They gave me candy and called me the light."[10] Of course, it is easy to inspire warm, reciprocal feelings in fiction and more difficult to capture them in real school time. Consequently, a documentary of Johnson's class may have had more the feel of the CPESS documentary than *Dangerous Minds.* Nonetheless, the affective message *Dangerous Minds* sends can inspire teachers to revision the way they relate to students and partially heal the fissures born of race and class inequality.

By reminding us of the gifts of ourselves we make and the gifts of our students we accept when we engage in authentic teaching and learning, the cinematically undistinguished Hollywood film has something of educational value to impart. Paraphrasing Richard Rorty's perspective in *Truth and Progress,* Carlin Romano (1998) writes that "Stories, not principles or definitions, lead to moral progress .... Instead of theories, we need 'sentimental education' of the sort that movies, journalism, and novels provide, which will expand the set of 'people like us'" (p. 28). *Dangerous Minds* offers a sort of "sentimental education" that guides educators to expand what historian David Hollinger (1995) calls "the circle of the 'we'" (p. 68). Unfortunately, this message is compromised by the racist stereotypes that afflict most of the African-American characters and by the depiction of Johnson as the only one who cares. The message is further attenuated by the absence of an historical context that would account for how racially coded unequal power relations played out in such a way as to make plausible the casting of communities of color as passive clients and a White educator as the savior of their children. This lack of context also affects the representation of Meier and her colleagues in *High School II.*

The White Image in the White Mind

LouAnne Johnson taught students enrolled in a special program for underachieving students and subsequently directed the program. Many of the students came from East Palo Alto, once a predominantly African-American community where there had been major battles over education in the 1960s and 1970s. Ravenswood High School was built there in 1958 with gerrymandered boundaries designed to enroll all the Black students in a very large, affluent high school district. Subsequent to the failure of sustained Black community efforts to achieve desegregation, a movement for community control in the late 1960s succeeded at Ravenswood in removing unsympathetic teachers, strengthening the academic program, and producing dramatic increases in attendance, grade averages, and college admissions. These gains were compromised, however, in 1971 when the school board turned Ravenswood into a magnet school designed to attract countercultural White students. Five years later Ravenswood was closed. Black students were bussed to the remaining schools in this far-flung district, becoming a small minority in each. This completely ruptured the connection between schooling and community aspirations, and academic failure for African Americans became the norm (Lowe, 1992).

If White district officials did not have the power to terminate the experiment in community control, there might have been no need for Johnson's special program, and her students would not have had to rely on what appeared to be a single advocate. Similarly, had the community control effort in New York City survived, it is unlikely that Deborah Meier would have emerged as the rescuer of city children and of urban public schools. Meier, however, helped make herself indispensable by supporting the teachers' union that undermined community control. The silence of the films on these matters of history makes it appear natural that White educators are the heroes. Such a perverse sense of the normal is fed by public amnesia. Whites typically bring to the films no memory of African-American and Latino struggles for just schools or White resistance to these efforts. Given this vacuum, the films merely confirm Whites' self-image as the benefactors of other people's children.

In the end, no matter how great the energy expended and personal sacrifices made by Meier and Johnson, their stature as saviors of kids of color depends on massive failure stemming from the educational disenfranchisement of the students' communities. For the foreseeable future, of course, White teachers will predominate in most urban schools. Paradoxically, perhaps apolitical teachers, like LouAnne Johnson, who care for their students and respect their parents, are more likely to see the need for fundamentally redistributing educational power than politically progressive educational reformers who are ideologically committed to the right of Whites to run schools for African-American and Latino students.

NOTES

1. *My Posse Don't Do Homework* also tends to portray Johnson as the lone fighter for students, but the ugly racial dynamics of the film are absent. The one really offensive teacher is a White man whom Johnson accuses of racism.
2. For precise phrasing of these habits, see Meier (1995), *The Power of Their Ideas*, p. 50.
3. Meier (1995), in fact, writes that "A good school for anyone is a little like kindergarten and a little like a good post-graduate program ..." (p. 48).
4. Also, given CPESS's high-powered leadership and visibility, it would not be surprising if the school has attracted external funding that exceeds the possibilities of most urban schools.
5. This is also true of the one conference that includes a White student.
6. The one faculty meeting that takes place without Meier being present does indicate that all felt free to speak and air their disagreements. Two Black faculty members argued quite eloquently for a rigorous approach to literature that would prepare students adequately for college work and make it possible for them to succeed on the advanced placement test. None of the White teachers spoke in support of this position, but seemed to be more interested in thinking about English in an interdisciplinary way. The discourse was certainly democratic, but given that the majority of teachers were White, one wonders whether the freedom of a minority to register its opinions mattered when it came to making policy.
7. One could also argue, of course, that legitimacy derives from the choice of parents to send their children to Central Park East. The option to choose from a number of different schools, however, does not mean that there is an opportunity to choose a good school. Central Park East at least has the reputation of being a good school.
8. In the book, the student Johnson visits is Gusmaro Guevarra whose infraction was a refusal to do homework. Johnson speaks to the parents in Spanish with somewhat different words of praise than in the film (1993, p. 167). In an analogous situation in the book, Callie West misbehaves and Johnson communicates through a note to Callie's parents that she knows Callie will read. Johnson said, "I wrote a note telling Mr. and

Mrs. West how much I enjoyed having Callie in class, that she was a bright and charming student with a delightful sense of humor" (pp. 63–64). The results were so positive that Johnson wrote to all the parents, finding positive things to say about even the most difficult students.

9. In the book, the student is Shamica Stanton. Also, the real name of the school is Carlmont.

10. The students do not do this in the book, but Johnson makes clear that students' appreciation of her through their letters and, in one case, a ceramic teddy bear accompanying a note of gratitude, are the reason for her return.

REFERENCES

Anderson, J. D. (1988). *The education of Blacks in the south.* Chapel Hill: University of North Carolina Press.

Bromwich, D. (1994, September 19, 26). Unsentimental education. *The New Republic, 211,* 39–43.

Delpit, L. D. (1986). Skills and other dilemmas of a progressive Black educator. *Harvard Educational Review, 56*(4), 379–385.

Hollinger, D. (1995). *Postethnic America: Beyond multiculturalism.* New York: Basic Books.

James, C. (1994, July 6). 25 years later, Wiseman goes back to school. *The New York Times,* p. C14.

Johnson, L. (1993). *My posse don't do homework.* New York: St. Martin's Press.

Lowe, R. (1992, April). *Benign intentions: The magnet school at Ravenswood High.* Paper presented at annual meeting of the American Educational Research Association, San Francisco.

Lowe, R., & Kantor, H. (1995). Creating educational opportunity for African Americans without upsetting the status quo. In E. Flaxman & A. H. Passow (Eds.), *Changing populations, changing schools: Ninety-fourth yearbook of the National Society for the Study of Education* (pp. 186–208). Chicago: University of Chicago Press.

Maslin, J. (1995, August 11). If teacher is Pfeiffer, can youths be all bad? *The New York Times,* p. C3.

Meier, D. (1968, March–April). From a Harlem school. *Dissent, 15,* 131.

Meier, D. (1995). *The power of their ideas: Lessons for America from a small school in Harlem.* Boston: Beacon Press.

Romano, C. (1998, July 27–August 3). Rortyism for beginners. *The Nation, 267,* p. 28.

Walker, E. V. S. (1993). Caswell County Training School, 1933–1969: Relationships between community and school. *Harvard Educational Review, 63*(2), 161–182.

Wilmington, M. (1995, August 11). Mindless "dangerous" glosses over the urban grit. *Chicago Tribune,* p. H7.

Epilogue

13

Responding to Reform:
Images for Teaching
in the New Millennium

Gail E. Burnaford
David Hobson

In a nation fond of reforming, the end of the 20th century arguably wit-
nesses the most comprehensive reform agenda ever undertaken. Few
schools remain untouched by new standards, structure, or ideas about
practice.

—McLaughlin and Oberman (1996, p. ix)

Reform and Image: Examining the Connection

Images of Schoolteachers in America takes us back in time, to rethink the images that have confronted us from the media, from popular culture, and from
our own histories. How is teaching different than it was 50 or 100 years ago?
How have the roles and responsibilities of teachers shifted, throwing into relief the inconsistencies, paradoxes, and ironies of the familiar imagery of
teachers? What kinds of teachers will we need and what kinds will we have in the
new century?

The future for the teaching profession may seem dismal. Teachers struggle with
reform initiatives that are often top-down and temporary, as administrators scram-
ble to produce results and achieve standards. Teachers are required to demonstrate
how their teaching addresses specific district and state goals and are often required
to match classroom assessments to learning standards set for them outside the

classroom and away from the needs of their particular children. Whereas researchers acknowledge teaching as a complex phenomenon, some districts insist on
scripted learning that deprives teachers of their capacity to create and adapt teaching to their students. And, all the while, teachers face numerous challenges as they
work with increasingly diverse populations and see great cultural and linguistic
variations in their classes. They also must meet the needs of children with disabili-
ties who enter classrooms in increasing numbers. In addition, teachers are being
asked to learn new ways of instruction that encompass technological changes. Certainly, the current conditions of schooling and forces of reform pull teachers in various directions.

Reform initiatives and new theories about how children learn have challenged
stereotypes and expectations of teachers. Teachers are writing grants, trying out innovative curriculum, and forming partnerships with community organizations to
improve children's learning. Public and private foundations are supporting reform
initiatives in schools, particularly in urban centers; teachers collaborate with each
other and with their university colleagues by engaging in research to learn more
about how to improve education. Reform, therefore, becomes renewal for many
teachers as they themselves take on these new challenges.

However, in order for this renewal to take place, professional development is a
priority. McLaughlin and Oberman (1996) explain,

> The new classroom practices that reformers imagine, often described as
> "teaching and learning for understanding," assume fundamental change in
> the ways teachers interact with students. Not surprisingly, teachers' ca-
> pacity and opportunity to enact this complex, far-reaching reform agenda
> have taken center stage. At root, the problem of reform is a problem of
> teachers' learning—understanding how to translate new standards, curric-
> ula, and theories of learning into effective educational experiences for all
> their students. (p. x)

Classrooms are changing as teachers explore new ways of "teaching for understanding." Schools, moreover, look different as more and more teachers plan and work together, team teach, and coach each other as peers in order to better meet the needs of
students. There are different ways to address professional development, with teachers
taking leadership in their own growth and learning. Moreover, teacher-preparation
programs are examining more realistic, grounded, and research-based ways to ensure
new teachers' success as they assume their roles in the classroom.

Nonetheless, reform efforts themselves have introduced a complicated dance—between professionalism, featuring the independence of teachers, and centralization of
authority to achieve high standardized results. However, questions remain about how to
deal with such tensions: How can standards be contextualized in individual classrooms
with children who cannot be easily categorized and labeled? How much diversity
among teachers' practice will be tolerated? How will the actual daily routine of a
teacher be shaped by these new demands and new roles in education?

As we have tried to understand what new images for teachers might look like, we found repeatedly that there was a certain bipolar approach to imagining teachers' roles and images (Howard, 1989). On the one hand, teachers seem to have less control over their classrooms as mandates for how and what they teach are handed down from central offices. On the other, teachers are seeing themselves as researchers engaging in systematic inquiry, publishing, and sharing their work in their schools and at conferences. While we see top-down "teacher-proof" curriculum being implemented, we also see whole language philosophy making an even stronger presence in schools; there are many classrooms in which teachers chose to have children read real literature and create a print-rich environment. Yet in districts where teachers are required to implement 10-week progress tests that will be compared across classrooms, teachers also may be encouraged to integrate the arts and take advantage of museums, symphony concerts, and poetry readings—developing a rich curriculum with outcomes that will not be featured on standardized tests. Regardless of the images we conceive for teachers, they will most certainly be asked to make sense of and work within a system in which a multitude of tensions will affect their professional lives.

Today's teachers will need different competencies than those of their colleagues who worked in the typical classroom of the past. Currently held learning theories repudiate an "empty vessel"/transmission-of-knowledge approach. They suggest that teachers must teach for understanding by helping children help to construct knowledge for themselves (Brooks & Brooks, 1993). Schlechty (cited in Brandt, 1993) asserts that the teacher in the new millennium will play the role of an inventor of engaging work. Teachers are learning how to facilitate learning that occurs as students sit in front of a computer screen. Also, teachers are assuming a new role of legal expert as litigation becomes increasingly common in school-based cases (McIntyre & O'Hair, 1996). They are learning political, ethical, and managerial roles as they advocate for children who have many needs—physical, emotional, and academic. All of these teachers' roles—stemming from research, reform, and demands for accountability in an ever-widening domain—paint a picture of the changing nature of teaching.

In this climate of reform, we recognize the need to revisit the old images that have dominated our understanding of the teaching profession. We also acknowledge the need to construct new images that re-imagine what it means to be a teacher. In this chapter, we present four images that address essential aspects of teaching as we move into the 21st century. These images reveal new ways of looking at the work of teaching that answer the call to reform, while maintaining the professionalism, creativity, and opportunity that brought us to teaching in the first place.

Teachers as Artists in the New Millennium

Twenty teachers gathered in a room at the Chicago Department of Cultural Affairs in early 1998. They were there to learn about the particulars of quilting from a textile artist —to imagine how they might return to their classrooms and design, make, and exhibit a quilt with their students. The quilt was to be a Millennium Quilt—one that would help the city of Chicago and the Chicago Public Schools celebrate the birth of the 21st century. By summer, they returned to that same room and shared the quilts that they and their students had produced (Chicago Department of Cultural Affairs, 1998). Each quilt told a story; each quilt had a theme that revealed something about students' memories, hopes, and images of the future. What was going on there?

The picture of a teacher reorganizing her classroom to make possible the planning, construction, and exhibition of a quilt disturbs the traditional image of how teachers think and what they do. Quilting is a process of collaboration and multiple perspectives. It is a rethinking of pattern and a reconstruction of events and memories. It requires planning, and yet it is spontaneous. It evokes response, and yet it is a rendering holding its own truths.

The painter Chuck Close uses the imagery of quilting to describe how he views his artwork (Greenberg & Jordan, 1998). He notes that in quilting, often described as "women's work," there is a commitment to the entire form, with an awareness of a sense of "all-overness." He urges a "sense of belief in a system. If I just keep making these marks and maintain the same attitude, and have some kind of overall vision in mind, I will eventually come out at the other end having built an image" (Close, 1998).

This quilting imagery is consonant with the practice of teaching. As we examine new images for teaching, we recognize that teachers too see the "all-overness" of their process; they too see each child as important to the whole and realize the essential need for staying true to that commitment in order to help children succeed. Now, more than ever, teachers are making metaphoric quilts in their classrooms that bring together the needs and interests of vastly different children who speak a variety of languages and represent a continuum of cultural and educational experiences. In addition, teachers are building new roles for themselves; they are revisioning their professions in new ways, and they, too, will "eventually come out at the other end having built an image."

Images in the media and from teachers' recollections do not hold up as we examine the new roles that teachers are playing in classrooms and schools across the country. And yet "women's work"—metaphorically making the quilt—suggests, to the contrary, that we need to continue to return to the old images and rework them as new challenges present themselves. Teachers are challenging the stereotypical images of drill sergeant, mother, or schoolmarm that have been discussed in this book. Reform efforts to improve the quality of schooling require that teachers assume professional roles, not just replay traditional versions of what it means to be a teacher.

Gage (1978) addresses the notion of teaching as an art in *The Scientific Basis of the Art of Teaching*. He writes: "As a practical art, teaching must be recognized as a process that calls for intuition, creativity, improvisation, and expressiveness—a process that leaves room for departures from what is implied by rules, formulas and algorithms" (p. 15). It is this dimension of creativity and improvisation that we find intriguing, especially in this age of systematic reforms that seem to standardize and regularize the practice of education.

What happens when we think of re-imaging the teacher as an artist (Rubin, 1985)? When a teacher engages in the curriculum as an artistic endeavor, the dynamic shifts. She is no longer the expert, the deliverer of information. Instead, she is a co-creator with students. Artistic representations of learning embrace both sensory and intellectual dimensions. They reveal what children are learning and how they are perceiving their world. The teacher is a partner in that process of discovery and articulation of meaning.

Artists and arts organizations have begun to play more of a role in schools. As a result, these days there are spaces called studios in schools, and students participate in reading and writing workshops as well as in woodshop and home economics workrooms. Students compose portfolios that reflect their best work or their work over time. Such terminology stems from the world of art and influences teachers as they revise their roles in classrooms.

The conception of teachers as artists has a past and recent history (see Eisner, 1985; Rubin, 1985); however, applications of artistic methods to classroom practice are beginning to be applied more widely. Teachers can choose from an array of literature on professional development to understand their teaching as an artistic endeavor (Chancer & Rester-Zodrow, 1997; Ernst, 1994; Greene, 1995; Hargreaves, 1989). Gallas (1994) discusses the "languages of learning," noting that children not only write and read their way to understanding, but also sing, draw, and dance as a means of learning and then exhibit what they know. Teachers are learning more about how the multiple intelligences can inform their teaching and strengthen their students' understanding of subject matter (Campbell, Campbell, & Dickinson, 1998; Gardner, 1983). We are realizing that assessment need not be merely with paper and pencil. The world of art suggests a variety of ways that children can represent their learning. Daniels and Bizar (1998) point out that individuals need to be creative and that "expression, in all of its manifold forms, is a key to learning and thinking" (p. 9).

Chuck Close (1998) asks: "Why make art? Because I think there's a child's voice in every artist saying, 'I am here. I am somebody. I made this. Won't you look?' We are turning this on its ear and saying there's an artist in every child who says the same thing: 'I am here ... won't you look?'"

What then does this approach to teaching mean for re-imaging teachers as artists? It suggests that teachers are more engaged in the doing and so are their students. Neither are passive recipients of curricular materials; they are creators of those materials. Jackie Murphy, Chicago teacher and artist, speaks of a classroom in which art is integrated as one in which the "air is full of possibilities." The teacher-artist role also suggests an adult in the classroom who is comfortable with ambiguity and flexibility. She may not have the outcome precast. Singer-teacher Amy Lowe reports that she is learning to "build the muscle of improvisation." Eighth-grade teacher Wendy Anderson asserts that an artistic approach to her work "helps me teach the way I want to teach—from whole to part, more depth than breadth."

In *Art as Experience,* Dewey (1934) wrote what the arts have to teach us about our lives. More recently, Jackson (1998) explains in his book, *John Dewey and the Lessons of Art,* how we can use Dewey's writings and our own arts experiences to make us better teachers:

> The arts, Dewey tells us, reveal the rewards of bringing an experience to fruition. They reveal what it takes to fashion works whose form and structure are holistic and unified, yielding a reaction ... that is at once satisfying and fulfilling. In this way, they hint at what life might be like if we sought more often to shape ordinary experience in an artistic manner. (p. 6)

It is this goal—to shape the ordinary experience of schooling in an artistic manner—that characterizes teachers who see their work as art, not simply skill or science. Furthermore, they accommodate more demanding standards of accountability. As these teacher-artists honor self-expression, the arts also becomes a medium for appraisal of learning, whether students engage in quilting—or painting—or improvising—or dancing.

Teachers as Researchers: Knowledge Producers in Reforming Schools

> I've been a teacher for over 30 years. I have done it all, I think. What is left? Well, I can mentor new teachers ... I can always do that. But, if I don't start doing my own research, I think I will just have to call it quits. I have something more to contribute—why hasn't anyone ever asked me?
>
> —Sixth Grade Teacher

Traditionally, educational research was characterized by an order of progression, a linear three-step process: university researchers designed, carried out, and analyzed various studies in education; specialists in curriculum and policy worked with the results to construct plans for educational change; and finally, teachers implemented those plans in classrooms (Houser, 1990, p. 56).

Enter the teacher-research movement. The linear process has undergone a significant change in recent times such that "teachers lead as well as follow. They act autonomously, often initiating each vital function of the research project. In this sense, teacher-research is a significant departure from all previous research roles" (Houser, 1990, p. 59). When teachers become researchers, "the classroom becomes a place of inquiry, where questions are explored in meaningful contexts and teacher and students collaborate to seek answers .... By becoming researchers, these teachers take control over their own classrooms and professional lives in ways that confound the traditional definition of teacher ...." (Bissex & Bullock, 1987, p. xi).

Interest is a starting point for inquiry of any sort, a necessity perhaps, whether it occurs in the lives of children or teachers. As Dewey (1933) pointed out, "Individual effort is impossible without individual interest" (p. 444). A fresh and welcome development in educational research has been the validation of inquiry that is drawn from the interests of classroom teachers rather than, as has been the traditional pattern, from the interests of university professors. Curiosities from the everyday classroom experiences of practitioners are fueling inquiry in the burgeoning teacher-researcher movement and are providing a contemporary image of the classroom teacher as "practitioner-inquirer" rather than perpetuating the exclusive claim of the university professor as the "scientist-theorist" of the educational research past.

Katy Smith, English teacher-researcher, discusses her new role during a classroom inquiry project on American culture. She describes her stance as a "guide on the side" instead of a "sage on the stage" (Smith, 1993, p. 37). In Smith's class, the teacher and students construct knowledge. Together they are questioners, problem solvers, and initiators of curriculum. "As students become co-researchers, teachers can see themselves as co-learners. All take ownership of the exploration; students are no longer specimens to be researched. They are part of the research team" (Burnaford, Fischer, & Hobson, 1996, p. xii).

Paradoxically, the teacher-research movement began many years ago and exerted various degrees of influence in the past 30 or 40 years. However, this movement continued even as waves of reform and centrally mandated edicts washed over schools, demanding uniformity and conformity to lessons and pedagogy invented outside the classroom. How is it that teachers have persisted in maintaining this image for themselves as researchers who have something to say about how children learn and how teachers teach?

The answer is two-fold. First, teachers are researchers. Conducting classroom inquiry is part of what it means to be a teacher. Now and before, as teachers deliberate how and what shall be taught, they learn to use methods of teacher research and are guided by their discoveries. Inquiry becomes a way of life and a way of teaching, not just a technique for gathering bits of discrete information (Flake, Kuhs, Donnelly, & Ebert, 1995). Moreover, at different times, teacher research has been acknowledged and supported.

Writing in 1999, Cochran-Smith and Lytle maintain that the current wave of renewed interest in teacher research is just about 10 years old. By the 1990s, professional teacher organizations, such as the National Council of Teachers of English, supported teacher research by publishing teacher work and encouraging teacher conference presentations. The *Harvard Educational Review, Teaching and Change,* and other journals have also begun to publish reports of research, including narratives of classroom experience, written by teachers. There is a Teacher As Researcher Special Interest Group associated with the American Educational Research Association, and there have been numerous International Conferences on Teacher Research.

Teachers and administrators currently are beginning to rethink their acquiescence to university-based research initiatives that do not beneficially affect the teaching and learning that occurs in their schools. Teachers are joining research teams as collaborators who have something to contribute to the work of research.

Universities are offering coursework in teacher research to better prepare teachers to conduct systematic inquiry that will improve their practice (Burnaford & Hobson, 1995; Hollingsworth & Sockett, 1994; Zeichner, 1994).

If this movement continues, the image of teacher as researcher will certainly transform what the media, parents, community leaders, and reformers think about school reform. If teachers accept their role as knowledge producers, and not merely knowledge users, they will have the capacity to rewrite how schools participate in reform. This image is a compelling one for policymakers and local leaders. The question then becomes: To what extent will teachers seize this chance to shape their profession?

Teachers as Navigators: Technology in 21st-Century Schooling

It seems obvious that teachers are assuming new roles as technology permeates our culture and, ultimately, our schools. It may be that we are, for the moment, empty of imagery for this new technologically grounded teacher because it is not clear how classrooms will look and how technology will actually shape teaching and learning 50 years from now. Some have envisioned classrooms where there is no need for a teacher, as long as students have access to a computer.

Teachers' roles may shift in very real ways when technology becomes commonplace in classrooms, but there is no evidence that teachers are so easily dispensed with in the educative process. B. F. Skinner's work in the early 1950s influenced the development of teaching machines and programmed instruction—translated into Computer Assisted Instruction (CAI) and other models. While educators then seemed to embrace Skinnerian principles, they quickly learned that children are not automatons. The tedium of individualized, computer-driven rote-learning strategies cannot substitute for relationships built between students and teachers.

Now we are into an age of easy access to information; this new technology is seductive. Software programs abound as resources for teachers and children. However, we wonder if some educators are mesmerized by the lure of Skinnerian theory? One research study claims that *Reader Rabbit,* an early-childhood reading software program used in more than 100,000 schools, caused a 50% drop in creativity. At a research site in that study, it appeared that after children used the program for 7 months, the children were "no longer able to answer open-ended questions and showed a markedly diminished ability to brainstorm with fluency and originality" (Oppenheimer, 1997, p. 52). Nevertheless, as Cuban notes, "Schooling is not about information. It is getting kids to think about information. It's about understanding and knowledge and wisdom" (cited in Oppenheimer, 1997, p. 61). Much discussion and analysis need to occur about how teachers can creatively address the issue that Cuban raises.

In a comprehensive study by the National Center for Education Statistics (NCES, 1999), only 20% of teachers surveyed reported feeling very well prepared to integrate educational technology into classroom instruction. Teachers are being asked to bring up test scores, teach in new and different ways, and learn the technology that is intended to transform their classrooms. The influx of new technology has been compared to the attempt to board a train while it is traveling at high speed (Rice, 1984). If teachers are to be the navigators, they will need support and encouragement to get on the train.

In the new millennium, technology in schools introduces an even more compelling challenge. Relationships between students and teachers are being redefined because of the Internet. The Web offers a new world of information—some accurate, some false, some hazardous, some enlightening. Students and teachers are busy navigating this landscape and experimenting with how their findings play a role in schooling. Are students in danger of developing "hypertext minds," in which they can access bits of information from a variety of sources, but have little ability to sequence and deepen this information with context? If there is such a danger, what does this mean for our image of what teaching is and should be?

The Apple Classroom of Tomorrow research, sponsored by Apple Computer, notes that teachers appear to pass through five stages as they learn to integrate technology: entry, adoption, adaptation, appropriation, and invention (Sandholtz, Ringstaff, & Dwyer, 1997). If we are to get to the innovator image for teachers, we need to work on ways to move through the first four stages of learning with technology.

Encounters with information via technology also raise issues of morality that invite teachers to engage students in the dialogue about whose information, for what purpose, and in whose interest it is distributed? The Internet "teaching machine," while it does constitute a delivery system for data and inquiry, has no soul. It does not model, as a teacher does, curiosity, questioning, and grounded decision making. Teachers help students to make meaning and to create real knowledge, not merely consume it. What's more, students identify with the human qualities of a teacher.

On the positive side, navigating the newest software, the Internet, and the school curriculum can present a view of a classroom that is embedded in collaborative inquiry. Teachers are more accessible to their students through e-mail than ever before. They can provide responses to student work, receive assignments, and facilitate discussions without ever entering a classroom. Contrary to the Skinnerian image of solitary terminal users pacing themselves and learning without talk, the new navigation offers options for multiple users who are engaging in conversation while they are exploring.

It is clear is that the physical classroom must accommodate and make space for the virtual classroom in the new century. The space for learning is ever widening. The traditional image of Norman Rockwell's classroom teacher standing at the front of the room speaking to a captive audience does not mesh with the new generation's encounter with teachers who must navigate in and around computer terminals. Information wends its way into the classroom from a plethora of sources all over the world. The teacher, then, is forced to find new ways to work in a classroom that has virtually no walls. Therefore, we have chosen the image of "navigator" to illustrate a new role for teachers integrating technology.

We have observed groups of teachers and ourselves as we have learned to use a new program or integrate a new mode of technology. We are busy helping each other, talking across the lab to others, discovering treasures, and sending messages to those who may or may not be in the room. A redefining of what it means to be a teacher involves a careful consideration of the implications of technology for collaborative learning in classrooms. The teacher-navigator, may guide the group, but the group gathers its energy from the expanded classroom and from its members. In this adventure, teachers can be the gateway to change (Cuban, 1986).

Teachers as Collaborative Learners: Challenging the Tradition of Isolation

Much of the lore surrounding the profession of teaching maintains that teachers have been, and continue to be, isolated in their solitary classrooms. The image of the lonely teacher behind a closed classroom door permeates discussions of school change and the culture of teaching (Hobson, 1996; Lieberman & Miller, 1984; Lortie, 1975). We would contend that imagery of teaching for the 21st century must challenge this assumption. New ways of working, with administrators, with students, with parents and community, and with peers, are placing different demands on classroom teachers.

In a study sponsored by the National Center for Educational Statistics, teachers reported relatively strong collegial support for their work; many (63%) surveyed strongly agreed that other teachers shared ideas with them that were helpful in their teaching. A good many teachers (55%) also felt supported by the school administration (NCES, 1999, p. vi). The same teachers reported that school-based collaborative activities produced positive and long-lasting change. Such collaborative opportunities—including teacher networks, mentoring, team teaching, and common planning meetings—were sources for professional development in which teachers saw themselves as lifelong learners (p. 29).

It is becoming less and less acceptable to retreat into the sanctuary of one's classroom; contemporary teachers are called upon to plan curriculum, facilitate team meetings, coordinate staff development, and interact with community participants in schooling (Monson & Monson, 1993). Teacher educators are integrating team models into their programs of teacher preparation, and administrators are working with teachers to design partnerships as a means of evaluating teacher performance (Black, 1993; Walen & DeRose, 1993).

We cannot underestimate the challenge inherent in rethinking isolationist patterns within the profession. Although team teaching is much studied in the literature as a construct, little research has been devoted to just how teaming changes teachers and the ways in which they interact with other adults. Arnold and Stevenson (1998) note that a "plethora of research, theory, and recommended practice has been published about interpersonal relationships. Unfortunately, very little of that data is devoted to interdisciplinary team organization in schools" (p. 161). The literature on teaming in the field focuses largely on structural and organizational procedures, scheduling, and the responsibilities of team members (Dickinson & Erb, 1997; Erb & Doda, 1989), rather than on group development skills and how the image of teaching may be changed. A new image of teachers as collaborators must be framed by case studies and teacher stories about how such teaming really works.

We examined the process of teacher collaboration while working in a summer institute in which teachers, for the first time, were teamed with colleagues in other schools. One participant commented: "Seeing great minds working together makes me realize I never want to be behind a closed classroom door again." Others, however, struggled with the new paradigm. It seemed very difficult to break patterns that may have been developed over a lifetime of teaching. One teacher remarked, "I am so used to being the only adult in the room." Another commented, "We didn't really team. We just broke into small groups (with the students) and did our thing with our groups—no teaming required. If there's no public accountability, a group does not necessarily have to be a team. Maybe I need a workshop on teaming."

The teaming organization allowed participants to look more closely at themselves as teachers and as learners. Many used this opportunity for personal reflection on themselves and their ability to collaborate: "I sometimes felt I was too bossy. Was that how the others wanted it or was it my fault?"; "It was very difficult for me to listen in the beginning. None of us was really listening to each other. That made communication very difficult and made the differences in ideas even more obvious"; "I have a tendency to jump in before students have played out all of their thinking."

In this context, the teachers were experiencing the very same thing that their students do. They were placed in what we call a "cooperative learning group," in which they were asked to make decisions, negotiate, and listen to each other—just as students are asked to do. The institute challenged them to experience what they were being asked to facilitate in their own classrooms: Professional development moved away from the telling and into the realm of doing and being.

The teachers began to realize that they, too, had much to learn and they were part of a diverse professional community, just as students are members of ethnically, culturally, and socially diverse classrooms. One participant seemed to summarize: "I am taking away ... a reminder that teachers are a lot like students. They are engaged in a process and they are at many stages along the continuum." Another declared, "Schools would be wise to invest money into team teaching. Resource stuff is not effective. Double us up instead!" These teachers had moved beyond the closed doors, admitting that they were in unfamiliar territory, but would rely on the support of this new-found network of teachers and principals to move forward.

If we see teachers as collaborators, the image of the solitary adult standing in front of a classroom of students will not be sustainable in the new millennium. The new image of a teacher may be that of an actor in a repertory theater—never a one-man show and always dependent on co-actors, be they students or colleagues. However, Daniels and Bizar (1998) note effective collaboration processes are not the result of chance; the teacher must have the opportunity to model processes for working together that their students will need to practice in their own lives.

Caveats and Contexts

Each of the new images of teaching we have explored involves alternative ways of seeing who the teacher actually might be in a classroom. Especially, we have noted how images and new structures for teaching arise from current research on learning as socially mediated and participatory (Salomon & Perkins, 1998). These emerging definitions of teacher compel us to think of ourselves not as isolated orators, but as collaborative and socially dependent learners in that complex redefined construct called school. In this complexity, learning involves engagement with cultural artifacts, tools, and other information sources that challenges teachers to rethink their role as resource in the technology lab and the museum (Salomon & Perkins, 1998). Moreover, learning may bring community members, artists, and parents into teaching roles along with the traditional solitary teacher in a classroom. Perhaps, in the new century, this long-held progressive view of learning in classrooms will prevail as definitions of "teacher" and "classroom" evolve that previously did not exist in traditional schools.

The teacher images described in this chapter stem, in part, from what we have experienced and, to some extent, from what we believe to be possible. However, notwithstanding their desires, many teachers encounter difficulties as they strive to create new roles for themselves. To illustrate, the teachers who participated in the Millennium Quilt Project demonstrated both the possibilities and the tensions inherent in a complex vision of teaching. They had chosen to reach beyond what they known and have done in the past by learning new skills and thinking like the artists, in fact, becoming artists themselves. They have taken risks in the company of new friends in order to try extraordinary ways of creating curriculum with students. Nevertheless, they have faced administrative barriers, criticisms, and confusions.

As districts explore the possibilities of teacher research as an approach to long-term staff development, administrators must examine the conflict inherent in schooling in the present society: the autonomy of teacher research groups to grow, learn, and change classroom practice contrasted with the demands for standardization and conformity of practice. In a study about the viability of teacher research as having a permanent role in the future, participating teachers asserted that this movement will not be sustained unless it receives the support needed from school districts to become an organic part of the life of schools (Bennett, 1993). School leaders, legislators, and central office administrators who see themselves as responsible for reform that is speedy, widespread, and easily observable apparently still do not fully understand or accept inquiry as a means of learning for both adults and students.

Similarly, it seems clear that there are substantial barriers to the successful integration of technology in many public schools. Teachers frequently are hampered in their efforts to meaningfully help students access information through this medium. In some schools, technology is secluded in labs to which few students have regular and consistent access. Many teachers still are not familiar enough with the capacities inherent in the technology to be able to plan and develop technological teaching strategies that make sense to them (Blanton, Moorman, & Trathen, 1998). Moreover, some teachers are aware of the tide, but often cannot figure out how to "cybersurf" in their classrooms, and others, we believe, continue to ignore the potential of technology.

New roles and their correspondent images will continue to evolve and to be shaped by the decisions that teachers make for themselves and with others. In a sense, images of teachers for the future rest on how teachers define their own autonomy to pursue new visions for themselves—as artists, researchers, technological navigators, and collaborators—in balance with their obligations to students, schools, and communities (Hawthorne, 1986). These sets of choices confront teachers at the start of each day, at the start of each year. The teachers can make new images for themselves for the beginning of the new century. Still, "until the parameters of teacher autonomy are defined, new roles for teachers cannot be realized" (Monson & Monson, 1993, p. 19). But can such parameters ever truly be defined? For us, it is the ongoing possibilities in the act of teaching and within the teaching profession—of creating and recreating teacher images for ourselves in the future—that provide the excitement.

REFERENCES

Arnold, J., & Stevenson, C. (1998). *Teachers' teaming handbook.* Orlando, FL: Harcourt Brace.

Bennett, C. K. (1993). Teacher-researchers: All dressed up and no place to go? *Educational Leadership, 51*(2), 69–70.

Bissex, G. L., & Bullock, R. H. (1987). *Seeing for ourselves: Case-study research by teachers of writing.* Portsmouth, NH: Heinemann.

Black, S. (1993). How teachers are reshaping evaluation procedures. *Educational Leadership, 51*(2), 38–42.

Blanton, W. E., Moorman, G., & Trathen, W. (1998). Telecommunications and teacher education: A social constructivist review. In P. D. Pearson & A. Iran-Nejad (Eds.), *Review of research in education 23* (pp. 235–275). Washington, DC: American Educational Research Association.

Brandt, R. (1993). On restructuring roles and relationships: A conversation with Phil Schlechty. *Educational Leadership, 51*(2), 8–11.

Brooks, J. G., & Brooks, M. G. (1993). *In search of understanding: The case for constructivist classrooms.* Alexandria, VA: Association for Supervision and Curriculum Development.

Burnaford, G., Fischer, J., & Hobson, D. (1996). *Teachers doing research: Practical possibilities.* Mahwah, NJ: Lawrence Erlbaum Associates.

Burnaford, G., & Hobson, D. (1995). Beginning with the group. *Action in Teacher Education, 17*(3), 67–75.

Campbell, L., Campbell, B., & Dickinson, D. (1998). *Teaching and learning through multiple intelligences* (2nd ed.). New York: Allyn & Bacon.

Chancer, J., & Rester-Zodrow, G. (1997). *Moon journals: Writing, art, and inquiry through focused nature study.* Portsmouth, NH: Heinemann.

Chicago Department of Cultural Affairs. (1998). *Chicago schools quilts millennium project.* Chicago.

Close, C. (1998, June 20–September 13). *Chuck Close audio tour.* Exhibit at the Museum of Contemporary Art, Chicago.

Cochran-Smith, M., & Lytle, S. L. (1999). The teacher research movement: A decade later. *Educational Researcher, 28*(7), 15–25.

Cuban, L. (1986). Principaling: Images and roles. *Peabody Journal of Education, 63*(1), 107–119.

Daniels, H., & Bizar, M. (1998). *Methods that matter: Six structures for best practice classrooms.* York, ME: Stenhouse.

Dewey, J. (1933). Why have progressive schools? *Current History, 38,* 441–448.

Dewey, J. (1934). *Art as experience.* New York: Capricorn Books.

Dickinson, T., & Erb, T. (Eds.). (1997). *We gain more than we give: Teaming in middle schools.* Columbus, OH: National Middle School Association.

Eisner, E. W. (1985). *The educational imagination: On the design and evaluation of school programs.* New York: Macmillan.

Erb, T. O., & Doda, N. (1989). *Team organization: Promise, practice, and possibilities.* Washington, DC: National Education Association.

Ernst, K. (1994). *Picturing learning: Artists and writers in the classroom.* Portsmouth, NH: Heinemann.

Flake, C. L., Kuhs, T., Donnelly, A., & Ebert, C. (1995). Reinventing the role of teacher: Teacher as researcher. *Phi Delta Kappan, 76*(5), 405–407.

Gage, N. L. (1978). *The scientific basis of the art of teaching.* New York: Teachers College Press.

Gallas, K. (1994). *The languages of learning: How children talk, write, dance, draw, and sing their understanding of the world.* New York: Teachers College Press.

Gardner, H. (1983). *Frames of mind.* New York: Basic Books.

Greenberg, J., & Jordan, S. (1998). *Chuck Close up close.* New York: DK Publishing.

Greene, M. (1995). *Releasing the imagination: Essays on education, the arts, and social change.* San Francisco: Jossey-Bass.

Hargreaves, D. J. (Ed.). (1989). *Children and the arts.* Philadelphia: Open University Press.

Hawthorne, R. K. (1986). The professional teachers' dilemma: Balancing autonomy and obligation. *Educational Leadership, 44*(2), 34–35.

Hobson, D. (1996). Learning with each other: Collaboration in teacher research. In G. Burnaford, D. Fischer & D. Hobson (Eds.), *Teachers doing research: Practical possibilities* (pp. 93–108). Mahwah, NJ: Lawrence Erlbaum Associates.

Hollingsworth, S., & Sockett, H. (Eds.). (1994). *Teacher research and educational reform: Yearbook of the NSSE.* Chicago: University of Chicago Press.

Houser, N. O. (1990). Teacher-researcher: The synthesis of roles for teacher empowerment. *Action in Teacher Education, 12*(2), 55–60.

Howard, J. (1989). On teaching, knowledge, and "middle ground." *Harvard Educational Review, 59*(2), 226–239.

Jackson, P. W. (1998). *John Dewey and the lessons of art.* New Haven, CT: Yale University Press.

Lieberman, A., & Miller, L. (1984). *Teachers, their world, and their work: Implications for school improvement.* Arlington, VA: Association for Supervision and Curriculum Development.

Lortie, D. (1975). *The schoolteacher: A sociological study.* Chicago: University of Chicago Press.

McIntyre, D. J., & O'Hair, M. J. (1996). *The reflective role of the classroom teacher.* Belmont, CA: Wadsworth.

McLaughlin, M. W., & Oberman, I., (Eds.). (1996). *Teacher learning: New policies, new practices*. New York: Teachers College Press.

Monson, M. P., & Monson, R. J. (1993). Who creates curriculum? New roles for teachers. *Educational Leadership, 51*(2), 19–21.

National Center for Education Statistics (NCES). (1999). *Teacher quality: A report on the preparation and qualifications of public school teachers*. Jessup, MD: U.S. Department of Education.

Oppenheimer, T. (1997). The computer delusion. *The Atlantic Monthly, 280*(1), 45–62.

Rice, R. E. (1984). Evaluating new media systems. In J. Johnston (Ed.), *Evaluating the new information technologies* (pp. 53–71). San Francisco: Jossey-Bass.

Rubin, L. J. (1985). *Artistry in teaching*. New York: Random House.

Salomon, G., & Perkins, D. N. (1998). Individual and social aspects of learning. In P. D. Pearson & A. Iran-Nejad (Eds.), *Review of research in education 23* (pp. 1–24). Washington, DC: American Educational Research Association.

Sandholtz, C., Ringstaff, C., & Dwyer, D., (1997). *Teaching with technology: Creating student centered classrooms*. New York: Teachers College Press.

Smith, K. (1993). Becoming the "guide on the side." *Educational Leadership, 51*(2), 35–37.

Walen, E., & DeRose, M. (1993). The power of peer appraisals. *Educational Leadership, 51*(2), 45–48.

Zeichner, K. M. (1994). Personal renewal and social construction through teacher research. In S. Hollingsworth & H. Sockett (Eds.), *Teacher research and educational reform* (pp. 66–84). Chicago: University of Chicago Press.

Contributors

William Ayers is distinguished professor of education and university scholar at the University of Illinois at Chicago. Before his academic career, he was an early childhood educator and social activist. He is the author of *The Good Preschool Teacher, A Kind and Just Parent,* and *To Teach: The Journey of a Teacher.* He is co-editor with William Schubert of *Teacher Lore* and co-editor with Patricia Ford of *City Kids, City Teachers.* He has published numerous chapters in books as well as articles in various journals including *Action in Teacher Education, Cambridge Journal of Education,* and *Harvard Educational Review.* His scholarly and practical work centers on urban school improvement, teacher education, and the ethics of teaching.

Gail E. Burnaford is associate professor and Director of Undergraduate Teacher Education at Northwestern University. She has taught both high school and junior high English/language arts and preschool. Her research interests are teacher action research, multicultural children's literature, and integrating the arts across the curriculum. She has published articles in *The Middle School Journal, Music Education Journal, Action in Teacher Education,* and the *Journal for Research in Middle School Education,* as well as the book, *Teachers Doing Research* (Lawrence Erlbaum Associates, 2000) with David Hobson and Joseph Fischer. Her latest book, *Renaissance in the Classroom: Arts Integration and Meaningful Learning,* is also in press with Lawrence Erlbaum Associates.

Mary Eaton has a bachelor's degree in American studies from Brandeis University and is presently studying for a master's degree in theology at Episcopal Divinity School in Cambridge, Massachusetts.

Sara Efron is assistant professor in the Educational Foundations Department of National-Louis University. She has worked as a curriculum consultant and has been teacher and academic coordinator at Solomon Schechter Day School, coordinator at Kohl Teacher Center in Wilmette, director of a program for learning-disabled children at a summer camp, and a high school and junior high teacher of Hebrew language and literature. Her scholarly interests are moral education, curriculum, and literature; and she has published in *The Journal of Moral Education* and *Religious Education.*

Joseph Fischer is a professor of education and one of the founding instructors of the Graduate Field-Based Program in the Interdisciplinary Studies Department at

National-Louis University. He has had a long relationship with the Chicago public schools and continues to work as a consultant involved with staff development and literature. He has lived and studied for many years in South America. His research interests include teacher centers and comparative education, and he has co-authored the text *Teachers Doing Research* with Gail Burnaford and David Hobson.

Nancy Stewart Green is professor emeritus of the Educational Foundations Department of Northeastern Illinois University. She has a long involvement with the Chicago Teachers' Center, working with the Chicago public schools. Her scholarly interests include the teaching profession, gender issues, and the history of education; she is co-author of *Cultures of Curriculum* with Pamela Joseph, Stephanie Bravmann, Mark Windschitl, and Edward Mikel; and has published in *The Journal of Teacher Education, History of Education Quarterly, Catalyst: Voices of Chicago School Reform,* and *Chicago History.* She currently lives in Seattle and is adjunct faculty at Antioch University Seattle.

Stan Hiserman is adjunct instructor at Antioch University Seattle and a facilitator of positive school change, community involvement, and democratic governance in schools and communities in the Seattle area. As a community volunteer, he was co-founder and board chair of Powerful Schools, a coalition of four public elementary schools and two neighborhood organizations in southeast Seattle. He started his professional life as a counselor providing individual and group psychotherapy and co-developing an adult day treatment program in inner-city Seattle, and has had a long career as a cabinetmaker.

David Hobson is a professor in the Interdisciplinary Studies Department of National-Louis University. He was the founder and long-time director of the Graduate Center for Human Development and Learning at Fairleigh Dickinson University. As a former middle and high school social studies teacher, he has taught psychology and sociology to adolescents and helped found the Student Action Movement. He has published in the field of human development and social relations and is co-author of *Teachers Doing Research* with Gail Burnaford and Joseph Fischer.

Pamela Bolotin Joseph is chair and faculty member in the Programs for Experienced Educators at Antioch University Seattle. She also has been a social studies and language arts teacher in high school and junior high and a member of a board of education. Her research interests include curriculum studies, moral education, the teaching profession, and teacher research. She has published in *The Journal of Moral Education, Social Education, Theory and Research in Social Education,* and *The Journal of Teacher Education.* She is co-author of *Cultures of Curriculum* with Stephanie Bravmann, Mark Windschitl, Edward Mikel, and Nancy Green.

Benjamin Kantor is a graduate of Brandeis University, where he received a bachelor's degree in African/African-American studies and women's studies. He is currently a director of promotions and publicity and on-line disk jockey at www.RadioBoston.com, an Internet radio station in Boston.

Josh Kantor has a bachelor's degree in Spanish literature from Brandeis University and is a reference librarian at the Harvard University Law School Library.

Ken Kantor is professor in the Curriculum and Instruction and the Reading and Language Departments of National College of Education, National-Louis University. He has taught English on the high school level and has been a faculty member at Bowling Green State University and the University of Georgia. He has published chapters in *Teaching and Thinking About Curriculum: Critical Inquiries* (edited by J. Dan Marshall and James Sears) and *The Arts, Curriculum and Teaching: Reflections From the Heart of Educational Inquiry* (edited by G. Willis and W. Schubert). He also has published in *The Journal of Curriculum Theorizing*.

Nancy Lerner Kantor is coordinator of the Faculty Development Program in General Internal Medicine at Cook County Hospital, Chicago, Illinois.

Anne Kiefer is a retired faculty member from the Interdisciplinary Studies Department at National-Louis University. She worked both with teachers receiving master's degrees in curriculum and instruction and with teachers in interdisciplinary ESL programs. She has been a teacher and high school principal, administrator of ESL and bilingual programs, and a project director of staff development and preschool Title VII programs. Her research interests include English as a second language, bilingual education, and teacher renewal.

Robert Lowe is professor of education at Marquette University. A founder and former editor of the journal *Rethinking Schools,* he is an educational historian who focuses on issues of equity and has been co-editor of the journal *Educational Foundations.* He is currently working on a book (co-authored with Howard Fuller) provisionally entitled *Race, Class, and Teaching: A Social History of Teachers in Milwaukee.* He also is the co-author of *Public Schools in Hard Times* with David Tyack and Elizabeth Hansot.

Mary Phillips Manke is associate dean at the University of Wisconsin-River Falls and formerly was associate professor of interdisciplinary studies at National-Louis University, and of educational foundations at Minnesota State University, Mankato. Her research interests include the social foundations of education, qualitative research, and Asian immigrants in rural Minnesota. She has published in numerous journals including the *Journal of Research in Rural Education, Educational Studies,* and *Educational Foundations.* She is the author of *Classroom Power Relations: Understanding Student–Teacher Interaction.*

Edward R. Mikel is a core faculty member in the Experienced Educator Program at Antioch University Seattle and program director of Graduate Programs in Education. He has worked for many years with the St. Louis School District and has taken various leadership roles in working for democratic schools and school reform. He has written for the journals *Democracy and Education* and *School Review,* as well as the book *Democratic Teacher Education: Possibilities, Prospects, Problems, Paradoxes,* edited by John Novak. He is co-author of *Cultures of Curriculum* with Pamela Joseph, Stephanie Bravmann, Mark Windschitl, and Nancy Green.

Author and Name Index

Subject Index